"Why does so much Christian teaching f: transform lives through the impartation of liv edgeable and passionate Christian teacher and reach the heart of the person with the heart of the Bible through the power of the Holy Spirit. This wise and well-written book helps correct this pedagogical tragedy and should be read by all Christian teachers and preachers."

Douglas Groothuis
Professor of Philosophy, Denver Seminary

"I know of no one who passionately weds what he teaches in the classroom with what he practices in ministry better than Gary Newton. *Heart-Deep Teaching* is for all kinds of teachers who want to connect deeply with students and develop as individuals and teachers themselves. The personal and ministry examples Gary shares are worth the price of the book. If you want to develop personally as a teacher by learning from Jesus himself; if your desire is to effect heart-deep change by understanding how people learn; and if you are looking for tested and proven practices rooted in one teacher-practitioner's forty years of experience, this book is for you."

William A. Heth
Professor of Biblical Studies, Taylor University

"This book meets a crucial need in today's churches. Thousands of faithful people teach Bible studies each week. Yet they often do not know how to teach the Bible to transform lives. Writing from years of teaching and pastoral experience, Gary Newton guides readers in the exciting journey of getting to the heart of the text to get at the heart of readers."

Paul House
Professor of Divinity, Beeson Divinity School of Samford University

"*Heart-Deep Teaching*, written by an experienced teacher, offers an insightful teaching-learning framework for helping students of all ages respond deeply to Bible-based lessons. Teachers are encouraged to model being Bible learners themselves as they develop learning experiences that resonate with student needs and motivation. Newton raises the right questions about teaching in a Christian setting and provides guidance and examples for teachers from start to finish in the lesson planning process. I enjoyed the wide range of personal stories throughout each chapter that helped me picture in my mind the various phases of lesson design and teaching."

Klaus Issler
Professor of Christian Education and Theology,
Talbot School of Theology, Biola University

"Gary Newton has tackled an immensely critical need in the church today – how to change superficial teaching ministries into ones that impact the hearts and lives of both teachers and students. Combining insights from biblical studies, education, and his many years of ministry experience, Gary shows us a better way for teaching the Bible to transform lives. He challenges us and shows us how to dig deeper in God's Word, open our own lives to God's teaching, and create more interactive teaching/learning experiences that the Holy Spirit can use to form and transform our students. This book is a great gift to the church, and I recommend it highly for all who care about the impact of their teaching."

Kevin E. Lawson
Director of Ph.D. and Ed.D. programs in Educational Studies
at Talbot School of Theology, Biola University,

"Gary Newton is a gifted educator and offers crucial insights about the teaching and learning process. This book helps us see that the essence of discipleship is a lifelong process of tying together the content of Scripture with life and character transformation. Such insights are desperately needed in the church today."

Jim Plueddemann
Professor and Chair of Mission and Evangelism
Trinity Evangelical Divinity School

"Gary Newton thinks that too much ministry too shallowly engages the Bible for too little impact. I couldn't agree more. Having once been his office neighbor I can testify that this book more fully articulates a passion that he has lived and taught for as long as I've known him. Not only does Gary identify the problem without mincing words, he coaches us how to be used by God's Holy Spirit for teaching that changes lives. For all of my YFC colleagues who aspire to be faithful Bible teachers, let this book help guide your practice."

Dave Rahn
Senior Vice President and Chief Ministry Officer, Youth for Christ/USA

"In a world characterized by ignorance of any source of authority other than personal perspectives, Gary Newton's *Heart-Deep Teaching* provides an insightful process for discovering the Big Ideas from biblical passages and finding ways to aid learners to be transformed by the Holy Spirit through applying the Scripture to their hearts, to the core who they are."

Mark H. Senter III
Professor of Educational Ministries
Trinity Evangelical Divinity School

HEART-DEEP

DEEP

GARY NEWTON

TEACHING

ENGAGING STUDENTS FOR TRANSFORMED LIVES

B&H
ACADEMIC
NASHVILLE, TENNESSEE

Published by B&H Publishing Group
Nashville, Tennessee

Dewey Decimal Classification: 220.07
Subject Heading: TEACHING \ BIBLE—STUDY
AND TEACHING \ CHRISTIAN LIFE

Scripture quotations from the Holman Christian Standard Bible® Copyright
© 1999, 2000, 2002, 2003, 2009 by Holman Bible Publishers. Used by
permission.

Scripture citations marked NASB are from the New American Standard Bible.
©The Lockman Foundation, 1960, 1962, 1968, 1971, 1973, 1975, 1977.
Used by permission.

Scripture quoted by permission. Quotations designated (NIV) are from THE
HOLY BIBLE: NEW INTERNATIONAL VERSION®. NIV®. Copyright ©
1973, 1978, 1984, 2011 by Biblica. All rights reserved worldwide.

Printed in the United States of America
4 5 6 7 8 9 10 11 12 • 21 20 19 18 17
VP

Contents

DEDICATIONS

There are several very special people to whom I would like to dedicate this book. The first two have been significant mentors throughout my adult life modeling and teaching me the substance of *Heart-Deep Teaching*. James Reapsome has continued to influence my life ever since I served as his Youth Pastor in Marietta, Pa., and Ted Ward has continued to invest in my life since I studied under him at Trinity Evangelical Divinity School.

I also want to dedicate this book to my wife, Joy and my three boys, Joel, Ben, and Peter, who have been such a blessing to me through the years. I pray that each of them will continue to follow Jesus from the deepest corners of their hearts.

ACKNOWLEDGMENTS

I want to express my sincere appreciation to the many people who have helped me with this book, starting with the editorial team at B&H Publishing Group, including Jim Baird, Chris Cowan, and Dean Richardson. Alexis Jones and Abbi Palsma from Crown College did an exceptional job editing the first drafts of my manuscript. Rose Laugerman from Waconia, Minnesota, did an exceptional job producing the graphic diagrams for my book. I am also indebted to Crown College for their encouragement and financial support for this project and to Huntington University for providing a writing sabbatical.

CHAPTERS SUMMARY

The book *Heart-Deep Teaching* contains four parts and 12 chapters.

Part I of the book, "Explaining the Problem," contains chapt. 1, which explains the problem of "Shallowness in Biblical Teaching" in the church. The author identifies six faulty but commonly held principles that often influence Christian curriculum writers and teachers. Examples are given to illustrate the erroneous nature of each principle.

Part II of the book, "Preparing the Heart of the Teacher," includes three chapters to help the teacher understand the process of "heart-deep teaching." It is imperative for teachers to understand and personally apply the biblical, philosophical, and educational principles at the core of "heart-deep learning" in order to design a strategy to teach others.

Chapter 2, "Understanding the Mystery of the Heart," examines the term *heart* from a biblical, theological, and philosophical perspective. Writers such as Dallas Willard shed light on this topic. Attention will be given to the nature of the person, the role of God's Word, and the essence of discipleship as the transformation of the whole person.

Chapter 3, "Mapping the Journey to the Depths of the Heart," considers educational research dealing with the taxonomies related to each of the four aspects of the person: affective, cognitive, volitional, and behavioral. The purpose of this chapter is to help the teacher understand how to move deeper in each of the domains to change the heart of the person.

Chapter 4, "Digging Deeper into the Word for Yourself as a Teacher," challenges the teacher to develop a personal habit of studying the Bible inductively, without always relying on a teacher's manual or commentary. Changing the heart of the student begins with the teacher's modeling the process of "digging deeper into the Word." This process of inductive Bible study includes: analyzing the detail of the text; establishing an analytical outline; identifying the major theme, principles, and the Big Idea; applying the Big Idea to life; setting specific, personal goals; and establishing accountability measures for accomplishing those goals. Only by moving deeper through the cognitive, affective, volitional, and behavioral levels of learning can the teacher model the process of heart-deep learning for students.

Part III, "Designing Deeper Learning Experiences," contains four chapters dealing with how to design learning experiences that will facilitate a change in students at the deepest possible level. These chapters spiral through the sequential order of the steps identified in chapter 3 related to the taxonomies of learning in each of the four dimensions of the person.

Chapter 5, "Looking at the Biblical Text Through Students' Eyes," explains how teachers can apply their study of the biblical text to their students' context. At this stage of preparation, teachers will learn how to explore the things students struggle with emotionally, intellectually, volitionally, and behaviorally connected to the Big Idea. By thinking through the Big Idea from the perspective of the frustrations, concerns, and ambiguities of the students, the teacher is more likely to connect at a deeper level with the students. This chapter will focus on how to read a text from the students' perspective, looking for illustrations, connectives, parallels, stories, and applications that could clarify and illuminate the discovery process.

Chapter 6, "Setting Goals to Encourage Deeper Student Learning," explains how teachers can set goals for their lesson based on the Big Idea and major principles of the biblical text related to the needs, interests, and contexts of their learners.

Chapter 7, "Understanding How People Learn," explains the role of sensory experience in the learning process and the value of interactive experiential learning in accomplishing deeper learning outcomes.

Chapter 8, "Designing Learning Experiences that Encourage Heart-Deep Learning," will explain a variety of multisensory methods of instruction along with the process of how to design effective learning experiences to accomplish goals. The intentional connection between the purpose and goals of the lesson and the design of the learning experiences will be emphasized.

In Part IV, "Structuring the Lesson," chapters 9 through 12 deal with how to organize and structure the lesson to accomplish heart-deep learning. Each of the chapters represents a different phase of the lesson from beginning until end.

Chapter 9, "Priming Students' Heart Pumps," focuses on how to create an emotionally and relationally warm environment conducive to sharing from the heart. Various strategies will be discussed for how to relate to the real concerns and needs of students. Using the "backside of the Big Idea" as a springboard for student reflection, suggestions are given on how to get students to explore their thoughts and feelings related to the biblical theme. The goal of this part of the lesson is to stir up students' passion for truth and to prime their hearts to learn and change.

Chapter 10, "Getting Students to Dig Deeper into the Word," discusses how to equip students to wrestle with God's Word at deeper levels by guiding them to discover truth from the biblical text for themselves. This chapter is based on the assumption that people of all ages learn at a deeper level when they take responsibility for learning. Teachers will be encouraged to use more student-centered teaching approaches such as discovering, investigating, problem-solving, storytelling, acting out passages, questioning, active listening, group assignments, and researching. Teachers will learn how to provide adequate structure for such learning experiences to ensure that students will find the necessary details and principles from the biblical text. Special attention is given to strategies to help students discover and articulate the Big Idea in their own words. By integrating active learning methods with systematic Bible study principles, teachers will avoid the error of biblical superficiality.

Chapter 11, "Stimulating Student Heart Talk," focuses on strategies to challenge emotional and volitional reflection and application in students' hearts. Based on the Big Idea they discover, the students will be challenged to reflect creatively on its implications for their lives. Students will be encouraged to share inhibitions, fears, hesitations, and attitudes they encounter in applying the Big Idea. Benefits and blessings of applying the Big Idea are also identified and discussed. In this section of the lesson, students will be challenged to wrestle with the implications of the Big Idea to their lives at the deepest level possible.

Chapter 12, "Encouraging Heart Change in Life," explains the last but most often ignored part of the lesson. Most teachers are satisfied if students merely identify a few general ways of applying the Big Idea to their lives. The focus of this chapter will be to suggest ways to get students to set and actually accomplish personal or group goals based on that to which they have committed their hearts in response to the Big Idea of the text. This chapter will cover goal-setting strategies, planning for change, implementing plans, accountability structures, and assessment. Trust and confidentiality are essential components of an environment that encourages heart-deep change.

Conclusion: "The Challenges and Benefits of Heart-Deep Teaching" provides a summary for the book discussing the challenges and benefits of heart-deep teaching. This last chapter suggests reasons many teachers might hesitate to teach at a heart-deep level. It takes considerably more preparation time, personal integrity, and interpersonal involvement on the part of the teacher. This type of teaching might even scare away some students who would rather remain at a nominal level of Christian growth. Yet the benefits far outweigh the cost. While Jesus never hid the cost of discipleship, He continually reminded His followers of the joys of obedience. The conclusion of this book discusses the joys and benefits of heart-deep teaching in an attempt to motivate teachers to teach at a deeper biblical and educational level.

INTRODUCTION

While many books on teaching the Bible focus on the mechanical details of techniques, methods, and strategies, this one focuses on depth of learning. The purpose of this book is to help those involved in teaching the Bible learn how to engage students in the process of learning—to discover and obey truth from God's Word themselves. The goal of teaching is to engage the learner in following Christ at the deepest level possible as he or she grows in Christlikeness.

PART I

EXPLAINING THE PROBLEM

Chapter 1

Shallowness in Biblical Teaching

"Get Your People Pumped!"

That was the title of the training event the ministry team leaders in our church chose to attend. They picked it above all others because it was close by and promised them hope in turning around our stagnant ministry programs.

We were greeted with colorful banners and exciting music. The circus atmosphere quickly woke us up after our early morning, one-hour drive. Soon we were captured by the frenzy of a crowd of excited people swaying to the music from the loud worship band. When the main speaker took the stage, he captured the attention of the audience with jokes, affirmations, and drama.

Suddenly we were told to form small groups based on a number printed on our handouts. After a few minutes of bedlam, each participant settled into a circle of strangers to engage in a formatted "get to know one another" activity. Just when some connections were being made, we were thrust into a new learning activity. This time it was a brief skit, followed by a clip from a contemporary movie showing the desperate needs of people in our culture. While I don't remember the details of all the experiences of the day, I do remember the Bible lesson theme. The focus of the lesson was Jesus' illustration from Matt

7:24–27 of building a house on the rock rather than on the sand. A dramatic skit on stage etched that theme in my mind forever. Using huge LEGO bricks, two teams built similar houses on different foundations. One built on a pile of foam balls and the other on a pile of bricks. When a large industrial fan was turned on, accompanied by fierce storm sounds from the audience, the result was graphic. The house on the foam balls fell with a crash, and the house on the bricks stood firm.

We were then formed into new small groups near our seats to speculate what the different foundations represented from the dramatized story. While the text was displayed on a screen with a PowerPoint image, little direction was given to the small groups as to how to analyze Jesus' illustration. In fact, the groups were asked to focus mainly on the dramatic presentation to discover what the sand and the rock might represent.

The leader roamed around the small groups looking for a consensus from the groups in answer to the main question. He then called the groups together to sing that old Sunday school song, "The Wise Man Built His House upon the Rock." Then he asked the groups in a loud voice, "Who is the Rock?" To which the crowd responded, "Jesus!"

He repeated the question and asked the audience to respond at least four times. The scene reminded me of a high school pep rally.

The seminar concluded with the small groups coming up with creative ways to help people in their various ministries reach out to unbelievers and draw them to Jesus as their foundation instead of the superficial foundations of the world. Some of the more creative groups were asked to present their plans in front of everyone. In conclusion, we were challenged to go back to our churches and more intentionally design strategies to reach people who did not know Jesus.

While my leaders definitely picked up some valuable ideas and methods to pump up their people, I left the seminar with a deep sadness.

It wasn't because of the new and creative ideas and methods. As an educator I know how important it is to engage the learner in the lesson. My sadness came from the superficiality of the whole learning experience. I was disappointed by the lack of depth relationally, educationally, and theologically. The whole experience left me feeling empty.

Is it possible to be pumped up, yet empty?

The real heartbreaker for me was the superficial and inaccurate way Scripture was used. A more thorough analysis of Matt 7:24–27 within its immediate scriptural context would reveal that Jesus was challenging His audience to a different theme from the one identified by the seminar leader.

(Before reading any further, see for yourself. Answer the question posed by the seminar leader, "What did Jesus use the sand and the rock to represent?" Start reading in v. 13 of chap. 7 to understand a little more of the context of this illustration in vv. 24–28.)

It is clear after studying the context and the specific words Jesus used in vv. 24–27 that to build one's house on the rock had deeper implications than a simple declaration of a belief in Jesus. In vv. 15–20, He challenges His followers to look out for false teachers who will wear sheep's clothing to cover up their real identity as wolves. He concludes the illustration in v. 20 with the statement, "By their fruit you will know them." His point is that we have to be wary of people who claim to be His followers but do not display any evidence in their lives. The issue is deception. In vv. 21–23, Jesus goes on to explain that it is not those who say they follow the Lord who will get into heaven but only those who "do the will of my Father." Jesus' next illustration, of the houses erected on sand and rock, builds on the two previous illustrations. The context reemphasizes the obvious point of the story of the two foundations. There is no stability in simply calling Him "Lord" or doing religious deeds for Him. Rather, security only comes to those who build their homes on the rock, by acting on or putting into practice His words. The central theme of this passage is not simply to believe in Jesus as the rock. Rather, Jesus is challenging superficial believers to understand that the only way they can be secure is not merely by listening to His words but by putting them into practice. Believing in Jesus means listening to Him closely and doing what He says. Even a child can understand this principle.

As Christian educators we must be careful not to distort or water down the message of the Word of God in an attempt to be relevant or overly simplistic.

A generation ago the major problem with biblical teaching was that it often lacked cultural relevance and practical application. In both secular and religious education, content was taught as an end in itself. Wilhoit used the term "transmissive approach" to describe this traditional schooling model of education that "put a high value on the retention of factual information."[1] Yet as a result of the influence of secular educators such as John Dewey and religious educators such as Larry Richards, there has been a shift of focus from content itself to using content to enable students to "make sense out of the world" or, for Christians, to guide them in their Christian pilgrimage.[2] For the most part this shift made

---

[1] Jim Wilhoit, *Christian Education and the Search for Meaning* (Grand Rapids: Baker Book House, 1986), 88.

[2] Ibid., 90.

education more useful and practical by focusing more on process and application. This has been largely positive for the church. It has engaged more students in active learning and applying biblical truth to their lives. Yet, as with any major change, there is a tendency for the shift to go too far. The focus on process to the neglect of content is a shift neither Dewey nor Richards would embrace. Both of them maintained a high value on both content and application. In many Christian education settings, biblical teaching has become too shallow biblically, relationally, and educationally. In an attempt to pander to the needs of busy teachers and students who crave instant gratification, we have abandoned the high biblical standards for "correctly teaching the word of truth" (2 Tim 2:15). In an attempt to be relevant and practical, we have sometimes glossed over the objective facts and principles of the biblical text. In an attempt to produce visible tokens of student learning, we have ignored the need for more lasting fruits of changed character.

To address this problem of superficiality in Christian teaching, I have identified six faulty but commonly held principles that may influence our approach to teaching the Bible within our culture: (1) All fun activity equals good learning. (2) All interaction equals good learning. (3) Keeping students busy is more important than accurately teaching biblical facts and principles. (4) Simple points are more important than biblical depth. (5) Since most people learn through their experience, experience must be the basis of truth. (6) Accomplishing measurable behavioral objectives is more important than changing students' character.

While each of the statements may contain an element of truth, each also contains serious errors that fall short of scriptural teaching standards that will transform a person's heart and life into the likeness of Jesus Christ. These statements may serve as warnings to each of us to evaluate carefully our presuppositions about teaching and learning before we begin to teach.

Partial Truths of Good Learning

1. All Fun Activity Equals Good Learning

While the enjoyment of a learning experience almost always increases the level of student learning, not all fun activity can be equated with good learning. Students can have a good time and learn negative values. Children could have a lot of fun playing a game such as dodgeball, but if a few children were allowed to cheat without being confronted, the overall experience could certainly be negative for many of the participants. It is even possible that the children who had the most fun could be those who were cheating.

Youth pastors often make this mistake in designing fun activities for their students. They sometimes design fun excursions like trips to amusement parks, sports activities, or movies, purely as fun events to attract unchurched students. In themselves these events could be designed as positive learning events. Yet if they are not organized well with biblical goals and objectives, they could easily degenerate into opportunities for the students to learn negative values and behavior. Fun activity is of great value when it affirms biblical principles.

2. All Interaction Equals Good Learning

One of the most positive developments in Christian education in the last 50 years is the growth of small groups. More intimate settings with a smaller group of children, students, or adults allow people of all ages the opportunity to interact and learn more effectively. In order to grow as a disciple of Christ, each believer needs to be connected to a small group of fellow believers in order to confide in others. Yet not all small groups are positive learning environments. Not all interaction, even within a church or parachurch setting, is necessarily positive. Gossip, backbiting, criticism, cockiness, and cliquishness can squelch the learning within a small group. Not all interaction promotes positive learning.

A small group of adults getting together regularly may spend a great deal of time sharing personal concerns and needs, but if the effect of the communication within the group doesn't reinforce biblical values and principles, the learning is more likely to be negative. If what the adult participants take away from their Bible study has no connection to what the text actually says within its grammatical and historical context, they could be seriously deceived. If a group allows its members to gossip repeatedly about other people in the church, they could subtly contradict the principles they profess.

It is not always healthy for a group to get together and simply share their feelings and perceptions about the Bible. If they fail to examine the facts and principles of the biblical text itself, they may fail to learn the truth God has for them in His Word. Recently I was observing a youth group in which the leader divided the large group into several small groups to discuss their observations from the scene of Jesus feeding the five thousand. Their guide was a list of generic questions designed to help the students identify the observations, meanings, and applications from the story. Yet without any real leaders within the groups or an intentional focus of the questions, most of the small groups missed the main point of the whole passage. Little attempt was made before they broke up to guide students toward the most significant discoveries in the text. As a result, the students focused on random details and insights rather than Jesus' main intention in this dramatic event. As valuable as the students' ideas are, little is gained if what they learn has nothing to do with the central meaning of the text. In fact, what they learn may even be contrary to God's Word if it is based on inaccurate observation or interpretation. Inductive group Bible study needs to be structured in some way through the carefully designed questions of a leader or in a written guide to ensure that the participants are moving toward the intended meaning of the text or story. This guidance will help ensure that the participants arrive at a right understanding of the truth of the text. While interaction is necessary for effective learning, it must reinforce biblical values and principles. Heart-deep teaching must go beyond just good discussions and personal sharing.

3. Keeping Students Busy Is More Important Than Accurately Teaching Biblical Facts and Principles

This subtle error in educational practice stems from the mantra of "active learning" that is continually repeated by curriculum guides and trainers. While active learning is extremely important for learners of all ages, it should never minimize the value of the biblical text. In training teachers, I have observed that some spend more time thinking up creative learning activities than they do researching and thinking about the main biblical point they are trying to teach. Many pick a creative, active learning experience related to a theme before studying the biblical text they will use to teach it. As a result, the text often appears to supplement the activity rather than provide the rationale or principle behind the activity. In such cases there is a tendency to alter the biblical text's main idea to fit the illustration or activity.

Teachers and curriculum writers must spend enough time digging deep into the Word of God to discover the necessary facts, principles, and Big Idea of a text before designing creative activities to help their students learn at a heart-deep level. Even then, teachers must assess the outcome of the activity to make sure the students will go away accomplishing the biblical goals of the lesson rather than just focusing on the activity. Student activity, disconnected from principles derived from God's Word, does not result in heart-deep learning.

4. Simple Points Are More Important Than Biblical Depth

With the tantalizing options of technology available today to make presentations clear, concise, simple, and impacting, some teachers are substituting simplistic, predigested points pillaged from the Internet for truths taken from their experiences with God and their personal study of His Word. Sometimes the mystery and ambiguity of God's revelation is sacrificed at the altar of time, language, and text message-patterned attention spans. Without minimizing the educational value of keeping things as simple as possible, simple points should always illuminate rather than hide biblical truth.

Jesus was the master of communicating simple points, yet His simplicity never came at the expense of depth. While each of His parables and stories had a simple Big Idea, His simplicity was never a mask for "dead-end" thinking. Jesus' simplicity served as a "trailhead" to mark the beginning of the path that learners should take to change their hearts, minds, wills, and actions. Jesus' simple stories and pointed challenges served as catalysts for "heart-deep" change rather than simple points to take home and put on a shelf. Take for example Jesus' story of the Good Samaritan. It would have been difficult for people to listen to Jesus tell this simple story and walk away without their hearts being changed. We must never be satisfied with a simple, polished, professional, PowerPoint presentation that impresses our audience without challenging people to a change of heart.

5. Since Most People Learn Through Their Experience, Experience Must Be the Basis of Truth

While most people learn through their experience, the basis of truth is not our experience. Truth is truth whether or not anyone experiences it. It does not mystically become truth through our experience. While it is important for us to experience truth in order to know it personally, the validity of truth does not depend on our experience.

In John 14:6, in response to a question from one of His followers about heaven, Jesus declares, "I am the way, the truth, and the life." Jesus is making an objective statement about the nature of truth: He is the truth. The validity of this statement does not depend on whether people actually experience Jesus. Jesus is the way, the truth, and the life whether anyone follows Him or not. Yet if people are to know truth, they must know and experience Jesus personally. People do not get to heaven by simply acknowledging the fact that Jesus is the way to get there. That would be as absurd as saying an alcoholic could be delivered from his addiction by simply acknowledging that he or she has a problem.

In order to understand this fallacy, we must separate "the nature of truth" from "how we know truth." The "nature of truth" is objective and propositional. Yet "how we know truth" is both objective and subjective. While the nature of God is objective and propositional, knowing God has both objective and subjective experiential elements.

Jesus explains this principle in His response to the many Jews who had begun to follow Him. He says, "If you hold to my teaching, you are really my disciples. Then you will know the truth, and the truth will set you free" (John 8:31–32 NIV). In order to be true disciples of Jesus, we must know the truth personally, a task that demands a personal, experiential response of holding to Jesus' teaching. The result of this deep, heart-motivated response of obedience to Jesus is true freedom. While the basis of truth is objective, knowing truth demands a response that is both objective (He tells us clearly what to do) and subjective (we must do it experientially). Yet the fact that we must experience truth in order to know it does not mean our experience is the basis of truth.

In order to understand the dynamics of heart-deep teaching, we must affirm the value of both objective, propositional truth and the experiential way we come to know truth. Heart-deep teaching depends on both.

6. Accomplishing Measurable Behavioral Objectives Is More Important Than Changing Students' Character

While few teachers would say they believe this statement, their practices in the classroom may prove otherwise. Time restraints, large classes, lack of consistency in teachers, and shallow relationships often make it appear as if all teachers care about is getting the students to accomplish short-term objectives. While short-term, measurable objectives are important, they should never displace the long-term goals of changing character. Intentional "heart-deep teaching" demands that the teacher plan both short- and long-term goals and objectives around the overarching mission of changing students' character.

It is too easy for a high school Sunday school teacher, in a lesson on witnessing, to be satisfied if each of the students shares his or her faith story with one person that week. As good as that accomplishment may be, it must be followed up with a variety of other learning experiences if it is to change the hearts of the students toward their unsaved friends. In the same way, children may be able to draw cute pictures in children's church about helping their parents with the dishes or taking out the garbage, but if they seldom help their parents at home, the exercise has little value.

There is no question about the value of encouraging students of all ages to put into practice the goals and objectives of a lesson. Yet teachers must be intentional about sequencing various learning activities challenging the mind, the emotions, the will, and the actions of their students. Behavioral objectives must never be isolated from the other dimensions of the person that also influence the heart to change. Rather, they need to be integrated with objectives from these other dimensions to produce a change in heart.

Teachers need to plan strategically to use an assortment of short-term and long-term learning activities to accomplish their learning goals and objectives with the ultimate goal of changing the hearts and character of their students. They should never be satisfied with mere external tokens of change.

In this chapter we have identified six faulty principles influencing Christian education practice that contribute to the problem of shallowness in biblical teaching today:

- All fun activity equals good learning.
- All interaction equals good learning.
- Keeping students busy is more important than accurately teaching biblical facts and principles.
- Simple points are more important than biblical depth.
- Since most people learn through their experience, experience must be the basis of truth.
- Accomplishing measurable behavioral objectives is more important than changing students' character.

The solution to this problem of superficiality in teaching is not simply to unload a large quantity of "predigested" content on the students. Rather, the solution demands a return to the biblically based goals of education that focus on transforming the hearts and entire lives of people. **The goal of Christian education must be to transform the heart so that every aspect of the person becomes progressively more Christlike.** Anything less denies the radical transformational power that Christ gave us through His grace and Holy Spirit. Learning must penetrate the surface of the mind, the emotions, the will, and behavior. Heart-deep teaching must affect the innermost core of the person.

Application Questions

1. Identify an experience you have encountered related to each of these common yet faulty principles of teaching the Bible:

All fun activity equals good learning.

All interaction equals good learning.

Keeping students busy is more important than accurately teaching biblical facts and principles.

Simple points are more important than biblical depth.

Since most people learn through their experience, experience must be the basis of truth.

Accomplishing measurable behavioral objectives is more important than changing students' character.

2. What are some of the causes of superficiality in biblical teaching in our culture?

3. How would you characterize the depth of biblical teaching you have experienced at the different stages of your life from childhood until the present?

4. Identify and describe a Bible teacher from whom you learned much and under whose teaching you experienced life change.

5. How would you characterize the level of biblical and personal depth at which you normally teach?

6. What would you need to change in your life and ministry in order to teach at a deeper level and to reflect a stronger personal commitment to biblical truth?

PART II

PREPARING THE HEART OF THE TEACHER

The most important part of teaching a lesson from the Bible is preparation. If teachers fail to prepare their hearts to teach, they will be ineffective in partnering with the Holy Spirit in influencing students' lives. As we will soon discover, the biblical concept of the heart includes the mind, emotions, will, and actions. When teachers fail to prepare each aspect of their hearts at the deepest possible level before teaching, they risk coming across to others as merely a tinkling bell.

Chapter 2

Understanding the Mystery of the Heart

Most people define the "heart" based on a popular view gleaned from television, movies, songs, or even sermons. It is usually thought to be closely related to the emotional center of the personality. The heart is said to be "touched" when people see a tear–jerking movie, listen to a challenging sermon, hear a passionate story, remember an empathetic experience from the past, or experience a traumatic event. People speak of moving information from the head to the heart, as if data travel through the channels of our minds for a while before mysteriously infiltrating our emotions. We want to explore that mystery in this chapter. We will attempt to study the heart from a biblical, theological, and philosophical perspective with particular attention to the nature of the person, the role of God's Word, and the essence of the process of discipleship.

Use of the Term *Heart* in Scripture

Throughout the Old and New Testaments the term *heart* represents the innermost part of the whole person, including the core of a person's emotions, volition, thinking, and intention. While different passages and contexts in Scripture may focus on one of these aspects of the heart over another, there is no warrant to limit the term *heart* in Scripture to the emotions.

Hebrew View of the "Heart"

The Hebrew mind-set does not make the radical distinctions the later Greek philosophers made between the various faculties within the person. While the OT uses "heart" both literally and metaphorically, it primarily refers to the whole person.

When used in a literal sense, the heart is the source of strength and life (Ps 38:10; Isa 1:5). When the heart is strengthened, the person is rejuvenated, as demonstrated in Gen 18:5 when Abraham feeds and encourages the three visitors from heaven. The text literally says that the bread would strengthen or sustain their "hearts" (Gen 18:5). Yet the term "hearts" refers here to their whole persons, not simply a specialized part of them. When a person's heart is strengthened, the whole person is revitalized.[1]

Even when used in a metaphorical sense in Hebrew Scripture, the heart is viewed as the "seat of man's feeling, thinking, and willing." A whole range of dynamic feelings of joy, pain, peace, and excitement is attributed to the heart (Deut 19:6; 28:47; Jer 4:19; Prov 14:30). A wide range of knowledge and understanding also originates in the heart (1 Kgs 3:12). That includes both good and bad and concrete and speculative thinking (Prov 10:20; Jer 4:19). The will or intentions of man also come from the heart (1 Kgs 8:17; Exod 36:2). Actions, whether good or evil, proceed from the heart. It is clear from the OT that the heart is the deepest place within the person where thoughts, feelings, decisions, and attitudes originate.[2]

When Moses challenged the Hebrew people to "love the LORD your God with all your heart, and with all your soul, and with all your might" (Deut 6:5), he was not emphasizing three distinct parts of the person. Rather, he was stating a fundamental principle of what God expects of each of His chosen people. God commands His followers to love Him with the whole self. The words "heart," "soul," and "might" represent different, overlapping aspects of the person, all focusing on the principle of the complete self. The Hebrew words had different meanings than we give them in contemporary language. Warren Wiersbe explains how these different aspects of the self, mentioned by both Moses and Jesus, focus on the essence of the person. *Heart* encompassed the deepest aspect of the whole person including feelings, will, and intellect. *Soul* was the name used to label an organism that was alive and breathing. *Might* referred to superlative effort or diligence in applying oneself to a goal.

---

[1] Colin Brown and Lothar Coenen, *The New International Dictionary of New Testament Theology*, 3 vols. (Exeter, Devon, U.K.: Paternoster Press, 1975), 114.

[2] Ibid., 181.

The use of these three terms together described the multidimensional ways in which we are to love God. We are to love Him with every faculty within us, with all of our lives, and with all diligence. When Moses explained next that "these words that I am giving you today are to be in your heart" (Deut 6:6), he used the term *heart* not in order to distinguish it from *soul* and *strength* but rather to emphasize that our love for God should be embedded at the core of our being. *Heart* was understood to be the deepest and most comprehensive term for everything we are and all that we have.[3]

Jesus' Use of "Heart"

Jesus reinforced this principle by His lifestyle and teaching. When asked by the expert in the law what he must do to inherit eternal life, Jesus replied, "Love the Lord your God with all your heart, with all your soul, and with all your strength, and with all your mind; and your neighbor as yourself" (Luke 10:27). By restating Moses' ancient command to the people of Israel, Jesus was emphasizing that His message was based on the teaching of Moses. Just as Moses expected followers of Yahweh to love Him with everything that made up who they were as people, so did Jesus. The lawyer's attempt to justify himself with his self-righteous attitude simply reflected how far he and the nation of Israel had fallen short of God's requirement. The story of the good Samaritan graphically showed how offtrack the lawyer and the religious leaders of his day were. Through this simple story, Jesus demonstrated what deep, heart-based faith in God involves.

Much of Jesus' teaching focused on explaining and illustrating this "heart-deep faith." In an attempt to contrast "heart-deep faith" with the teachings of the religious leaders of His day, Jesus often prefaced His comments and stories with, "You have heard that it was said, . . . But I tell you . . ." (Matt 5:43–44). Jesus would then go on to explain God's brand of "true spirituality," to use Francis Schaeffer's term.[4] Godly spirituality is rooted in the deepest core of the person: the heart.

Throughout the Sermon on the Mount, Jesus explained this deeper level of spirituality as an inner transformation affecting outward lifestyle. His teaching focused on the transformation of the heart. Those who were pure in heart were blessed (Matt 5:8), while those who fantasized in their hearts (lusted) about adulterous acts had already "committed adultery . . . in [their hearts]" (Matt 5:28).

---

[3] Warren W. Wiersbe, *The Bible Exposition Commentary: Old Testament* (Seattle: Biblesoft), Commandment V. 5.

[4] Francis A. Schaeffer, *True Spirituality* (Wheaton, IL: Tyndale House, 1971).

Jesus taught that actions, whether good or bad, flow out of the heart (Matt 12:34; 15:18–19; Luke 6:45). Yet He observed that some people honored Him with their lips while their hearts were far from God (Matt 15:8–9). Jesus used the term "hard-hearted" to describe both His enemies and followers at times when they refused to understand and respond to Him at a deep, heart level (Mark 8:17; 16:14; John 12:40). He taught that Satan is actively influencing people at the deep, heart level when they refuse to understand or obey God's Word (Matt 13:19; John 13:2). On the positive side Jesus challenged His disciples not to allow their hearts to be troubled or become fearful when difficulties come (John 14:1,27). He expected His followers to apply His teaching to change even the way they dealt with the inevitable disappointments of life. This transformation was to radiate from the inner core of their mind, emotions, and intentions to affect their behavior and lifestyle.

Paul's Use of "Heart"

Paul follows Jesus in His use of the term *heart*. He does not equate the heart primarily with the emotional side of the person. In fact, as R. K. Bultmann points out, the Greek term used for *heart* was translated not only to "heart" but also to "mind." The term often meant "heart" and "mind" synonymously. Paul used the term more accurately translated as "the self as a willing, planning, intending self."[5] This holistic definition of the heart is seen clearly in Paul's explanation of why the Jewish leaders were deceived in the way they looked at Jesus: "But their *minds* were closed. For to this day, at the reading of the old covenant, the same veil remains; it is not lifted, because it is set aside only in Christ. Even to this day, whenever Moses is read, a veil lies over their *hearts*" (2 Cor 3:14–15, emphasis added). The fact that their lack of understanding was found in both their minds and hearts shows the close connection of these aspects of the person.

Paul often used these two terms as almost parallel in content. When Paul describes the downward moral slide of the Gentiles in Romans 1 and 2, he relates it to both mind and heart (Rom 1:28; 2:5). In a similar way Paul described both mind and heart as being hardened (Rom 1:28; 16:18; 2 Cor 4:4; 11:3). When discussing the solution to the fate of the sinful person, Paul explained that both heart and mind must be illuminated or transformed (Rom 12:1,2; 2 Cor 4:6). Rather than focusing on the radical distinctions between these two faculties, Paul emphasized their complementary nature. The heart

---

    [5] Rudolf Karl Bultmann, *Theology of the New Testament* (New York: Scribner, 1951), 220.

involves a dynamic interplay between the various components of the person. It is certainly not used by Paul to imply a radical dichotomy from the mind.[6]

Light can be shed on Paul's use of the term *heart* by examining how he used the Greek term *nous*, translated as *understanding* or *mind*. Yet, "in English there is really no equivalent for '*nous*.'"[7] It was used not so much as the cognitive center of the person but rather as the center of one's *acting*. *Mind* is not an abstract faculty that can be defined by its physical or mental capacities alone; rather it is the deepest place within the person where God reveals Himself and man initiates his reflections and actions. By definition the transformation of the mind necessitates a transformation of the whole person including emotions, affections, and behavior. The *mind*, according to Paul, was used in a similar way to how *heart* was used, as the determiner of behavior and action. In this way, *heart* and *mind* overlap in their function. Paul saw the *heart*, or the innermost part of the person, involving an intimate connection of understanding, will, soul, spirit, and conscience. Rather than a separate part of the person, the heart represents the person in his thinking, feeling, and choosing. The heart, mind, and will are interconnected in the term *heart* in Paul's writings and throughout the NT.[8]

Paul does not set forth a belief that there are two distinct aspects of the person, the inner and the outer man, but rather that the person is made up of both the inner and the outer man. Instead of presenting a dichotomous view of the person, Paul emphasizes the need for both the inner and the outer man to be filled with the Spirit and to be under submission to the lordship of Christ.

Ridderbos explains this connection between inner man and outer man as related to two ways sin affects a person's life, as found in Romans 1, Ephesians 4, and Rom 7:14–25:

> First of all, the corruption of sin in the "inner man," the "nous," the "heart," which from there extends itself in the (sinful acts of the) "outer man," in his "body," and his "members." With the second idea the reverse sequence is in the foreground; the external man, the body, the members, appear to have been brought under the control of sin in such a way that the inner man, too (the nous, the heart, the will), is unable to offer resistance to the superior power of sin in the body.[9]

---

[6] Ibid., 220.

[7] Herman N. Ridderbos, *Paul: An Outline of His Theology* (Grand Rapids: Eerdmans, 1975), 117–19.

[8] Ibid.

[9] Ibid., 114.

While there may be differences between the inner and the outer man, sin can be introduced in either or both. The same is true with righteousness. Just as thoughts, feelings, inclinations, or reflections about good or bad could be initiated through the inner man, they also could be initiated through the external environment as perceived by the faculties of the outer man. Hebrew religious education revolved around a balance of these two elements of the person. While the Hebrews were challenged to love the Lord their God with all their heart, soul, strength, and mind, they were also immersed in a community and culture designed to reinforce those same godly values. When this balance between the inner and outer person was distorted, the process of religious education broke down. When devotion to God became merely external and ritualistic, God was displeased, challenging them to return to a "heart-based" faith. True religion was intended to be a passion of the heart expressing itself in both holiness and social justice. Both the internal and external aspects of the person were essential to Paul.[10]

The concept of "heart-deep" teaching presupposes that the goal of teaching is to affect the deepest part of the person. This change in turn will influence every aspect of the person. While it is possible to dissect the various aspects of the person and to analyze each part, we must be careful not to focus on one aspect over the unity of the whole person. Since God looks at the person as a whole, we too must view the person as a whole.

Too often the church has failed to teach biblical truth in a way that emphasizes its multidimensional nature designed to influence the whole person: emotions, volition, mind, and behavior. A shallow view of truth which simply transmits biblical or theological facts and principles falls short of transforming the heart of the person.

Other NT Writers' Use of "Heart"

Other NT writers reinforce the meanings for the term *heart* that we found in Paul's writings. One of the clearest statements about the centrality of the heart is found in Heb 4:12, "For the word of God is . . . sharper than any double-edged sword, penetrating as far as the separation of soul, and spirit, joints and marrow. It is able to judge the ideas and thoughts of the heart."

In discussing the impact of God's Word within the person, the author of Hebrews describes His Word as cutting through the biological and philosophical dichotomies of the person to deal with what is really going on at the core of the person. Rather than focusing on *emotions*, the author emphasizes *ideas* and

---

[10] Ibid.

thoughts when using the term *heart* in this context. The heart is the place deep within the person where motives, intentions, thoughts, and passions germinate into actions (Heb 4:12–13).

Often, when I read Scripture, I sense the Holy Spirit cutting through the outer layers of my heart to get me to see something I have never seen before. Just yesterday, when I was having my quiet time with the Lord, the Spirit convicted me from Psalm 109 of my lack of prayerfulness. Within the context of the psalm, while David is lamenting the fact that his enemies are tormenting him, he characterizes himself a man of prayer. As I reflected on that psalm and David's defense before God and his enemies as a "man of prayer," I wondered whether I could honestly consider myself a man of prayer. The more I thought about David's character and steadfastness in the midst of persecution, the more I became aware of my own need to make prayer a more central part of my life. As a result, I have been committed not only to spending more time in prayers of praise to God but also to be bolder in my prayers for other people during the day. When the Holy Spirit convicts through His Word, He affects our intellect, our emotions, our wills, and our actions. He changes our hearts.

In Rev 2:23, John uses the term *heart* in a similar way, showing the close connection between one's heart and one's intelligence and will.[11] Here the Son of God is presented as the One who "examines" people's minds and hearts and gives people what they deserve based on what they have done. *Heart* is intimately connected to cognition, volition, and behavior. Similar to the Hebrew text, God is seen as the judge with penetrating eyes gazing deep within the person to evaluate his real identity. His judgment takes into account the thoughts of the heart and its expression in action.

A dangerous tendency within some theological systems separates beliefs in the mind from actions of the body. Some even go as far as to say that salvation has nothing to do with our actions since it depends totally on what we believe. This dogma is based on the fundamental doctrine of justification by grace alone through faith. Yet while our works have no instrumental value in securing our salvation, true belief will eventually result in more Christlike behavior. While we can do nothing to merit our salvation, Scripture teaches that our response to God in salvation involves every part of our person: our minds, emotions, will, and behavior. The fundamental doctrine of grace alone must be applied to the whole person. It is dangerous to base salvation on a false dichotomy related to the nature of the person. Does Scripture separate the

---

[11] Cleon Rogers Jr. and Cleon Rogers III, *The New Linguistic and Exegetical Key to the Greek New Testament* (Grand Rapids: Zondervan, 1998), 619.

mind from the heart, will, and actions? Does transformation only affect the mind? Does the gift of salvation by the Father through His Son only regenerate the mind? Does God's grace not transform the innermost part of the whole person in salvation? Should not salvation be expected to transform the inner core of the person and behavior?

NT writers use the term *heart* to depict the deepest part of the person, the inner man, or what others call "the real person." In the NT the heart is the place at the core of the person where the most important dynamics of one's life originate. Thoughts, understandings, desires, perceptions, reasoning, imaginations, intentions, conviction, purpose, meaning, and faith all have their roots in the heart. True transformation of the heart affects every part of the person including behavior and lifestyle.

Henri Nouwen reaffirms the nature of the heart as the center of our quest for intimacy with God. In a thoughtful book, *The Way of the Heart*, Nouwen suggests that understanding the nature of the heart and submitting the heart to God are at the core of both intimacy with the Father and effectiveness in ministry.

> From the heart arise unknowable impulses as well as conscious feelings, moods, and wishes. The heart, too, has its reasons and is the center of perception and understanding. Finally, the heart is the seat of the will: it makes plans and comes to good decisions. Thus the heart is the central and unifying organ of our personal life.
>
> Our heart determines our personality, and is therefore not only the place where God dwells but also the place to which Satan directs his fiercest attacks.[12]

From a theological perspective the heart is where spiritual action takes place. As the center of the person, the heart is where God connects with humankind and humankind reciprocates. The heart is the seat of prayer and power for ministry.

Philosophical Insights on the Heart

Philosophers, as well as theologians, have much to contribute to the question of the nature of the heart. They have wrestled with the complex issues relating to the nature of the person and the dynamics of how the various components

---

[12] Henri J. M. Nouwen, *The Way of the Heart: Desert Spirituality and Contemporary Ministry* (New York: Seabury Press, 1981).

of the person relate to one another. The insights of Dallas Willard in his book *Renovation of the Heart* seem particularly relevant to the purpose of this book.[13]

As a philosopher, Willard explains what he considers to be an orderly process by which the heart of every believer in Jesus Christ can be transformed into the likeness of Christ. His insights on this process may prove helpful not only to encourage personal growth but also to guide us as heart-deep teachers.

Willard begins with a fundamental assumption that one's destiny depends on what goes on in one's heart. "What is in our 'heart' matters more than anything else for who we become and what becomes of us."[14] Whether a person believes in God or not, his heart affects everything else about him. This characteristic makes the person humanly distinct from the rest of God's creation. The inner heart forms volitional intentions that influence actions. When God has His home in the center of one's heart, one's whole life is transformed into His likeness. Willard defines this as the process of spiritual formation. This pilgrimage toward Christlikeness, however, is not something we earn by good works or human effort but rather by God's grace. Yet our participation and diligence in pursuing the process of growth are not antithetical to grace. Our initiative in obedience works hand in hand with God's grace. As Willard explains:

> This, I freely admit, is contrary to a view of grace as passivity that is widely held now. But the God-ordained order of the soul under grace must be discovered, respected, and cooperated with, if its God-intended results for spiritual growth are to be attained.[15]

As long as human diligence and God's grace are held as antithetical assumptions in the process of spiritual formation, spiritual growth will be hindered. Willard's model of "the renovation of the heart" is grounded on the principle that people will find God only when they seek Him with their whole hearts.

According to Willard, the heart is the place deep within us, at the core of our being, "from which outlook, choices, and actions come."[16] The terms *heart*, *spirit*, and *will* all refer to the same component within the person while describing different aspects.

Will refers to that component's power to initiate, to create, to bring about what did not exist before. *Spirit* refers to its fundamental nature as distinct and

---

[13] Dallas Willard, *Renovation of the Heart: Putting on the Character of Christ* (Colorado Springs: NavPress, 2002), 41.

[14] Ibid., 16.

[15] Ibid., 25.

[16] Ibid., 14.

independent from physical reality. And *heart* refers to its position in the human being, as center or core to which every other component of the self owes its proper functioning.[17]

When people become followers of Christ, they essentially make a decision from the center of their beings to give their whole selves to Christ. This decision from the heart or will involves every aspect of the person. Both Luke 10:25–28 and Ps 16:7–9 emphasize this multidimensional nature of a commitment to love God with all one's heart, soul, mind, emotions, and strength and to love our neighbors as ourselves. Willard points out that Scripture clarifies the perceived mystery of the nature of the person by explaining the components of this process of spiritual transformation. He identifies six basic aspects of human nature:

1. Thought (images, concepts, judgments, inferences)
2. Feeling (sensation, emotion)
3. Choice (will, decision, character)
4. Body (action, interaction with the physical world)
5. Social context (personal and structural relations with others)
6. Soul (the factor that integrates all of the above to form one life)[18]

By aligning these six dimensions of life with God's purposes, a person will grow and become Christlike in character and action. Only as the "heart" is committed to love and submit to Christ will life transformation happen.[19]

Willard emphasizes the integration of the various components of the person revolving around the love of God. As a person seeks God with his whole heart, he becomes more and more aligned with the will of God. As a person commits his will and disciplines his thoughts around God's revealed Word, character changes. The transformed heart motivates behavioral change which in turn influences the people and the environment around the person.

Although the *person* could be described in many different ways, we will represent it as being made up of at least four aspects: intellect, emotions, volition, and behavior. The center, where they all intersect, will be defined as the heart of the person. The heart is the place where the deepest changes are made in all other aspects of the person. The heart is where the deepest learning takes place, resulting in transformation. Transformational changes, by definition, are understood as interconnected, integrated, and overlapping with cognitive,

---

[17] Ibid., 29.
[18] Ibid., 30.
[19] Ibid., 39–41.

emotional, volitional, and behavioral functions of the person. Such an understanding of the nature of the person seems most consistent with the principles from God's Word.

The Role of God's Word in Illuminating the Heart

As mysterious as the human heart may seem to us, Scripture clearly explains the process of how we are to nurture a pure, malleable heart for God. As Willard points out, the problem is not that the heart is so mysterious but that we so often fail to follow God's guidelines related to cultivating a heart for God.

Early in life I learned this principle the hard way. When I was a sophomore in college, I bought my first car: a tiny French 304 Peugeot. While it looked somewhat cool, how it worked was always a mystery to me. Even the European symbols on the dashboard baffled me as to what they represented. Yet in my idealistic naïveté, I never studied the auto manual to find out what the symbols meant or what needed to be done to the car for regular maintenance. I figured that I could just learn that on my own. While I did eventually learn my lesson, it came at the expense of a blown transmission and engine. What was a mystery to me was clear in the manual. Since the same oil was used for both the engine and the transmission in this model, it was absolutely necessary to change the oil every 1,500 miles. I realized that the problem was not the mystery of the Peugeot but rather my naïve self-sufficiency.

One of the clearest passages of Scripture explaining how to nurture a malleable heart for God is found in the first four chapters of Hebrews. After establishing Christ's superiority over every created being in chapters 1 and 2, the author goes on in chapters 3 and 4 to explain how we can maintain a soft heart toward Him. The warnings throughout chapters 3 and 4, "not to harden your hearts," are accompanied by a series of principles instructing us how, including: Hear His voice and soften your heart (3:15), combine hearing with faith (4:2), hear and believe (4:3), do not disobey Him (4:6), and make every effort to enter that rest (4:11). These principles point to the fact that in order to maintain a soft heart toward the Lord we must listen to what God says, believe, and do what He says.

These first four chapters culminate in the statement in Heb 4:12:

> For the word of God is living and effective and sharper than any double-edged sword, penetrating as far as to the separation of soul and spirit, joints and marrow. It is able to judge the ideas and thoughts of the heart. No creature is hidden from Him, but all things are naked and exposed to the eyes of Him who to whom we must give account.

In this text God's Word is the means by which we maintain a soft heart toward God. If we listen to, reflect on, and obey God's Word, the Holy Spirit will cut through every part of our being to reveal and judge the innermost thoughts, ideas, and intentions of our hearts. As we become more and more open to the scrutiny of God's Word, His presence motivates and empowers us to obey His Word in our daily lives.

When we are tempted to become discouraged or humiliated by our own failures and disobedience, God's Word gives us a reason not to hide from God's gaze. As the author of Hebrews explains:

> Therefore, since we have a great high priest who has passed through the heavens—Jesus the Son of God—let us hold fast to the confession. For we do not have a high priest who is unable to sympathize with our weaknesses, but One who has been tested in every way as we are, yet without sin. Therefore let us approach the throne of grace with boldness, so that we may receive mercy and find grace to help us at the proper time. (Heb 4:14–16)

The sting of the purging sword of God the Father's gaze and His Word is buffeted by the gracious intercession of God's Son who understands firsthand our deepest struggles. This objective fact, relating to the character of the Godhead, gives the believer absolute confidence in opening the depths of his heart to God.

The Role of the Holy Spirit in the Teaching and Learning Process[20]

When most people sink their teeth into a soft slice of bread, they seldom take the time to reflect on the process of how the bread was made. Even if they can identify the sweet aroma of the yeast, they probably will not stop to appreciate the central role of that yeast in the bread-making process.

So it is with the Holy Spirit. Although He is the major catalyst to the educational process of learning and growing toward Christlikeness, the Holy Spirit's role is often ignored or, at the least, taken for granted. "The often neglected person in the teaching-learning process is actually the most important."[21]

---

[20] Gary C. Newton, "The Holy Spirit in the Educational Process," in Michael J. Anthony, *Introducing Christian Education: Foundations for the Twenty-first Century* (Grand Rapids: Baker Academic, 2001), 125–29. Used by permission.

[21] C. Fred Dickason, "The Holy Spirit in Education," in *Christian Education: Foundations for the Future*, ed. Robert E. Clark, Lin Johnson, and Allyn K. Sloat (Chicago: Moody, 1991), 121.

Without understanding and actively seeking the Holy Spirit's cooperation in our teaching, our efforts will fall short of raising up godly men and women who display the fruits of Christlikeness. A. W. Tozer makes this point in this timeless statement: "For the gospel is often preached and accepted without power, and the radical shift which the truth demands is never made. . . . The 'creature' is changed but he is not new."[22] Without intentionally cooperating with the Holy Spirit in the teaching-learning process, teachers will fail to accomplish spiritual results. In order to take advantage of the Holy Spirit in the teaching-learning process, we need to understand who He is, His role in the educational process, and how He works through the various aspects of the learning experience.

Who Is He?

In order to understand the significance of the Holy Spirit in the educational process, we must come to an understanding and appreciation of His distinctive nature as the Third Person of the Trinity. While He possesses all the attributes of God, He has a distinctive role and purpose.

Jesus introduces us to the Holy Spirit as teacher in John 14:26: "But the Helper, the Holy Spirit, whom the Father will send in My name, He will teach you all things, and bring to your remembrance all that I said to you." Jesus goes on to say that when "the Spirit of truth comes, He will guide you into all the truth; for He will not speak on His own initiative, but whatever He hears, He will speak; and He will disclose to you what is to come. He will glorify Me; for He will take of Mine, and shall disclose it to you" (John 16:13–14 NASB).

The Gospels refer to Jesus as teacher over seventy times, and "teaching was a major component of his ministry on earth."[23] After Jesus ascended to the Father, the Holy Spirit took on a similar role as teacher in the lives of the disciples. Following Pentecost, when the Holy Spirit was given to the church, His role became central in teaching the disciples and reminding them of all the things Jesus taught them during His earthly ministry. His teaching role would be of primary importance to the growth and health of the body of Christ. His ministry expanded Jesus' ministry to any of His disciples willing to be filled with His presence and power. Not limited by time or space, the Spirit can work in many places at the same time. He is able to fill each believer and develop an intimate relationship with His followers in every age. Intimacy with the Holy Spirit draws a person into an intimate relationship with Jesus Christ. The Holy

---

[22] Roy B. Zuck, *Teaching as Jesus Taught* (Grand Rapids: Baker Books, 1995); A. W. Tozer, *The Divine Conquest* (Bromley: STL, 1979), 34.

[23] Zuck, *Teaching as Jesus Taught*, 24.

Spirit testifies on behalf of the Son and brings glory to Jesus Christ through His words and actions.

Roy Zuck, in his book *Spirit-filled Teaching*, identifies six titles given to the Holy Spirit that directly relate to His ministry of teaching. We will examine five of these names to help us understand the nature of the Holy Spirit as a teacher: the "Spirit of wisdom and understanding, Spirit of counsel and power, Spirit of knowledge and the fear of the Lord, Spirit of truth, and Counselor."[24] The first three titles are introduced in Isa 11:2 in describing the Spirit that rested on Jesus during His earthly ministry. The other two are identified by Jesus. As we examine these titles given to the Holy Spirit, our goal will be to discover specific aspects of His identity that make Him such a great teacher. His role as a teacher is intimately connected to His identity as a person.

The Spirit of Wisdom and Understanding. This first title given to the Holy Spirit relates to His intellectual capabilities. The Hebrew word used here for *wisdom* means "skill, experience or expertise," and the word for *understanding* means "discernment and perception."[25] The deep intellectual capabilities of the Holy Spirit are not primarily esoteric but relate to practical, everyday situations and problems. The Holy Spirit brings God's insights and discernment to the ordinary decisions and problems we face. Because of His nature as God, He alone is the ultimate source of wisdom and understanding for humankind.

The Spirit of Counsel and Power. The second title in Isa 11:2 is the "Spirit of counsel and power." This name reflects His identity as not only the One who is the ultimate source of advice but also the One who empowers His people to put His advice into practice. As the teacher today, the Holy Spirit provides humankind with unlimited resources for both of these needs.

The Spirit of Knowledge and the Fear of the Lord. Knowledge and fear of God are closely linked throughout Scripture. The Holy Spirit's character models the intimate connection. The Holy Spirit has been an inseparable member of the Trinity from eternity past. His knowledge of the Father and the Son is based on an intimate relationship involving both objective and subjective elements. The Spirit not only knows everything there is to know about the Father but also knows Him personally and experientially. While the nature and character of God the Father and the Son are objective and never change, the Spirit's relationship to the other two persons in the Trinity is both passionate

---

[24] Roy B. Zuck and Charles R. Swindoll, *Spirit-Filled Teaching: The Power of the Holy Spirit in Your Ministry*, Swindoll Leadership Library (Nashville: Word Publishing, 1998), 12.

[25] Ibid.

and intimate. This provides a perfect model of the relationship we can have with the Father and the Son today.[26]

The close connection between the knowledge of God and the fear of God is seen most clearly in Prov 1:7: "The fear of the LORD is the beginning of knowledge." A distinctive of the Hebrews' religion in comparison with that of the Greeks was their close association between the fear of God and the love of God.[27] To the Hebrews there was no dichotomy between a healthy respect for God and drawing close to Him in a loving relationship. An intimate relationship and knowledge of God are reserved only for those willing to respect Him as the sovereign Lord. Once again the Holy Spirit represents the perfect manifestation of this respectful relationship.

The Spirit of Truth. This fourth title given to the Holy Spirit related to His role as an educator is found in John 14:17; 15:26; and 16:13. The fact that Jesus introduced Him to His disciples as the Spirit of truth emphasizes the Holy Spirit's role as the source of truth. This would be especially significant for His followers after the ascension since the leader they depended on as "the way, the truth, and the life" was no longer with them. Again in John 15:26, Jesus prophesies that the Spirit of truth will "testify about Me." A major part of the Holy Spirit's role would be to bear witness to the truth about Jesus and to lead the disciples into all truth. The truth that Jesus speaks of here is objective, based in Himself and His Father. The Holy Spirit testifies to this objective truth. This stands in stark contrast with the prevailing educational philosophy of this age, which defines the Holy Spirit as our inner light that reveals subjective truth within each individual.[28] Contrary to the popular belief that the Holy Spirit's voice is primarily a subjective expression of a person's inner spirit, the Bible teaches that the Holy Spirit represents an objective manifestation of the truth of God that never contradicts biblical truth. While the Spirit often expresses Himself in subjective ways within an individual, His voice can be tested as to its authenticity by comparing it with truth from the Word of God in Scripture. The Holy Spirit's teaching never contradicts God's objective revelation of Scripture.

The Counselor. The fifth name given to the Holy Spirit in relation to His ministry of teaching is that of Counselor, Helper, or Encourager (John 14:16,

---

[26] Henry T. Blackaby and Claude V. King, *Experiencing God: How to Live the Full Adventure of Knowing and Doing the Will of God* (Nashville: Broadman & Holman Publishers, 1994), 172–73.

[27] Colin Brown, *The New International Dictionary of New Testament Theology*, 3 vols. (Grand Rapids: Zondervan, 1975), 1:621–24.

[28] Marianne Williamson, *Illuminata: A Return to Prayer*, 1st Riverhead ed. (New York: Riverhead Books, 1995), 74–75.

26; 15:26; 16:7; 1 John 2:1). This role of the Holy Spirit in teaching lies at the core of the transformational process of learning. The Spirit not only speaks truth to His students but also comes alongside the learner initiating a personal, empathetic relationship. People are most receptive to truth when the teacher is both understanding and encouraging. This balance, between speaking truth and empathetic relationship, is a major factor in the Holy Spirit's effectiveness as a teacher.

By examining Scripture, we can identify several significant aspects of His nature and role as a counselor. The first major text relating to the role of the Holy Spirit as a counselor is found in John 14:16–17, where Jesus states, "I will ask the Father, and He will give you another Counselor to be with you forever. He is the Spirit of truth." The implication here is that the coming Holy Spirit will be a counselor to His followers just as Jesus was. Continuing in the same discourse, Jesus states in John 14:26 that "the Counselor, the Holy Spirit—the Father will send Him in My name—will teach you all things and remind you of everything I have told you." Jesus states a similar idea in John 15:26: "When the Counselor comes, whom I will send to you from the Father, the Spirit of truth who goes out from the Father, he will testify about me" (NIV). Jesus makes clear that the Counselor comes from the Father in the name of Jesus to represent the truth taught by Jesus. There is no room in Scripture for the false notion that the Spirit represents an independent testimony of truth revealed within an individual. The Spirit's advice and teaching come from the Father and represent the person and work of Christ.

This passage mentions at least two functions of the Holy Spirit as Counselor. He will teach the disciples "all things" and remind them of everything Jesus said to them while He was with them. Zuck suggests that the "all things" to which Jesus was referring did not include all truth wherever it could be found. That would eliminate all need for human teachers. Rather he states:

> They are all truths pertaining to God and His person and work. Knowledge of God and the full body of revealed truth is imparted by the Spirit to those Christians who are spiritually receptive to His teaching. "All the truth" (as the Greek literally reads) is not encyclopedic truth in general but all *revealed* truth, recorded in God's written word.[29]

For the disciples Jesus was addressing, "all things" probably referred to everything they needed to know to live a godly life.

---

[29] Zuck and Swindoll, *Spirit-Filled Teaching*, 24.

The fact that the Counselor would *teach* them all things implies not only the dissemination of information but also a process of helping the disciples understand and apply truth to their daily lives. As a counselor, the Holy Spirit would play a vital role in the subjective process of encouraging, helping, explaining, and coaching disciples, first to be open to the truth and then to grow in obedience to the truth. There is a close connection between teaching and counseling in the ministry of the Holy Spirit.

The second role of the Counselor is closely related to His role of teaching His disciples all things. Jesus said that the Counselor would also remind them of everything He had said while He was with them. What Jesus had in mind here was that the Holy Spirit would remind His early followers what He had taught them. While the disciples recorded many of Jesus' sayings as He spoke them, some of His teachings were recorded at a later time. The supernatural work of the Holy Spirit reminded the disciples of the actual words Jesus spoke to them and to the crowds. An accurate transmission of the words and sayings of Jesus would become the foundation of the teaching of the church. In a secondary sense the Holy Spirit could serve later generations of disciples by reminding them of the teachings of Jesus based on God's Word as it is recorded in Scripture. The Holy Spirit plays a vital role in the lives of Christ's followers today by reminding them of the principles and teachings of Scripture as they go through the normal activities of life. In this role the Counselor not only reminds the believer what to do but also encourages the believer to do the right thing.

Erroneous Conceptions of How the Holy Spirit Works as the Teacher

While it is obvious from Scripture that teaching is one of the major roles of the Holy Spirit, the process of *how* He teaches may not be so clear. By misunderstanding the process of how the Holy Spirit works, we risk misusing or failing to use the transformational power of God to change lives. Zuck identifies four erroneous concepts of how the Holy Spirit works in the teaching-learning process.[30] Becoming aware of these errors will enable us to identify false assumptions before they become ingrained in our patterns of thinking and ministry.

Human Teachers Are Unnecessary. This false view holds that since the Holy Spirit illuminates every believer individually, there is no need for us to be taught by a human teacher. This false idea comes from a misinterpretation of 1 John 2:26–27, which states:

---

[30] Ibid., 48–53.

> I am writing these things to you about those who are trying to lead you astray. As for you, the anointing you received from him remains in you, and you do not need anyone to teach you. But as his anointing teaches you about all things and as that anointing is real, not counterfeit—just as it has taught you, remain in him. (NIV)

Without studying the immediate context of these verses or looking at other biblical texts, one might come to the erroneous conclusion that because we have the Holy Spirit as our personal teacher, we don't need other teachers. Yet we must realize that John is writing to believers who are being seduced by false teachers promoting gnostic philosophical ideas. Instead of listening to these seductive false teachers, John tells the Christians to rely on the Holy Spirit's teaching, based on the objective testimony of Jesus' life and teachings. The same advice would be relevant today in a situation in which teachers were proclaiming doctrine contradicting the teaching of Scripture. "Though God uses human teachers, the learners must be sure their teachers are not counterfeit or false, and must remember that their divine teacher is the Holy Spirit."[31]

The Spirit Works Best When We Wing It. This erroneous view seems to be popular with teachers and ministers who don't like to plan ahead. Sometimes it becomes a way of spiritualizing laziness or a lack of preparation. A commonly used proof text for this view is Matt 10:19–20 NIV: "But when they arrest you, do not worry about what to say or how to say it. At that time you will be given what to say, for it will not be you speaking but the Spirit of your Father speaking through you." If this principle is generalized without looking at the immediate context, it could be taken to mean that we should not worry about what we are to say when we teach but rather just let the Spirit speak through us. Planning and preparing might be made to seem almost "fleshly."

Yet the context does not allow for such an interpretation. In this passage Jesus warns His followers that they will be handed over to local councils, governors, and kings to be tried. They are told not to worry about what to say when they are set before judges. Since they would not have either the time or the wisdom to know what to say, Jesus promises them that the Holy Spirit will give them the words. A possible application to a teaching context today might be when we are called at the last minute to teach. In such circumstances the Holy Spirit may supernaturally give us His words to speak. While this may

---

[31] Roy B. Zuck, "The Role of the Holy Spirit in Christian Teaching," in Kenneth Gangel and Howard Hendricks, *The Christian Educators' Handbook on Teaching* (Wheaton, IL: Scripture Press, 1988), 34.

happen in emergency situations, we must never use this principle to cover up for lack of planning or preparation.

The Holy Spirit Merely Adds the Zing. A subtle distortion of the work of the Holy Spirit in teaching occurs when teachers do all their preparation on their own and then ask the Holy Spirit "magically" to bless their efforts. Zuck calls this "adding a spiritual footnote" to our teaching.[32] It happens when we separate what we do as teachers from what the Spirit does. We think the Spirit works primarily when we ask for His power or blessing after we have done everything we can on our own. This view dichotomizes our work as a teacher and the work of the Holy Spirit. It reduces the Holy Spirit to the role of a "sacramental blesser" who takes the best we can do on our own and "zaps" it to make it produce spiritual results.

The Holy Spirit is not an "add-on" to our efforts in teaching. He must be intimately involved in everything we do related to our preparation and teaching. We should actively seek the help and power of the Holy Spirit for every aspect of the teaching experience. We should never reduce the role of the Holy Spirit to a mere "blessing" on the work we do as a teacher.

An Unnecessary Crutch. This view holds that if teachers were to teach with excellence, following all the correct methods, there would be no need for a "supernatural helper." While we might initially dismiss this view as an extreme liberal position, it is practiced in our churches and Christian schools more than we may realize. A more subtle form of this view simply takes the work of the Spirit for granted. While acknowledging the value of the Holy Spirit in the teaching process, we fail to partner actively with Him. "Those who appreciate the importance of educational theory and practice, of methods and materials, of curriculum and equipment, sometimes tend to overlook the supernatural element so essential to dynamic Christian education."[33] No matter how skilled, educated, or experienced we are as teachers, we must seek the Holy Spirit's total involvement in every aspect of the teaching-learning experience. His work should never be taken for granted.

As Larry Richards reminds us in a classic statement from his book *A Theology of Christian Education,*

> There are two ways we can distort God's role in the ministry of Christian education. The first is to discount it, and to see Christian growth as simply a natural process. The second is to make it a magical

---

[32] Zuck and Swindoll, *Spirit-Filled Teaching*, 51.
[33] Ibid., 52.

thing, demanding that God work against all natural processes and intervene in spectacular ways.[34]

If we are to use the power of the Holy Spirit in our teaching, we must build our educational practice on a biblical understanding of His role in the teaching-learning process.

A Biblical View of the Role of the Holy Spirit in the Teaching-Learning Process

The Holy Spirit desires to play a major role in every aspect of the teaching-learning process within Christian education. However, His influence may be limited by our unwillingness to draw on His wisdom, truth, and power throughout our teaching experience. By understanding the depth and breadth of His involvement as the Teacher, we should be more apt to seek actively His help in every part of the process. The Holy Spirit ministers through at least five elements of the teaching-learning process: the teacher, the learner, the Word, the participants, and the environment.

The Teacher. The first avenue through which the Holy Spirit works is the teacher. God chose to fulfill the Great Commission—to make disciples of Jesus—at least in part through teachers (Matt 28:19–20). Paul instructs Timothy to pass on his teachings to reliable men who in turn would teach others (2 Tim 2:2). God has chosen to use gifted men and women to be used by the Spirit to teach His truth to others. While in one sense all Christians have a responsibility to teach others what they have learned, some Christians are gifted by the Holy Spirit with special abilities to teach.

Teaching is included in each of the lists of spiritual gifts in the New Testament (Rom 12:3–8; 1 Corinthians 27–31; Eph 4:7–13; 1 Pet 4:10–11). In Eph 4:12 (NASB) the gift of teaching is closely related to the role of a pastor/teacher: "for the equipping of the saints for the work of service, to the building up of the body of Christ." The Holy Spirit uses gifted pastor/teachers to prepare, equip, or train believers to serve one another within the body of Christ. Spiritually gifted teachers seem to have a holistic ministry in Scripture, teaching God's Word in a way that changes both individual lives and communities. Teaching that is anointed by the Holy Spirit focuses on teaching disciples to obey everything Jesus taught (Matt 28:20). "The spiritually gifted teacher helps the Spirit-directed learner to understand and apply the Word of God in the context of the community of other spiritually gifted

---

[34] Larry Richards, *A Theology of Christian Education* (Grand Rapids: Zondervan, 1975), 323.

Christians."[35] Such a teacher must possess not only a thorough knowledge of God's Word but also an ability to communicate it to people in such a way as to equip them to apply the Word in their lives and their relationships. The Holy Spirit uses the spiritually sensitive teacher to orchestrate every aspect of the learning experience toward the Spirit's goals. As Jim Plueddeman states, the gift of teaching is the "art of compelling interaction between the various elements within the teaching-learning environment."[36] The Holy Spirit works most effectively through teachers who are gifted by God to oversee all aspects of the teaching-learning environment in order to stimulate others to learn and obey truth.

In addition to being gifted to teach, Christian teachers must be walking in the Spirit to be used effectively to accomplish His purposes. Fruitfulness in ministry is directly connected to our intimacy with Christ through the Holy Spirit (John 15:1–17). Scripture indicates that Christian teachers will be held to a high standard of godly living (Jas 3:1). In order for teachers to be fully used by the Holy Spirit, they must be committed to holy living. As Paul states in 2 Tim 2:20–22:

> In a large house there are articles not only of gold and silver, but also of wood and clay; some are for noble purposes and some for ignoble. If a man cleanses himself from the latter, he will be an instrument for noble purposes, made holy, useful to the Master and prepared to do any good work. Flee the evil desires of youth, and pursue righteousness, faith, love and peace, along with those who call on the Lord out of a pure heart. (NIV)

Although the Holy Spirit often uses many different people and means to teach, those most apt to have a fruitful teaching ministry are supernaturally gifted as teachers and have an intimate relationship with Jesus.

Spirit-led teachers will cooperate with the Spirit throughout each phase of the planning, preparation, presentation, and follow-up for teaching. They will maintain a soft heart toward the prompting of the Holy Spirit and a continual attitude and practice of prayer. If the Holy Spirit is indeed the catalyst to effective teaching, then prayer opens the door to the knowledge, wisdom, and power for an effective teaching ministry.

Yet a teacher should never allow prayer to cover up poor teaching methods. Since all truth is God's truth, we must use the wealth of knowledge available

---

[35] James Plueddeman, *Education That Is Christian* (Wheaton, IL: Victor Books, 1989), 308.
[36] Ibid.

from the field of educational psychology in an effort to teach with excellence.[37] As Paul challenges us from his own statement of purpose in Col 1:28: "We proclaim him, admonishing and teaching everyone *with all wisdom*, so that we may present everyone perfect in Christ." To teach with wisdom implies using not only the best content but also the wisest methods to ensure that our efforts will partner with the supernatural work of the Holy Spirit in transforming students' lives.

The Learner. The second area of the Holy Spirit's ministry related to the teaching-learning process is that of the learner. No matter how gifted or spiritual a teacher may be, learning and growth toward Christlikeness will not take place unless a learner allows the Holy Spirit to work in his heart. Even Jesus' teaching ministry was limited at times by the hardness of His students' hearts (Matt 13:15,53–58). He even rebuked His disciples for not having soft hearts toward what He was trying to teach them (Mark 8:17–21). A learner must have an open heart to the Holy Spirit in order to learn.

According to Roy Zuck in his classic study on the work of the Holy Spirit in teaching, the Spirit of God actively involves Himself in the learner's heart in three ways: conviction, indwelling, and illumination.[38] When a learner's heart is open to God, the Holy Spirit instigates the conviction of sin (John 16:8). Through the indwelling of the Holy Spirit, a believer may learn the things of God, even without a teacher present, as needs arise (1 John 2:27). Indwelt by the Spirit, believers are taught through the illumination of the Holy Spirit. In Eph 1:18, Paul prays concerning believers, "That the eyes of your heart may be enlightened," so that they may know on an experiential level the blessings of Christ. This illumination or enlightenment is the supernatural work of the Spirit whereby He enables the learner to perceive what God has revealed through His Word.

In order for learners to know and understand spiritual insights and apply them in their lives, they must have soft hearts toward Jesus Christ. When their hearts are soft before God, they are sensitive to the conviction of the Holy Spirit, causing them to confess sin and turn from sinful practices. The indwelling presence of the Holy Spirit allows them to enjoy the abiding presence of the Counselor to instruct, encourage, comfort, and admonish. As believers diligently study the Word, the Spirit illuminates scriptural principles for them to use in their daily lives. By continually seeking the fullness of the Holy Spirit each day, Christians open themselves up to all the power of God available for them to live holy and godly lives (Eph 5:18; 2 Pet 1:3).

---

[37] Arthur Frank Holmes, *All Truth Is God's Truth* (Grand Rapids: Eerdmans, 1977).

[38] Roy Zuck, *Spiritual Power in Your Teaching* (Chicago: Moody Press, 1972), 45–52.

The Word. The revealed truth of God, the Word of God, is the third element in the teaching-learning process. Because of its objective nature, the Word provides the foundation for the work of the Holy Spirit. Second Timothy 3:16–17 (NASB) says: "All Scripture is inspired by God and profitable for teaching, for reproof, for correction, for training in righteousness; so that the man of God may be adequate, equipped for every good work."

Inspiration relates to this initial act of God sharing His truth in the original writings of Scripture. This revelation of God was not "made by an act of human will, but men moved by the Holy Spirit spoke from God" (2 Pet 1:21 NASB). Since Scripture is directly inspired by God, it must be used as the final test of truth by which believers distinguish truth from error. In using the term "sword of the Spirit" to refer to God's Word, Paul emphasizes the Holy Spirit's aggressive use of the Word in accomplishing God's purposes (Eph 6:17 NASB). Growth takes place as both teacher and learner interact with and obey the Word of God.

Interpersonal Interaction. The fourth element the Holy Spirit works through in the teaching-learning process is the interaction between participants in the learning situation. While the Holy Spirit often works in a person's heart individually, He also works in the interpersonal context of small groups and relationships. When the Holy Spirit first came to the church at Pentecost, He baptized the whole group of believers (Acts 2:1–4,41). After the influx of about 3,000 believers, the new church established a close learning community centered on the teaching of the apostles (Acts 2:42–47). The close, loving relationships within the church provided a vehicle for the Holy Spirit to move in a way that could never have been accomplished through a series of individual encounters with God. An interesting example of this principle can be found in Paul's prayer in Eph 3:16–19:

> I pray that out of his glorious riches he may strengthen you with power through his Spirit in your inner being, so that Christ may dwell in your hearts through faith. And I pray that you, being rooted and established in love, may have power, *together with all the saints*, to grasp how wide and long and high and deep is the love of Christ, and to know this love that surpasses knowledge—that you may be filled to all the measure of the fullness of God.

Paul's prayer focuses not only on individuals understanding and experiencing the blessing of being Spirit-filled but also on the saints learning together. A certain element of His power and love can be understood only within the context of "other saints" who are seeking the fullness of God together. The healthy interpersonal dynamics of a class or group of Christians is an important factor in the Spirit's teaching ministry.

The nature of the church as the body of Christ suggests that it grows through its ability to learn and work together (Eph 4:11–16). A major part of the Holy Spirit's teaching ministry relates to the interpersonal relationships within the church and other learning environments.

The Environment. The fifth dimension of the Holy Spirit's work in the teaching-learning process is the environment. Environmental or contextual factors in Christian education may include such things as seating arrangement, lighting, temperature, visuals, room location or size, colors, distractions, or smells. While some of these elements may seem too common to relate to the supernatural work of the Holy Spirit, we must remember that God has used such physical elements to set the environment for spiritual learning throughout history. Learning experiences—Moses by the burning bush, Jews in the tabernacle or temple, Jesus and His disciples at the Sea of Galilee, the early disciples in the upper room, Paul and Silas in the jail at Philippi, or Paul and the philosophers in the Areopagus—illustrate the importance of the environment for the learning of truth. Both teacher and learner cooperate with the Holy Spirit by strategically designing the physical and aesthetic aspects of a learning environment to allow the Holy Spirit freedom to accomplish His purposes.

The Holy Spirit works as a catalyst for learning through each of these five elements. Although we may never totally understand the complexity of His role, we must continue to depend on His wisdom and power to teach and learn God's truth. For the teacher this means intentionally relying on the wisdom and power of the Holy Spirit in every step of preparation and teaching. It also means using the most effective teaching methods, tested through careful research. Only then, by walking in the Spirit, praying in the Spirit, and seeking His full presence, will both teacher and student effectively partner with the Holy Spirit in bearing fruit for the kingdom of God.

As the Holy Spirit softens the believer's heart to the words of Jesus, God's Word penetrates to the core of his being to instruct, encourage, motivate, and empower him to put the principles of His word into practice. God's Word is the authoritative instruction manual providing the disciple of Christ the knowledge of how to be transformed into the likeness of Christ.

The Heart of Discipleship

The essence of discipleship in both the OT and the NT is consistent. God has always had the same passionate desire for His people to love Him from the center of their beings. As the mystery of the Messiah was revealed with the coming of God's Son, the Father's purpose culminated in the Holy Spirit's empowerment for disciples to love the Father through following His Son from the depths of their hearts.

An assumption of this book is that the essence of God's will for all people is to give "as much of themselves as they can to as much of Christ as they can understand."[39] This response involves understanding, commitment, desire, and action. While it may begin small, even as small as a mustard seed, it will grow, develop, and produce fruit. The heart of the process of discipleship is in the heart of man, the center of a person's will, mind, and emotions. Any attempt to build disciples must focus on the transformation of the heart.[40]

Discipleship must be approached as an affair or relationship of the heart—a deep love relationship with Jesus Christ involving every aspect of a person's being. The relationship must be kindled through prayer and developmentally appropriate words and actions. Strategies must also be bathed in prayer and rooted in wisdom reflecting both biblical and social science principles. These strategies must focus on the spiritual formation and transformation of all aspects of the person from the inside out. By focusing on the transformation of the heart, we may avoid some of the superficial and unproductive "rabbit trails" that have sidetracked Christian education in the past. By focusing on the depths of the heart, we will open a vast new territory for the Spirit of God to renew. By introducing this journey of discipleship as a lifelong process of exploration and discovery, we will attract those who have been turned off by the superficiality of religious indoctrination.

Summary and Application Questions

1. How would you have characterized the "heart" before reading this chapter?

2. How has your understanding of the "heart" changed after reading this chapter?

3. What do preachers usually mean when they talk about the Word of God moving from the head to the heart?

4. Is this a correct use of the terms *heart* and *head* from a biblical and philosophical perspective? Why or why not?

5. What is the Hebrew concept of the "heart"?

6. How did Jesus use the term *heart*?

---

[39] Samuel M. Shoemaker, *How to Become a Christian*, 1st ed. (New York: Harper, 1953), 72.

[40] Willard, *Renovation of the Heart*, 14.

7. How did Paul use the term *heart*?

8. How did other New Testament writers use the term *heart*?

9. How did Dallas Willard use the term *heart*?

10. Explain the role of the Word of God in illuminating and transforming the heart.

11. Explain the role of the Holy Spirit in the teaching/learning process.

12. How is the "heart" central to understanding the nature and process of discipleship?

13. What does it mean to love the Lord with all one's heart?

14. Why is it so difficult for you to love God in this way?

15. What would you need to change in your life to love God this way?

Chapter 3

Mapping the Journey to the Depths of the Heart

Planning a road trip can be almost as exciting as the trip itself. When our three boys were younger, we planned a trip to Algonquin Park in northern Ontario, Canada, to go camping and fishing. Half the fun was the anticipation we experienced as we studied maps and gazed at moose pictures from *National Geographic*. While all our preparations didn't insulate us from some of the surprises along the way, such as coming face-to-face with a mother moose and her three calves, our plans did help us get to our destination. Without our careful plans we might have never realized that the best time to see moose was in the early morning. So it is with our journey to the center of the person; the better our preparation, the better chance we have to get to our goals.

Before we can design strategies to help others in this journey of discipleship, we must gain as much wisdom as possible about this journey to the center of the heart. Based on our definition of the heart as the focal point of our cognitive, affective, and volitional functions, this chapter will map out the process of going deeper in each of these domains. We will attempt to show the interrelationships of these domains in our journey to the center of the heart. Equipped with a better understanding of the process of the journey to the heart, we will be able to design wiser approaches to teaching and equipping others for a life of discipleship.

The journey to the heart can be compared to a journey descending the steps of ladders representing each of the domains (cognitive, affective, and volitional) toward the core of our heart. Each of the ladders represents the sequential steps a person takes toward heart-deep learning in each domain. While the Bible describes the process of knowing God and His Word at a deeper level, we can also clearly see the order and sequencing of the steps toward the heart from the collective observations of years of social science research. By integrating biblical and social science research, we can formulate a theory of how we respond to the Holy Spirit and His Word at progressively deeper levels of the heart.

Issler and Habermas have defined the ladders I am referring to as "levels of learning." We will be looking at four domains through which social scientists and educators explain the various taxonomies of the different types of learning. The Cognitive Level refers to knowledge and intellectual skills; the Affective Level refers to emotions and attitudes; the Dispositional and Volitional Level refers to values and tendencies to act, which intersects with all the domains; and the Behavior Level refers to physical skills and habits. While it may be helpful to separate these levels for purposes of analysis, we must realize that learning is much more "holistic and interrelated."[1]

For this reason we will depict our journey to the center of the heart as a descent, passing down through the four levels. This journey will circle progressively deeper into the depths of the person as the Holy Spirit acts as a catalyst in each of the areas of a person's heart. His role is to initiate and direct the whole range of learning as people respond to principles from God's Word. Working together with a teacher, fellow learners, and the environment, the Holy Spirit initiates and directs this process of heart-deep learning. Thus the Holy Spirit acts as a primary agent of teaching and learning in the process of discipleship in each of the domains.

The following diagram represents this journey to the center of the heart of the person. The journey passes through each of the dimensions of the heart including the mind, the emotions, and the will. The closer the journey progresses to the center of the heart, the more integrated the learning becomes. As the journey progresses deeper through the various taxonomies toward the center of the heart, the more difficult it becomes to differentiate between the various domains. Thinking, feeling, and deciding merge as both teachers and learners become more sensitive to the Holy Spirit in their journey toward transformation of the whole person. Obedient action based on the integration of thinking, feeling, and choosing becomes both the result and the catalyst for

---

[1] Klaus Issler and Ron Habermas, *How We Learn* (Grand Rapids: Baker, 1994), 29–31.

continued integration and deeper learning toward transformation. Obedient action or behavioral change reflects the continual transformation process within the heart. Good works, godly behavior, and fruitfulness proceed from the heart to affect the person's life, family, community, and world.

Cognitive Domain

For many years education focused primarily on the development of mental abilities in students and the teaching of knowledge. Even in the field of religious education, pastors and Sunday school teachers tended to focus on biblical knowledge and understanding more than character change or spiritual development. Teachers mistakenly assumed that spiritual growth happened most naturally through telling Bible stories and memorizing Scripture. With the more progressive educational ideas of Dewey in the beginning of the last century, there began a slow movement toward practical and experiential educational methods.

Heart-Deep
Teaching and Learning

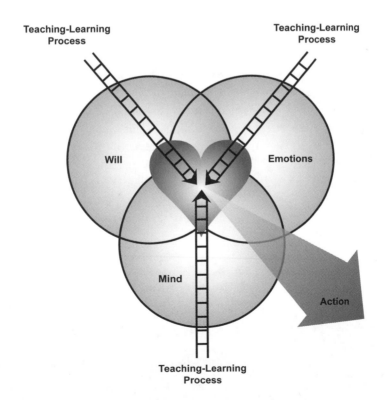

Today it seems as if we have moved to the other end of the spectrum by almost neglecting the cognitive area of development in favor of active learning experiences and "feel-good" activities. Perhaps a closer look at the various steps in the cognitive progression toward higher levels of learning will help us understand how to challenge heart-deep thinking. This, in turn, may rejuvenate our curiosity to discover a more systematic path to the transformation of the heart.

Benjamin Bloom provides us with a basic taxonomy of the cognitive domain, including six levels of learning. These levels include knowledge, comprehension, application, analysis, synthesis, and evaluation.[2] To these we will add the level the Bible calls "wisdom" to describe the highest level of thinking related to putting knowledge into practice in making decisions.[3] From a Christian perspective in line with a Hebraic way of thinking, the highest level of thinking always relates to practical application of knowledge. Thus the cognitive journey to the heart could be said to begin with knowledge and end with wisdom.

According to Bloom, the lowest level of the cognitive journey is characterized by simply recognizing or recalling previously known facts. According to Yount, "terms which focus on this level of learning include: to identify, to recall, to recognize, to name, to state, to reproduce, to list, to quote, and to match."[4] While this is only the first level, it is a necessary starting point for higher levels of learning. Yet so many times Christian educators, Sunday school teachers, and pastors fail to engage students in learning even at this level. The recognition, identification, and memorization of basic knowledge and principles begin the journey to the heart. Establishing a good start to the journey sets the stage for an exciting adventure.

According to Ford, the next five levels from Bloom's taxonomy could be categorized under the term "understanding."[5] This would separate the five more-advanced levels from the first level. The term *understanding* would then include Bloom's levels of comprehension, application, analysis, synthesis, and evaluation. Each of these levels moves toward a deeper level of understanding toward the heart.

---

[2] Benjamin Samuel Bloom, *Taxonomy of Educational Objectives: The Classification of Educational Goals*, 1st ed. (New York: David McKay, 1956), 18, 90–93.

[3] James Michael Lee, *The Content of Religious Instruction* (Birmingham, AL: Religious Education Press, 1985), 159.

[4] William R. Yount, *Called to Teach: An Introduction to the Ministry of Teaching* (Nashville: B&H, 1999), 140.

[5] Le Roy Ford, *Design for Teaching and Training: A Self-Study Guide to Lesson Planning* (Nashville: Broadman Press, 1978).

We can consider learning about evangelism as an example of this cognitive journey from knowledge to understanding. At the level of knowledge, students might identify a person trying to evangelize someone or simply memorize a definition of *evangelism*. Students could also recall a verse about evangelism or recognize a person who evangelized poorly. Other examples of demonstrating learning at this level might include naming a character from the Bible who was a good evangelist, stating an evangelism principle, reproducing a story of a positive evangelism experience, or listing five principles of good evangelism. Students could simply quote a saying from Jesus about evangelism or even match biblical characters with evangelism experiences they had. While these cognitive activities may be at a rudimentary level, they are certainly not insignificant in the process of moving toward heart-deep learning. In fact, basic levels of knowledge provide a necessary foundation for deeper learning.[6]

Jensen and Nickelsen give us a clear picture of Bloom's first level of learning with their "web of simple learning."[7]

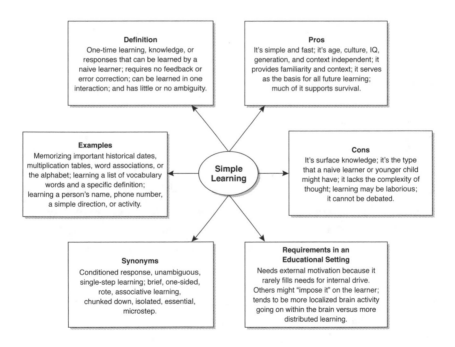

---

[6] Eric Jensen and LeAnn Nickelsen, *Deeper Learning: 7 Powerful Strategies for In-Depth and Longer-Lasting Learning* (Thousand Oaks, CA: Corwin, 2008), 8.

[7] Ibid.

According to Bloom, the largest category of intellectual abilities and skills is those that relate to "comprehension," in which the student, at some level, makes the knowledge more personally meaningful.[8] This is the most simplistic level of understanding, in which students begin to think through given information in concrete terms related to an immediate context. Relating to the topic of witnessing, this stage of intellectual reasoning might involve a student's discussing how he might share the gospel message to a friend at recess. Thinking at this level could be observed when students put things in their own words, translate a concept, or express their understanding of a particular story from Scripture.[9] It could also be observed when students begin to interpret observations or draw conclusions from data. It relates to a person's ability to move from specific situations to generalized abstract principles.

The next category of "application" is characterized by a person's ability to correctly use a principle in a new situation. Whereas applying a principle in an already rehearsed situation would suggest a "comprehension" level, correctly using the principle in a new, unrehearsed situation would suggest learning at the "application" level. Effectiveness at this level of learning would relate to a student's being able to apply principles in real-life situations.[10] The major distinction between comprehension and application relates to a person's ability to put learned principles into practice in new situations. In this way it is easy to see how learning could move from a simple cognitive domain to "doing." As we will see in every category, the deeper we get in the journey toward the heart, the more integrated learning becomes.

The next category of "analysis" focuses on the way the parts of the material are broken down and also on the organization of their relationships. It involves studying the various aspects of a principle, passage of Scripture, concept, or situation and breaking them down to bring further light and insight to the subject studied. According to Bloom, there are three sublevels of thinking within the category of analysis. The first sublevel relates to identifying the various elements in the learning experience. An example could be distinguishing a conclusion or major thesis in a biblical text from various supporting statements. Or it could relate to distinguishing between facts and suggestions given by a biblical author related to sharing our faith. The second sublevel relates to identifying the relationships, interactions, and connections between the elements identified. This skill is essential in identifying cause-and-effect relationships in

---

[8] Bloom, *Taxonomy of Educational Objectives*, 89.

[9] Ibid., 90–92.

[10] Ibid., 120–22.

arguments and in differentiating major and minor points in a stated case. The third sublevel relates to recognizing the organizing principles, which hold the parts together.[11] This intellectual skill is needed to analyze scriptural passages to come up with the central controlling thought. It involves recognizing the author's purpose and the structure used in making his argument. These three aspects of analysis—identifying the elements, identifying the relationships, and recognizing the organizing principles that hold it all together—make up the category of analysis. Analysis is crucial in discovering the main principles and Big Idea of a biblical text. The category of analysis is fundamental in the study of human behavior, theology, and Scripture.

The next category within the cognitive domain, according to Bloom, is "synthesis"—"the putting together of elements and parts so as to form a whole." At this level the student applies a unique element of creativity in pulling together what has been learned in the production of an original application of the facts, concepts, principles, and understandings learned. In this sense, this stage could be considered a culmination of learning up to this point. It involves sequencing what has been learned in a unique way to reflect the nature of both the subject material and the learner. Often termed "integration," this stage shows evidence that the student has pulled together the subject matter into a coherent whole and applied it in a unique way.[12]

An illustration of this level of learning would be when students pull together their research, experience, and insights to come up with their own strategy to share their faith in a previously unknown context. This would represent a fairly high level of cognitive learning. As students progress through the levels of deeper cognitive learning, they move closer to what the Hebrew Scripture defines as wisdom, the application and integration of truth into our lifestyles.

The last level in Bloom's taxonomy of cognitive learning is evaluation. This level is defined as "the making of judgments about the value, for some purpose, of ideas, works, solutions, methods, material, etc." The judgments must be based on some standard or criterion which is "accurate, effective, economical, or satisfying." Bloom explains that while there can be purely cognitive evaluations, this level of thinking often links up with other areas such as the emotional and dispositional domains. As we mentioned before, the higher we go on these taxonomies or the deeper we go toward the heart, the more integrative learning becomes.[13]

---

[11] Ibid., 144–48.
[12] Ibid., 162–64.
[13] Ibid., 185.

An example of this level of thinking might be when a group of students evaluate their effectiveness in witnessing based on established standards of effectiveness in sharing their faith learned in a class setting. Such an evaluation should be both accurate and as objective as possible, using either qualitative or quantitative judgments.

At the highest level of wisdom, cognitive learning is fully integrated with one's emotions, intentions, and actions. This level approaches the pinnacle of heart-deep learning in which biblical principles are integrated with the fabric of every aspect of the person. The person not only knows and understands truth but is also passionate about following truth, committed to following Jesus, and instinctively obeying the Holy Spirit moment by moment. While Jesus Christ is the only person who has ever lived such a life perfectly, this does not imply that we should not strive for such Christlikeness.

Affective Domain

The affective domain relates to attitudes and emotions within the person. When Krathwohl and his colleagues designed their taxonomy, they ordered it from simple to complex to relate to the degree of response an individual made to a particular phenomenon. Thus, at a simple level a person is simply "aware" of something and able to perceive it. At the next level a person decides to "attend" to the phenomenon or focus attention on it. Next he "responds" to it positively and then goes on to show even more initiative by "going out of his way" to respond to it. Later "he conceptualizes his behavior and feelings and 'organizes' these conceptualizations into a structure." As this structure becomes more and more characteristic of him, "it becomes his life outlook."[14]

We could illustrate this progression by using the earlier example of learning to witness to one's faith. Learning at the simplest level might be students sharing a time when they wished they could have shared their faith more freely: awareness. The next level of learning experience may be the students watching and describing how a person in a skit or video shared his faith with others: attendance. The next level could be demonstrated as the students find someone they respect sharing his faith and interview him or her: response. The next level could be evidenced when the students, on their own, venture out to share their faith with others. This level would progress to the last level as they

---

[14] Lorin W. Anderson, David R. Krathwohl, and Benjamin Samuel Bloom, *A Taxonomy for Learning, Teaching, and Assessing: A Revision of Bloom's Taxonomy of Educational Objectives*, Complete Ed. (New York: Longman, 2001).

thought through what they believed about sharing their faith and began to *conceptualize* their philosophy of witnessing. The more they thought through their strategy and put it into practice, the more they would progress to a stage in which witnessing would become an integral part of their lives. By following this simple progression of levels of affective learning, a person would move toward the transformation of the heart. As a person progresses deeper toward the heart, learning becomes more and more integrated with the other domains of learning, including cognitive, volitional, and behavioral.

Volitional or Dispositional Domain

The will is defined by Willard as the "executive center of the human self." From it, the whole self or life is meant to be directed and organized and must be if it is to be directed and organized at all. That is why we recognize the will to be the same as the biblical "heart" or "center." He goes on to explain that will and character are different. Character develops from the will. Will initiates what later becomes character after actions become habitual. When actions become habitual, they become instinctual and somewhat "automatic."[15]

The process often begins when a person thinks through his inappropriate actions after being convicted by the Holy Spirit, repents of sin, and realizes the forgiveness of God because of the sacrifice of Jesus Christ on the cross. He then turns from that sin, and obeys the Holy Spirit by taking the appropriate actions according to scriptural principles. As a person continues to turn from that sin and obeys the Holy Spirit, that response becomes habitual over time until it is ingrained into the person's character. What starts in the heart with the mind and the will eventually affects character. Regardless of the choices a person makes, decisions of the will eventually affect character.

This process is explained by Issler and Habermas in their adaptation of Watson and Tharp's research[16] on how habits are formed. In the first phase a behavior is generally uncontrolled. In the second phase—through influences of God, people, structures, or disciplines—a person gains control, step-by-step, over this area in his life. During this stage a new tendency or positive orientation is being developed toward this new behavior. In the third phase, if the practices and behaviors are continued over a long period of time, they become a "second nature" habit. They become a natural part of the character and lifestyle

---

[15] Dallas Willard, *Renovation of the Heart: Putting on the Character of Christ* (Colorado Springs: NavPress, 2002), 144.

[16] David L. Watson and Roland G. Tharp, *Self-Directed Behavior: Self-Modification for Personal Adjustment* (Pacific Grove, CA: Brooks/Cole, 1989).

of the person. If this fails to happen either because of strong temptation or personal weakness and the person regresses or falls, he usually needs continuous vigorous training in areas where he is struggling.[17]

While this three-step process may seem simple, most of us can identify with the struggle that goes on inside us when we commit our will to move in a particular direction. Whether it is an exercise regimen, a spiritual discipline, overcoming an imbedded habit, or implementing a resolution, changing our ingrained way of doing things is a challenge. Yet as Paul emphasizes in Rom 8:1–11, victory is possible through the grace of Jesus Christ coupled with moment-by-moment obedience to the prompting of the Holy Spirit. This three-step process provides us with a helpful structure in understanding growth toward a Spirit-controlled will.

This process of changing the will to become in sync with the will of God could be illustrated using the example of learning to have a passion for sharing one's faith. Step one could describe a person who had no desire or commitment to share his faith with anyone. Step two might describe a person whose heart was moved, softened, or convicted to share his or her faith with others. The initiating spark for this change in heart could be a person, an experience, a song, a movie, a retreat, a Bible passage, a sermon, or a convicting lesson. But whatever happened, the Holy Spirit used it to convict him or her to repent of an old way of thinking and turn around to follow Christ's lifestyle. It could have happened suddenly, or it could have happened over a long period of time, but when it happened, there was a change in heart resulting in a change of action. That experience with God initiated the person into the third stage. Then he began eagerly to share his faith with others. At this stage he had two choices. He could either maintain the lifestyle of support and spiritual stimulation that sparked the turnaround, or he could drift back into his past lifestyle. In order to maintain the commitment and practice of witnessing, he would have to continue to learn and practice sharing his faith regularly. By doing this throughout one's lifetime, witnessing would become ingrained into a person's character.

Behavioral Domain

The behavioral domain deals with psychomotor skills related to actions of the person. In this way the skills often become expressions of the heart of a person. They include biblical competencies such as praying, witnessing, talking, listen-

---

[17] Klaus Dieter Issler and Ronald T. Habermas, *How We Learn: A Christian Teacher's Guide to Educational Psychology* (Grand Rapids: Baker Books, 1994), 41–42.

ing, loving, serving, teaching, encouraging, and showing hospitality. As we grow toward a deeper experience with God in our hearts, one would expect that we would also express that in our actions as fruit. In many ways the higher levels of taxonomy for the behavioral level should reflect the growing expectations of a person growing in fruitfulness. Just as a new Christian worker might be expected to serve at one level, certainly a person who has walked with the Lord all his life would be expected to serve with increased excellence and fruitfulness.

Simpson's taxonomy for the behavioral levels[18] was summarized into three phases by Issler and Habermas:[19] Phase one relates to a student's "preparation" stage in which he becomes aware of things and their qualities and becomes prepared to perform the particular action. Phase two relates to "supervised practice" in which the student performs under the guidance of a skilled trainer. Phase three relates to the student's "increasing excellence in performance" and includes four substages: Stage One—performing with increased consistency, confidence, and proficiency; Stage Two—performing with a high degree of consistency, confidence, and proficiency; Stage Three—performing new but related tasks based on previously used skill; and Stage Four—creating new performances based on the understanding, abilities, and skills learned earlier.

As we design and analyze the process of heart-deep teaching, learning this taxonomy will be extremely helpful in understanding how people learn specific skills and behaviors, in particular in setting standards for learning in the area of ministry skills.

With the example of a person learning how to be a better witness, we could use this taxonomy to understand how to train people to serve at the highest level of excellence reflecting the deepest level of heart-deep learning.

In the first phase a new follower of Christ might become aware of the needs and desires of non-Christians and learn effective communication strategies for initiating relationships with them. He or she might engage in role-playing of typical encounters with non-Christians. In the second phase a person would do some witnessing with mentors present who would debrief and discuss the experience. In the third phase the student would become more and more proficient under the continued guidance and supervision of a mentor. As he gained more competence, confidence, and excellence, he would be given more freedom to try new tasks until he was able to master totally new situations on his own with fruitful results.

---

[18] Elizabeth Simpson, "Taxonomy of Objectives Psychomotor Domain" (Unpublished Manuscript, University of Illinois, Urbana, 1966).

[19] Issler and Habermas, *How We Learn*, 38.

By integrating the four taxonomies related to cognitive, affective, volitional, and behavioral domains, we can see their usefulness in helping us to move deeper toward heart-deep teaching through all levels within all domains. It may be helpful to picture the different domains as ladders descending to the depths of the heart of the person following the step-by-step process toward the core of one's being. The deeper we get, the more the ladders converge. The closer we get to the heart, the more the domains become integrated.

This understanding of the progressive journey to the depths of the heart will provide the conceptual basis of the sequential steps students must pass through, as they grow deeper in their walk with Jesus Christ. This pattern will be the basis of designing goals and objectives in each of the domains from simple to complex. It will guide us in exploring creative avenues to help people to discover and experience truth at increasingly deeper levels. Each of the following chapters will be built on the analogy of this progressive journey to the center of the heart. We will know when we near the end of the journey when both teachers and students reflect the Christ that they follow.

Questions and Applications

1. What are the four domains of learning? Briefly define each.

2. Describe what is meant by the journey to the center of the heart.

3. What is the role of the Holy Spirit in this journey to the center of the heart for the teacher and for the learner?

4. Outline the basic taxonomies for each of the four domains and give an example of learning from each level in each of the four domains based on Rev 3:19–20.

5. Explain why the Holy Spirit is so important in helping both the teacher and learner to learn the deeper truths from the Scripture above.

6. What do you think it would take to teach a student to understand and apply such a passage of Scripture to his or her life?

7. What are the values of studying and learning Scripture at this depth?

Chapter 4

Digging Deeper into the Word for Yourself as a Teacher

Hungering to Know God's Truth Yourself

Teachers face two dangers as they prepare for teaching. The first is that they may put more emphasis on how to relate to the students than on studying the meaning of the text. I have faced this temptation many times while preparing to teach. Instead of focusing on what the text intended to say to its original audience, I fix my mind on how to communicate specific ideas in the text to my students. The second danger that teachers may face is closely related to the first. As they get excited about their students and how to teach them these specific ideas from the text, they fail to apply at a heart level the central intent of the passage to their own lives. Thus the lesson bypasses the heart of the teacher only to become a professional objective to be accomplished in the lives of students. I have fallen into this dangerous pattern many times in my teaching and preaching career. Yet this practice leads to externalism, hypocrisy, and shallowness in teaching—the opposite of biblical standards of heart-deep teaching.

"Heart-deep teaching" must begin with "heart-deep learning" on the part of the teacher. Teachers must prayerfully ask the Holy Spirit to illuminate their minds, emotions, wills, and behaviors in light of the objective teachings of God's Word. They must engage all of their God-given faculties to discover what God is saying in the text within its grammatical and historical context and begin to apply those principles to their own lives. Teachers must begin by discovering and practicing the truth from the text before trying to apply and communicate it to their students.

Epistemological Foundations of Heart-Deep Teaching and Learning

The most important question to be answered before beginning the process of teaching others is defining the nature of truth in the biblical text or story. As important as students and their needs are, truth is more important. Pilate's question to Jesus at His trial, "What is truth?" pinpoints the most fundamental issue in life (John 18:38). While Jesus said, "I am the way and the truth and the life" (John 14:6 NIV), the rest of Scripture attests to the fact that OT and NT Scriptures are also truth.[1] The truth of Scripture promises to meet the deepest needs of humankind when applied accurately. Teachers need to start with God's Word in an attempt to get a firm grasp of what God wants them to teach their students. Understanding the essence of truth must be the first concern for the teacher before speculating about how to engage the learner.

While some insisted we are teaching *students* rather than *content*, we must be careful that our focus on students does not overshadow the objective truth and meaning of the biblical text. While it is important to focus on the process of what is going on in the hearts of our students, the students' perspective should not change the essence of the truth in Scripture. For this reason we must be diligent as teachers to pursue the accurate meaning of the text in its grammatical and historical context before trying to teach others. We also must be more humble about admitting our honest questions about the text when evangelical scholars and theologians throughout the history of the church have failed to come to a consensus about the meaning of some texts.

Teaching God's Word, however, goes beyond simply proclaiming truth to students. We teach students to know the truth. Yet, in another sense, it is not enough to teach students simply to know truth; we must help them obey and

---

[1] Douglas R. Groothuis, *Truth Decay: Defending Christianity Against the Challenges of Postmodernism* (Downers Grove, IL: InterVarsity Press, 2000), 81–82.

live the truth in their everyday lives. Some contemporary educators may dis-
agree, arguing that the deepest truth is discovered deep within the self, not in
some ancient text. Others would say that knowing propositional truth is impossible since both those who wrote the Bible and those who read it are subjective
beings. They might even say it is arrogant to teach students to know the truth.
Rather, they might say, we should engage students in the search for meaning to
come up with their own truth. With such a smorgasbord of approaches to the
question of what we should teach, how are we to choose what is right?

What makes this question even more complex is the fact that many
Christian ministers, professors, and teachers have drifted into postmodern
thinking in an attempt to minister to people absorbed in contemporary culture.[2] While supporting the need for Christians to engage in culture and to
understand how people think and reason within cultures, we must be careful
not to conform to the pattern of thinking in the world but rather be transformed by the renewal of our minds (Rom 12:1–2). From this text it is clear
that God is the primary agent transforming our minds, not our culture. We
are warned to be careful not to conform "mindlessly" to principles and practices of the system of the world. Yet how do we differentiate between what is
"of the world" and what is just part of culture? The key to discerning what
is right or wrong within any given culture depends on a clear understanding
of truth.

Many contemporary thinkers realize that epistemological beliefs lie at the
core of this dilemma. Epistemology deals with the nature of truth and how we
know truth. Yet so often we fail to separate these two aspects of this discussion.
Much of the confusion comes from thinking that both the nature of truth and
the process of how we know truth must be the same. Two questions illustrate
this dilemma. First, since we believe there is objective, propositional truth, does
that mean people necessarily learn truth best through rote learning and memorizing? Second, if we believe the best way people learn is through consistent
models, healthy experiences, and discovery learning, does that imply *all truth
is subjectively based on human experience*?

Several years ago I was attending a conference on teaching and learning,
listening to a lecture by a scholar who was deriding Christians because they
stood dogmatically on the belief that since truth was propositional they should
tell everyone else what to believe. His point was that "the Christians" were
violating every commonly accepted truth about learning theory in their epistemology. After a while I raised my hand and politely asked whether it would

---

[2] Ibid., 21.

be possible to be a Christian or a person of any other faith and believe strongly in propositional truth yet also hold a more progressive theory of how to teach. I explained the commonly accepted definition of *epistemology*, stating that it deals with both the nature of truth and how we know truth. After some reflection the presenter courageously took back some of his statements belittling "Christians" and acknowledged that he had seldom heard of strong Christians who did not dogmatically force their beliefs on their students. He reluctantly agreed that it would be possible to believe in objective propositional truth and yet practice more progressive methods of student learning.

In a culture that is increasingly more dependent on active learning, the church must acknowledge its failure to apply tested social science truth about teaching and learning in how we "did church" in the past. Without eroding our belief in the propositional nature of God's Word, we must explore creative ways to help people learn effectively within a rapidly changing culture. We need to use more engaging learning experiences such as self-directed learning, experiential learning, mentoring, teams, and interactions. We must take a more humble attitude toward what we believe as "absolute," realizing that some of the beliefs we may cherish the most are based more in our culture than in God's Word. While admitting that the church in the "modern era" made many overly dogmatic statements related to how truth should be applied, that does not justify throwing out the belief in the reality of truth. The church would be wiser if it acknowledged its mistakes in the past and reevaluated the process of how it should discern and teach truth.

I suggest a deeper and more thorough analysis of what we consider to be truth based on what the Bible states within its grammatical and historical context. We need to take the culture and context of Scripture seriously in order to be careful not to generalize laws and guidelines intended for particular audiences and apply them to people in other contexts. We must separate context-dependent instructions to a targeted audience from general principles related to all people in all times. This analysis is not easy. It demands biblical, historical, archaeological, cultural, and social science research to discern the intent of instructions. It demands a thorough understanding of God's central principles throughout Scripture to differentiate between universal truth and specific applications.

While a universal principle is true in every culture or time, specific applications may be radically different depending on many factors. An example can be found in the principle of honoring our elders. When I first taught students from a Chinese background, I was taken aback by their seeming lack of respect for teachers in their refusal to look me straight in the eye. It did not take me long to learn that in their culture looking an elder in the eye was a serious sign of disrespect. While they were seeking to follow the biblical principle of respect, their application of that principle was different from the Western practice of direct eye contact. We must look at truth in Scripture at a deeper level in order to differentiate between universal truth and specific applications.

Over the centuries some of these patterns of generally accepted applications of truth have taken on a life of their own. In some cases people seem more dogmatic about the specific applications of truth than truth itself. Jesus rebuked the Jewish leaders for a similar error in judgment and practice relating to honoring one's father and mother. Apparently they had dodged the commandment to honor their parents by giving money to the temple instead of supporting their elderly parents. Jesus rebuked them for this sternly, saying, "You have revoked God's word because of your tradition. Hypocrites!" (Matt 15:6). He followed this rebuke by quoting from Isa 29:13, saying that "these people approach Me with their mouths to honor Me with lip-service—yet their hearts are far from Me, and their worship consists of man-made rules learned by rote."

Jesus rebuked them because their hearts were far from Him: their worship consisted of following man-made traditions rather than God. Could it be that Jesus might give the same rebuke to the church today, chastising us for putting more emphasis on external religious traditions than God's never-changing truth?

These questions challenge the thinking of both teachers and students and demand careful, reflective responses. In order to engage in heart-deep teaching, we must understand the nature of truth and differentiate the unchangeable, eternal principles in Scripture from the specific applications directed to changing historical and cultural contexts. While we must design creative learning experiences, we also need to be careful that our methods lead us to discover truth rather than to obscure it. The unchangeable truth of God's Word sets people free.

Heart-deep teaching is built on the historically affirmed position of the church that God's Word is inerrant and fully trustworthy in its original manuscripts. As such, the Bible is the basis of our doctrine, teaching, and lifestyle. In order to apply truth to specific situations, we must examine texts and teachings within their cultural and historical contexts to differentiate between timeless principles and contextually dependent rules and instructions. We must continually ask deep questions such as what, why, for what reasons, and how. Teachers and students alike must do more than simply take in information. In order to learn, we must wrestle, interact, experience, practice, question, reflect, discuss, compare and contrast, and critique. The objective nature of God's truth does not mean that the best way to teach it is simply to preach or tell it. While truth is truth whether we experience it or not, the best way to know truth is through experiencing it in our lives.

While I was attending Houghton College in upstate New York, I taught freshmen skiing classes at a small ski slope on campus. In those days we used what was called "the stem turn" to initiate a turn going downhill. To negotiate a turn, students had to believe in a fundamental principle that took a lot of faith. They had to trust and follow my word, that by taking their weight off their downhill ski and slowly putting it on their uphill ski as they spread out the back of it, they could initiate a turn. Although this principle is true, it only becomes true for skiers as they put it into practice. Whether the skier could negotiate the turn had little to do with the truth of the principle. While the truth of the principle never changed, the proper application of the principle depended on the experience of the learner. If my students did not learn the turn, it was not the principle that was at fault but rather my ability to teach or the student's ability to learn. Once students experienced the feeling of spreading out the back of the uphill ski, transferring their weight to the uphill ski, slowly turning around, and drawing their skis together again in the opposite direction, they became much more assured of the validity of the turning principle. However, students who ended facedown in the snow, with legs spread in all directions, expressed serious doubts about either the truth of my theory or my ability to teach skiing.

While truth never changes, in order to learn it at a heart-deep level, we must experience it personally in as many dimensions of our being as possible through studying, interacting, wrestling, questioning, comparing, critiquing, and practicing.

Learning Truth Deeply Ourselves as Teachers

Most of us have experienced the frustration of trying to learn something from teachers who do not know how to practice what they are trying to teach. I remember taking a college class in counseling from a teacher who had exceptionally poor interpersonal skills. Almost everything he modeled in class violated the content he taught.

It is not enough for teachers of God's Word simply to know their material on a superficial level. Christian educators and those encouraging the spiritual development of others must be actively learning and applying truth at an in-depth level themselves before attempting to teach others. This involves studying, wrestling, searching, and discovering, as well as integrating, applying, and practicing truth. It is difficult to teach something we have not learned ourselves. The more passionate we are about an issue, the greater the chance those around us will catch that passion. The depth to which the teacher is personally connected to the subject often determines the depth to which the listener will respond. This is true in teaching almost any subject matter. If a history teacher was only interested in teaching facts, dates, and events, students would probably gain little passion to give their lives to historical research or exploration. Good history teachers not only help students learn the necessary facts but also inspire them to discover, explore, investigate, research, and publish. One of my favorite teachers in elementary school was a history teacher who taught me to love history by taking us through the adventures of the early Canadian explorers as they paddled the dangerous waters to discover the Northwest Passage to the Pacific. His passion for exploration was magnetic as he talked about his personal voyages in the Canadian northland. In a similar way our ability as teachers to communicate the riches of God's Word depends a great deal on how deeply we are emotionally, intellectually, volitionally, and practically involved in knowing and living out the principles from God's Word.

I found this out while experimenting with training methods to help college students tell effective stories to children. Initially I thought the best way to train students to tell good stories was to teach them the mechanical skills of storytelling. Yet my strategy changed after seeing limited success through this approach. Through trial and error I discovered that the best way to teach people to communicate through stories was to start by getting each student to think of something he had learned and was passionate about. The students were then asked to think about how they learned that lesson, noting the specific emotional, intellectual, volitional, and practical steps in the process. After some discussion most people were able to identify at least one major lesson they felt passionate about to share with the group. As they brainstormed about the specific ways they learned those lessons, compelling stories emerged that involved deeply personal details of their thinking, feeling, and inner wrestling. With a little guidance and encouragement these student teachers had no trouble sharing their stories. As the teachers illustrated the practical details of how they learned these deeply personal lessons, they came alive in the hearts of the listeners. Whether their approach was dynamic or quiet, the key factor of effectiveness, identified by the participants, was the passion and depth of their presentations. While passion should never be used by a teacher to cover up a lack of depth or knowledge, passion and depth are a compelling communication combination. There is no shortcut to displaying personal depth in teaching. It comes primarily through experiencing, reflecting, and exploring under the guidance of the Holy Spirit.

In this next section we will seek to understand how the teacher can model the process of personal discovery and exploration into the Word and the depths of the heart, allowing the Holy Spirit to break up the hard and callous compartments of one's inner being to allow the truth of God and His Word to permeate it. If the goal of Christian education is to transform the heart so that every aspect of the person becomes progressively more Christlike, then transformation must begin with the teacher. The teacher must be willing and committed to the difficult work of soil preparation of his own heart if he expects to bear fruit in the lives of his students.

Personal Preparation of the Heart of the Teacher

Having been a teacher all of my adult life, one of my greatest temptations has been to fail to take the time and effort to thoughtfully prepare my heart prior to my preparation for teaching. I sometimes get so excited about my teaching or preaching that I fail to wrestle with what God wants to do in my heart. It is much easier to tell someone else what to do than to do it myself first. While none of us wants to be labeled a hypocrite, the tendency toward hypocrisy is present in us all. That is probably the reason James warns people not to aspire to become teachers, since they "will receive a stricter punishment" (Jas 3:1). As teachers we must discipline ourselves to prepare our hearts by allowing the Holy Spirit to search, cleanse, and mold the deepest parts of our minds, emotions, and wills prior to teaching others.

This preparation involves approaching God and His Word with a humble, teachable attitude of the heart. It includes being open and honest before God with our minds, our emotions, our wills, and our behavior. It often begins with praise, thanksgiving, and confession following the pattern in so many of David's psalms (Psalms 9; 18; 19; 30; 51). Regardless of the structure of our prayer time, the most important ingredients need to be transparency and intimacy with God. We need to share with the Father our thoughts, feelings, behaviors, sins, doubts, questions, and praises. By systematically examining these aspects of the core of our being—our mind, our emotions, our will, and our behavior—we give structure to what otherwise might be a directionless activity. This reflective process not only disarms our pride and self-sufficiency but opens us up to listen to the Father and His Word. If teachers skip this mandatory step of preparation, they may risk perpetuating shallow hypocrisy.

By practicing this reflective time of preparing the heart, we will be in a position to be filled with God's presence and Word.

Getting a Big Picture of the Passage from the Word

After preparing our hearts before God, the next stage of preparation involves discovering what a text is saying within the larger context of the biblical passage. I usually begin by refreshing my memory of the details of the text by reading the introduction of the book in my study Bible. Then I read the entire book in which the passage is found. My goal is to discover the overall theme of the book and how the passage I am focusing on fits into that theme. Three questions that need to be answered from the text are: How does this passage fit into the overall theme of the book? What is the purpose of this passage within the theme of the book? How does this passage contribute to the main purpose of the book? The answers to these questions will help establish the Big Idea of the passage later in this discovery process.

Constructing an Analytical Outline of the Text

While this step often provides the most fruitful results from Bible study, few teachers take the time to practice it. It is much easier simply to focus on the insights from a teacher's manual or initial impressions from a general reading of the text. Such superficial approaches often miss the clear points made in the text by the Spirit-inspired authors. If we hold to biblical inerrancy, we must take careful notice of sentence structure, verb tenses, prepositions, conjunctions, and other details of the written word. A more precise analysis of the grammatical structure often provides the key to discovering the Big Idea and other important principles from the text. By taking the time to construct an analytical outline, you will gain insights as to how to help students discover similar insights through their own inductive studies.

While my approach for developing an analytical outline can be adapted to an individual's preferences in structure and layout, it contains guidelines necessary to ensure an objective analysis of the details of the text. It involves rewriting every word in the text in a way that shows the grammatical structure of how the words, phrases, and sentences connect with one another. It is usually best to do this on a computer where spacing and indenting are easier. When a computer is unavailable, I sometimes write an outline on a large notebook page where I can jot comments and applications at a later time. This is an analytical outline I made of Phil 4:4–9:

Rejoice in the Lord always.
I will say it again: **Rejoice!**
Let your graciousness be known to everyone.
    The Lord is near.
Don't worry about anything,
        but in everything,
            through prayer and petition
                with thanksgiving,
    let your requests be made known to God.

And **the peace of God,**
                which surpasses every thought,
            will guard your hearts
                and your minds in Christ Jesus.
        Finally, brothers,
            whatever is true,
            whatever is honorable,
            whatever is just,
            whatever is pure,
            whatever is lovely,
            whatever is commendable—
            if there is any moral excellence and
            if there is any praise—
    dwell on these things.
    Do what you have learned and
            received and
            heard and
            seen in me,
            And **the God of peace** will be with you.

You will notice how clear and organized are the structure and content layout of the passage. From such an outline it seems much easier to analyze the relationships between words and phrases.

The first guideline in constructing an analytical outline is to clarify subjects, verbs, direct and indirect objects, and other parts of speech showing the relationships between each of them. Indent to show secondary or modifying words or phrases and try to space them under the words they modify or relate to. Line up similar or parallel words, phrases, or parts of speech. Leave larger spaces between separate ideas or concepts. Separate or indent major themes to highlight them. Note transitional words or phrases implying cause and effect, rationale, consequence, or result (therefore, in order to, since, unless, if, then, etc.). Feel free to customize your outline using lines and arrows to show direction or connection between similar or related ideas. Highlight major words, phrases, or principles from the text. The purpose is not necessarily to follow a particular format but rather to be accurate in diagramming the connections between words and phrases in the text.

Often I make two or three revisions of my analytical outline before I am satisfied with its accuracy and clarity. Sometimes I ask a friend or mentor familiar with this method of analysis to give advice or suggestions. When I am satisfied with the outline, I go on to the next step.

Summary of How to Construct an Analytical Outline

1. Work with one paragraph, story, or segment from Scripture at a time.

2. Pictorially represent the major intentions of the author in a grammatical outline of the text.

3. Indent to show secondary or modifying words or phrases.

4. Identify and separate subjects, verbs, and objects on different lines.

5. Put modifying phrases or clauses under the words they modify or describe.

6. Line up similar or parallel words, phrases, or parts of speech under one another.

7. Leave larger spaces between separate ideas or concepts.

8. Clearly identify themes, major subjects, concepts, or principles.

9. Note conjunctions or transitional words or phrases implying cause/effect, purpose, rationale, consequences, or results (therefore, in order to, since, unless, if, then, etc.). *These are the keys to unlock the principles in the text and the Big Idea of the text.*

10. Define words you do not understand. Look up cross-references for similar word usage and background.

11. Highlight major words, phrases, and concepts.

12. Use lines and arrows to show direction and connections between similar or related ideas.

Discovering What the Text Says in Detail

Next the teacher must answer for himself the foundational content questions about what God was saying through the words of the original author of the text. This would include key words, key verbs, tenses of the verbs, lists, major and minor points, cause-and-effect statements, commands, repeated phrases, and word meanings. Details of the text are identified and analyzed. This is where I use my creativity and my pencil by circling, drawing connecting lines, showing relationships between words and phrases, and highlighting major or repeated words and phrases.

For example, on my outline of Phil 4:4–9, I observed a connection between "peace of God" in v. 7 and "God of peace" in v. 9, so I circled each and drew a line connecting them. I also circled "rejoice" twice in v. 1, realizing that it was both a key verb and a command. I also numbered the commands in vv. 4, 5, and 6 as 1, 2, and 3. It seemed clear that "rejoice in the Lord," "let your graciousness be known to everyone," and "don't worry about anything" were all related to receiving the "peace of God" in v. 7.

In vv. 8 and 9, I observed a similar structure of the text. There I saw two commands: "dwell on these things" from v. 8 and "do" from v. 9 that related to receiving the presence of the "God of peace." I drew a line between "dwell on these things" and the eight characteristics of the types of things we should dwell on. I connected the four verbs in v. 9: "learned and received and heard and seen" with what we are supposed to "do" related to the author's lifestyle. Then I drew a line connecting "dwell" and "do" with the gift of the "God of peace."

I doubt that I would have come up with these significant connections within the text if I had not constructed an analytical outline. From here I am much more informed as to the intent of the passage and the overall Big Idea. Yet before going any further, I look up the meaning of each of the significant words in a theological dictionary. I often write the meaning next to the word in the text or on another piece of paper so not to confuse the structural layout of the text. Key words that should be looked up in this text are "peace," "rejoice," "graciousness," "worry," "dwell," and each of the characteristics of things we are supposed to dwell on from v. 8. While this step takes time and effort, it is imperative if we are to understand the intent of the biblical passage.

An analytical outline provides a foundational structure from which to observe clearly the main details of the text. This outline creates a clear picture from which to gaze into the main components of any biblical passage. Robert Traina, in his classic book *Methodical Bible Study*, identifies four aspects of any biblical text that need careful analysis: "terms; the relations and interrelations between terms, or structure; the general literary form or forms; and the atmosphere."[3] The analytical outline provides an objective framework from which to search for these treasures that lead to the Big Idea of the text.

---

[3] Robert A. Traina, *Methodical Bible Study: A New Approach to Hermeneutics* (Grand Rapids: Zondervan, 1980), 53.

The *observation of terms* includes the definition of a term, the different kinds of terms, and the identity and inflections of terms. Defining terms means first of all explaining what the term means in its specific context. Second, it means identifying terms that have special significance and differentiating between literal and figurative terms. Third, it means identifying the grammatical categories for each word and inflections indicating "a change in form undergone by terms to indicate their case, gender, number, tense, person, mood, voice, etc. Inflections are especially significant in relation to nouns, pronouns, verbs, and adjectives."[4]

The second aspect of a biblical text that Traina says must be analyzed relates to *structure or the observation of relations and interrelations between terms*. The analytical outline provides the best way to graphically observe structure and relationships between terms. Terms are organized in various ways using phrases, clauses, sentences, paragraphs, groups of paragraphs, and larger segments and units organized around similar thoughts or expressions. The literary structure represented by the way these terms are organized is the major way the student of God's Word identifies the major theme and Big Idea of a passage.

Traina categorizes the ways terms can be organized structurally into 16 categories that can be used to identify the Exegetical Big Idea and the development of his arguments, rationale, or story line.

1. Comparison—an association of things that are similar (Heb 5:1–10)
2. Contrast—an association of things that are different (Romans 4)
3. Repetition—reiteration of the same words more than once (Leviticus: "holy")
4. Continuity—repeated use of similar terms or phrases (Luke 15)
5. Continuation—extended treatment of a theme more in depth (Genesis 13; 14; 18–19)
6. Climax—showing progress from lesser, to greater, to greatest (Exod 40:34–35)
7. Cruciality—organization around a pivotal point (2 Samuel 11–12)
8. Interchange—showing contrast or comparison (Luke 1–2)
9. Particularization and Generalization—movement from either the general to the particular or from the particular to the general (Matt 6:1–18; James 2)
10. Causation and Substantiation—progression from cause to effect or from effect to cause (Rom 1:18–32; Rom 8:18–30)

---

[4] Ibid., 35–36.

11. Instrumentation—stating the means to the end as well as the end itself (John 20:30–31)

12. Explanation or Analysis—an event or story followed by its interpretation (Mark 4)

13. Preparation or Introduction—setting the stage for what is to follow (Gen 2:24–25)

14. Summarization—pulling together what was stated earlier in a simplified format (Joshua 12)

15. Interrogation—a question followed by an answer (Romans 6–7)

16. Harmony—showing agreement using comparisons between similar things (Rom 1:18–3:20; 3:21ff.)[5]

The third aspect of the biblical text that those preparing to teach must examine is *the general literary focus of the text*. The literary focus determines how the reader should interpret what the author is saying. Traina identifies six categories of literary genre. The first category is *discourse and logical literature*, which includes explanations and discourses usually presented in an argumentative format to convince or instruct. The second category is *prose narrative*, which includes stories and biographical sketches often appealing to the emotions and imagination of the reader. The third category is *poetry*, usually characterized by being figurative, emotional, and complex, many times involving idioms that are difficult to interpret. The fourth category is *drama and dramatic prose*, which may include descriptions that emphasize some elements presented to emphasize particular characteristics or features. The fifth category is *parabolic literature*, which usually uses a physical narrative to illustrate a spiritual truth or concept (Matthew 13; Mark 4; Luke 15). The sixth category of biblical genre is *apocalyptic literature*, usually characterized by symbolism and predictive visionary language. Daniel and Revelation are good examples. Before trying to identify what the biblical author is saying in a text, the reader must identify the genre.[6]

The fourth element identified by Traina in the process of observing a biblical text is the observation of *atmosphere*. "By atmosphere is meant the underlying tone or spirit of a passage, which though intangible, is nevertheless real. The tone of the passage could reflect many different emotions such as despair, thanksgiving, awe, urgency, joy, humility, or tenderness." Observation

---

[5] Ibid., 50–55.

[6] Ibid., 68–71.

of the tone or atmosphere of the passage is an important clue to identifying the author's main passion and heart.[7]

The steps of inductive Bible study follow the natural progression of the steps of going deeper toward the heart explained earlier. They move from simple observation of facts to interpretation, to application, and to putting applications into practice. The steps need to follow this logical order to guard against impulsively speculating as to what God might be saying to us based on a faulty interpretation of the text. Before attempting to interpret the meaning of a passage, the Bible student must take the time and effort to construct an analytical outline and analyze the details of the text. While the focus so far seems to be primarily in the cognitive domain, most learners at this point are already beginning to open their hearts, including both emotional and volitional aspects.

For instance, at this stage in my study of the Philippians passage, I was already aware that there is a profound connection between my attitude in the midst of troubles and my ability to experience the peace of God. I was also becoming aware of the fact, stated in the text, that my experience of God's presence may be directly related to whether I am practicing what the apostle Paul modeled before his followers. The Holy Spirit was beginning to open my heart to what He wanted to change in my mind, my emotions, my will, and my behavior. Rather than jump to a premature conclusion about the meaning of the text, I wrote down my initial thoughts so that I could process them after more study and reflection. As important as these early insights were to me personally, I held off from premature conclusions about what God might be saying to me until I had answered the major question: "What is the Big Idea of the text?"

Identifying the Exegetical Big Idea of the Text

The major focus of this stage in the preparation process is to understand the primary lesson that God, through the biblical writer, had for the original readers. This will be referred to as the *Exegetical Big Idea* of the text, although in this chapter it will also be called simply the *Big Idea*. The noun *exegesis*, from which we derive the adjective *exegetical*, means "an explanation or a critical interpretation of a text."[8] This step of the inductive process focuses on discovering what the text means or how it should be understood or interpreted. Thus

---

[7] Ibid., 71.

[8] *Merriam-Webster's Collegiate Dictionary*, 11th ed., s.v. "exegetical."

the Exegetical Big Idea should explain the central meaning or interpretation of the biblical text.

Yet as Wilhoit and Ryken point out, "There is no single 'correct way' to formulate the Big Idea in a biblical passage."[9] While different approaches may be used by both biblical scholars and preachers to find and express the Exegetical Big Idea, there are common elements to most approaches.

Haddon Robinson, who popularized the concept of the Big Idea in preaching, states that the two questions central to identifying the Big Idea are: "What is the author talking about? and What is he saying about what he is talking about."[10] He prefers the term *subject* to refer to the theme or topic and *complement* for what the author says about the subject. While other authors use different terminology to describe the thesis statement or Big Idea, the main characteristic of the Big Idea is that it contains two parts, one identifying the main thing the author is talking about and the other describing the main thing he is saying about it. Robinson's terminology of Big Idea is used similarly to the way authors often use the term *thesis*, as a concise sentence that states something profound about a subject.

While I have been strongly influenced by Robinson's construction of the Big Idea, I like to use the term *principle* to describe the form in which Big Ideas from Scripture should be stated. A "principle is a comprehensive and fundamental law, doctrine, or assumption."[11] When stated as a principle, the Big Idea takes the form of an *axiom* or "a statement accepted as true as the basis for argument of inference."[12] In combining Robinson's components (a subject and something profound about the subject) with the definition of a principle in characterizing a Big Idea, it makes it more foundational, generalizable, and profound.

Principles should connect theology with practice in a way that promotes wise living. While they should dip deeply into theological insights, principles should also inform practical living. They should show the integral relationship between theory and practice, knowing God and living for Him. They should show how right belief impacts actions. Accurate and well-developed principles become the teacher's gold mine from which to draw insights for their own lives and the lives of their students. The process of discovering and developing good principles becomes the catalyst to heart-deep learning and teaching. Principles

---

[9] Jim Wilhoit and Leland Ryken, *Effective Bible Teaching* (Grand Rapids: Baker, 1988), 81.

[10] Haddon W. Robinson, *Biblical Preaching: The Development and Delivery of Expository Messages* (Grand Rapids: Baker, 1980), 41.

[11] *Merriam-Webster's Collegiate Dictionary*, 11th edition, s.v. "principle."

[12] Ibid., s.v. "axiom."

become the focus of what the student learns from Scripture, and the major principle of a given text becomes the Exegetical Big Idea of the Bible lesson. In an attempt to find the Exegetical Big Idea of a text, I have found that it often helps to identify a number of general principles from the text first before narrowing in on the Exegetical Big Idea.[13]

Some of the guidelines I use to help construct principle statements are as follows:

- Use first person plural—*we* or *us* rather than *you*.
- State the subject or theme and something profound about it.
- State it in one complete sentence.
- Don't just state a fact or give a list of ideas.
- Go beyond a statement of the obvious.
- Use simple rather than compound sentences.
- Use inclusive language.
- Use variety in sentence structure. Don't start each principle the same way.
- Use active rather than passive verbs.
- Don't sound preachy.

Some of the easiest ways to state principles are by using these phrases:

- "If we expect to . . . , it is necessary to . . ."
- "In order to . . . , we must . . ."
- "The best way to . . . is to . . ."
- "If we are to . . . , we should . . ."

When we ask questions of exegesis or the meaning of a text related to principles or the Exegetical Big Idea, we are asking "why," "how," and "so what" questions. They usually involve cause and effect, rationale, reasons, dangers, prerequisites, depth, implications, applications, and results. A major key to discovering these meanings is found in the grammatical layout of the text. Words such as *if, then, because, but, and, in order to, rather,* and *therefore* become markers signaling inherent meanings.

Examples of such key words in the Philippians passage are "but," "through," "with," and "and" in v. 6. Each of these words marks a potential statement of meaning within the text.

---

[13] I learned this practice of identifying principles from a biblical text from Dr. Walter Kaiser in a class I attended at Trinity Evangelical Divinity School. Since that mid '80s class, I have used this method to prepare for all my teaching and preaching.

Analytical Outline of Philippians 4:4–9

Rejoice in the Lord always.
I will say it again: Rejoice!
Let your graciousness be known to everyone.
   The Lord is near.
Don't worry about anything,
    but in everything,
      through prayer and petition
      with thanksgiving,
let your requests be made known to God.
      And the peace of God,
         which surpasses every thought,
       will guard your hearts
        and your minds in Christ Jesus.
   Finally, brothers,
    whatever is true,
    whatever is honorable,
    whatever is just,
    whatever is pure,
    whatever is lovely,
    whatever is commendable—
    if there is any moral excellence and
    if there is any praise—
dwell on these things
Do what you have learned and
   received and
   heard and
   seen in me,
     And the God of peace will be with you.

I like to indicate the meaning statements in a way that shows cause and effect, rationale, consequences, or implications relating to life. They should go beyond stating a simple fact to giving a principle of life, truth, or living. From v. 6, I identified a principle relating to "but" as, "*Rather than worry about your stresses, a better way to deal with them is to pray to God concerning them.*" I identified the principle relating to the word "through" as, "*By talking to God and actually pleading with God about our struggles, we can be assured of His supernatural peace.*" By noting the significance of the word "with," I found this principle: "*Giving God thanks in our prayers in the midst of difficulties helps us experience His peace.*" Finally, from the word "and," I identified one of the key principles in v. 6: *"When we take the time to rejoice in the Lord and pray rather than waste our time worrying, God's peace protects us."*

It is important to make sure you are not reading into the text in coming up with meanings or principles. The principles must be directly related to what the text says, based on your analytical outline and your analysis of the details of the text. However, they should be stated in a way that goes beyond the obvious. They should not merely repeat the text but make it even more clear, applicable, and meaningful.

The following statements represent other principles I developed from the Philippians text. See whether you can identify the details in the text that served as the basis for each one. Next, try to identify which principles could be considered as the Exegetical Big Idea of the text.

- No matter what emotions we may be experiencing, we should seek joy in our relationship with Jesus Christ (v. 4).
- The fact that the Lord is always by our side helps us be more relaxed in the midst of difficulty (v. 5).
- The best antidote for worry is prayer (v. 6).
- In order to experience God's presence and peace, we must bring our emotions, thoughts, and behavior under His lordship (vv. 4–9).
- Even in the midst of horrible circumstances, we can pray with thanksgiving because God is close to us and in control (vv. 4–7).
- Although we may not always understand how and when God answers prayer, we should pray about everything that concerns us (vv. 6–7).
- When we rejoice in the Lord and talk to Him about all our concerns, His peace guards our hearts and minds (vv. 4–7).
- When we discipline our minds according to God's Word and obey God consistently, the God of peace promises to be with us (vv. 8–9).
- What we think about influences our actions for either good or evil (vv. 8–9).
- It is easier to learn to practice godliness when we see others living it in front of us (v. 9).
- Experiencing God's presence and His peace involves more than just our emotions (vv. 4–9).
- The presence of God is experienced by those willing to discipline their minds and behavior according to God's Word (vv. 8–9).
- The peace of God seems to be intimately connected to the indwelling of the God of peace (vv. 7–9).
- While the peace of God may be beyond our human understanding, the path to experiencing it is simple (vv. 4–7).

At this stage in my inductive study of a scriptural passage, I try to identify as many principles as I can based on the analytical outline and a detailed study of the passage. This gives me a more objective basis from which to choose the major principle or Exegetical Big Idea. Once I list all the principles I can find from the text, I prioritize and arrange the statements in order from most significant to least. Interpretation of a biblical passage must begin with the major principle or Exegetical Big Idea and then proceed to the minor principles. The most significant principle reflects the major thing the biblical author is saying about the primary theme of the text. While minor principles may come from verses or sections within the passage, the Exegetical Big Idea or major principle must take into account the whole passage.

In Phil 4:4–9, I would choose the principle, "In order to experience God's presence and peace, we must bring our emotions, thoughts, and behavior under His lordship" as the Exegetical Big Idea. I could state the same concept in a similar principle, "Experiencing God's presence and His peace involves more than just our emotions." My reasons for choosing these principles are as follows:

- A major theme of the passage, *the God of peace* and *the peace of God*, declares the benefits of following the commands within the two main sections of the text.
- The five commands—rejoice in the Lord always, don't worry about anything, pray about everything, think only God-honoring things, and put into practice the things Paul taught—could be summarized as "bringing our thoughts, emotions, and behavior under His lordship."
- While some might argue that rejoicing is the major theme of the passage, it is only the first of five commands mentioned in the passage. The theme of the whole passage has more to do with experiencing God's presence and peace, and the thesis of the passage is that this takes more than just disciplining our emotions. I do, however, realize that because the text uses "rejoice" twice, the author is emphasizing it above the other commands. It could be that focusing our joy on Christ has a trigger effect on our thoughts and our behavior.

The following analytical outline and list of principles from Psalm 19 give us another example of how the structure of a passage gives clues to the principles found in the text. As we compare the principles to the structure and detail of the analytical outline, we can see where the principles come from in the text.

Analytical Outline of Psalm 19

The heavens   declare   the glory of God;
The skies   proclaim the work of his hands.

Day after day   they pour forth speech;
night after night they display   knowledge.

There is no speech or language where their voice is not heard.

Their voice goes out into all the earth,
their words   to the ends of the world.

In the heavens
he has pitched a tent
for **the sun,**
      which is like a bridegroom coming forth from his pavilion,
        like a champion rejoicing to run his course.
     It rises at one end of the heavens and
     makes its circuit to the other;

            nothing is hidden from its heat.

The law of the LORD is		perfect,	reviving the soul.
The statutes of the LORD are		trustworthy,	making wise the simple.
The precepts of the LORD are	right,		giving joy to the heart.
The commands of the LORD are	radiant,		giving light to the eyes.
The fear of the LORD is		pure,	enduring forever.

The ordinances of the LORD are sure and
             altogether righteous.

They are   more precious than gold,
            than much pure gold;

    they are   sweeter than honey,
         than honey from the comb.

    By them   is your servant warned;

    in keeping them   there is great reward.

Who can discern his errors?
>forgive my hidden faults

Keep **your servant** also from willful sins;

>may they not rule over me.

Then will I be blameless,
>>innocent of great transgression.

May   the words of my mouth and
the meditation of my heart

>>be pleasing
>>in your sight

>>O LORD
>>>my Rock and
>>>my Redeemer. (NIV)

Principles from Psalm 19

1. Since God has revealed Himself to all people through His creation, everyone has a responsibility to see and respond to God (vv. 1–6).
2. The predictability of the movement of the sun and the stars reflects the dependability, power, and faithfulness of God (vv. 1–6).
3. Just as no person can hide from the awesome heat of the sun, no person can hide from God's glory (vv. 4–6).
4. Because God's law is perfect, it has the capability of rejuvenating our souls (v. 7a).
5. Since God's commands are trustworthy, even a simple person can become wise by faithfully following them (v. 7b).
6. Contrary to the popular tenets of postmodernism, true joy doesn't come from following our subjective impulses but rather from following what is objectively right (v. 8a).
7. Since God's commandments are radiant, following them will light up the dark pathways of life (v. 8b).
8. Because God's judgments are perfect and true, the person who respects and follows His commands has nothing to fear (v. 9).

9. God's precepts can be more valuable to us than gold and sweeter than honey since they are not only absolutely pure but also will last forever (v. 10).
10. God's laws are a blessing only to those who follow them (v. 11).
11. Even when God's servants get off track, His commands come as a blessing to warn us of imminent danger (v. 11a).
12. Our response to the awesomeness of God's glory and the holiness of His law should be to bow humbly before Him for the forgiveness of our sins (vv. 11–14).
13. The true servant of the Almighty God will keep as far away from sinning as possible (v. 13).
14. While God does not expect us to be perfect, He does expect us to commit ourselves to obey His commands (vv. 7–14).
15. One way we can keep on the right track is never to be overcome by a willful, habitual sin pattern (v. 13).
16. God's revelation to us through His creation and His commandments demands that we strive to please Him through our thoughts and our words (vv. 1–14).
17. Our response to the awesomeness of God's glory and the holiness of His law should be to bow humbly before Him for the forgiveness of our sins and to follow Him in obedience (vv. 1–14).
18. As our Rock, God provides us with stability; as our Redeemer, God provides us with grace (v. 14).

As you examine each of the principles, you will observe many creative ways to state them. Some principles come from specific verses, and others come from the insights stated in specific sections of the psalm. Yet the principle chosen to reflect the Exegetical Big Idea of a passage should reflect the major thesis of the psalm as a whole. I would choose the statement: "Our response to the awesomeness of God's glory and the holiness of His law should be to bow humbly before Him for the forgiveness of our sins and to follow Him in obedience." Each of the three statements of this thesis relates directly to the major point of each of the three sections of the psalm, thus pulling the whole psalm together. After reflecting on God's revelation, in His creation and His law, the only logical response for humankind is to repent and to turn to God for forgiveness and then to follow Him in obedience. All the rest of the principles could be placed under this major Big Idea. The Exegetical Big Idea may be conceived as an umbrella that overshadows the other principles.

The Big Idea is defined as the main, overarching principle of any given text. While there may be many principles in a text, all the other principles usually fit under or relate to one major principle. As you can see, identifying the Exegetical Big Idea of a text is much more difficult than coming up with a minor principle. The Big Idea must be comprehensive, inclusive, and encompassing. Although there may be various ways of stating an Exegetical Big Idea, it is essential that it accurately reflects the major intent of the text based on thorough research and study. It is not enough just to borrow a Big Idea from a lesson quarterly or another biblical author. Teachers must go through this wrestling and learning process in order to know and understand the Big Idea at the depth needed to apply it effectively in their own lives. Only after wrestling through this process for themselves are teachers ready to help others to learn the Big Idea at a heart-deep level.

The process of coming up with an Exegetical Big Idea is the most difficult and complex component of preparation. No wonder teachers may hesitate to take the time and effort to commit themselves to this process. It involves all the cognitive processes identified for in-depth learning: observing, discovering, organizing, assessing, evaluating, critiquing, reflecting, hypothesizing, creating, and formulating. Yet this process provides a rich reservoir for both personal learning and creative ideas to help students learn more in depth.

Applying the Exegetical Big Idea
and Other Principles in Life

By the time a teacher has wrestled through the process explained in this chapter, application flows naturally. If one had jotted down personal insights throughout this process, he or she would likely have a long list of notes and reflection already recorded. What I usually do to stimulate more personal response at this stage is to go back to the Exegetical Big Idea and each of my principles and prayerfully ask the Holy Spirit for insight about what I need to work on related to each of them. By starting with the Big Idea, I make sure I focus on God's major purpose in His inspiration of the biblical author. Then I allow the Holy Spirit to use each principle to purge my thoughts, my emotions, my will, and my behavior. While I may respond in different ways depending on the focus of the principle, I have found it most helpful to state specific goals for myself in areas where God is challenging me.

The following statements relate to specific goals I as a teacher might jot down in my journal in regard to my Big Idea and some of the principles identified earlier. While the first statement is the principle, the second statement of each set represents a personal goal or prayer I might jot down in response.

Exegetical Big Idea

In order to experience God's presence and His peace, we must bring our emotions, thoughts, and behavior under His lordship.

I would reflectively ask the Holy Spirit to evaluate my emotions, thoughts, and behavior to reveal and purge me of all evil.

Other Principles

No matter what emotions we may be experiencing, we should find our joy in our relationship with Jesus Christ.

Lord, even though I am frustrated, help me to appreciate Your great love for me.

The fact that the Lord is always by our side helps us to be more relaxed and calm in the midst of difficulty.

Lord, help me appreciate the fact that You live deep within my heart.

The best antidote for worry is to pray.

I would spend time praying about my concerns.

Even in the midst of horrible circumstances, we can pray with thanksgiving because God is close by and in control.

Acknowledging before God my difficult circumstances, I would petition the Lord for my needs with thanksgiving.

It is easier to learn to practice godliness when we see others living it in front of us.

I would pray to be an example to my students so that I could say as Paul said, "Follow me as I follow Christ."

While the peace of God may be beyond our human understanding, the path to experiencing it is simple.

I would commit myself anew to follow the simple plan of praying instead of worrying.

While in a normal preparation time I may narrow my focus to applying the Exegetical Big Idea and a few of the related principles, these statements reflect the types of responses I could focus on related to each of the principles identified in the text. At this point in the preparation stage, teachers of the Word must be ruthlessly open to what the Holy Spirit wants to change in their lives before even attempting to help students learn similar principles.

Establishing Accountability Measures
for Accomplishing Goals

It is futile to set goals and never plan how you will accomplish them. If there is no planning or assessment of goals, it is unlikely the goals will ever be accomplished. If teachers expect their students to set goals related to the lessons they give, the teachers must practice this discipline in their own lives first. This takes time and integrity.

The first step in setting goals is to soften your heart before the Lord to make sure you are open and pliable to His will and direction. After reflecting on the implications of the Big Idea and other significant principles you have discovered from the text, ask the Holy Spirit to narrow His focus down to one or two major areas of concern in your life. This will be more manageable than a long list.

After choosing an area of concern to work on, brainstorm as to what is the root of the problem. A journal is helpful for writing down reflections and having dialogue with the Lord at this point. A journal entry based on the following Big Idea—"In order to experience God's presence and His peace, we must bring our emotions, thoughts, and behavior under His lordship"—might include the following reflections:

> Lord, You know that I do not feel particularly close to You this morning. I'm not sure why, because I truly desire to experience Your presence more fully in my life. As I have been reading and reflecting on this passage of Scripture, I am convicted of the fact that the only way I can experience Your presence and peace is by bringing my emotions, thoughts, and behavior under Your control. I realize that lately I have been bombarded with thoughts of resentment for what she did to me. While I have tried to forgive her, I don't think I really want to. I keep bringing back to the surface of my consciousness feelings of resentment and retribution. I know this is wrong. Yesterday I intentionally refused to look at her when I walked past her. How can that be forgiveness! Lord, please cleanse and purify my heart, break my will.

Reflections related to the Big Idea can take many forms. Sometimes I list specific concerns, temptations, or blessings related to the focus of the Big Idea. Honesty, transparency, and vulnerability are the most important elements of these reflections.

After sharing with the Lord these deeper thoughts, the next step is to set one or two goals related to the application of the Big Idea in your life. Personal goals I might set related to the issue I was dealing with might include:

- I will refuse to dwell on any negative thought.
- When a negative thought comes to my mind, I will immediately think of some of the good things she has done for other people.
- By narrowing my goals down to one or two short, clear, measurable actions, I will be more apt to accomplish them.

The last step is to find some way of keeping yourself accountable for accomplishing your goals. I have found that the best way to accomplish my goals is to write my goals down in a journal and to be accountable to a small group or a Christian friend. Other people use the Internet and texting to keep accountable with Christian friends. I use several relationships for different levels of accountability. Some things I am able to share in my small group while other things I am dealing with are reserved for the more intimate relationships with my wife or mature mentors. If you are serious about accomplishing a goal, you must hold yourself accountable to someone else. This principle keeps teachers both vulnerable and moldable.

Chapter Summary

When I follow these preparation steps in my teaching and preaching, the lesson planning and presentation seem to flow much more naturally. Each of the stages of this process seems essential in helping the teacher *learn* the lesson at a deep enough level to enable him to *teach* at a heart-deep level. Stages in a teacher's preparation should include getting a big picture of the passage from the Word, constructing an analytical outline, discovering what the text says in detail, identifying the Exegetical Big Idea and other principles, applying the Big Idea and other principles to life, and establishing accountability measures for accomplishing goals.

Only after thorough study of the text is the teacher ready to strategize how to contextualize the lessons for the students. Once teachers have made progress in applying the principles of the text to their own lives in specific ways are they ready to create a plan to help the students learn similar lessons from the biblical text.

Summary of the Steps of Personal Preparation

1. Getting the big picture of a biblical text
2. Constructing an analytical outline of the text
3. Discovering the details of what the text says from the analytical outline

4. Identifying the Exegetical Big Idea and other principles
5. Applying the Exegetical Big Idea and other principles to your life personally with specific goals
6. Establishing accountability measures for accomplishing your goals

Questions and Applications

1. Why is it important for a Christian to define the nature of truth?

2. How do postmodern philosophers tend to define truth?

3. How does the Bible define truth?

4. What two issues does the term *epistemology* deal with?

5. Is it inconsistent to believe in the objective nature of truth and also that people learn through their experience? Why or why not?

6. How can we avoid making overly dogmatic statements in applying commands in Scripture from other times and cultures to our present contexts?

7. What is an example of an overly dogmatic application of a biblical guideline to our culture today that may not be based on a solid principle?

8. Why must teachers learn and apply Scripture themselves before teaching others?

9. Following each of the steps of personal preparation listed at the end of this chapter, complete a thorough study of Eph 1:1–17.

10. What do you see as the value of studying a biblical text at this level before teaching it to others?

PART III

DESIGNING DEEPER LEARNING EXPERIENCES

Once the teacher has thought through the meaning of the biblical text, established an Exegetical Big Idea to guide the teaching-learning process, and made progress in applying the principles in the text to his own life, he is ready to think through how to design deeper learning experiences to challenge students to join him in discovering and applying the biblical principles to their lives. This process of designing deeper learning experiences involves four steps representing each of the following chapters: "Looking at the Biblical Text Through Students' Eyes," "Setting Goals to Encourage Deeper Student Learning," "Understanding How People Learn," and "Designing Learning Experiences that Encourage Heart-Deep Learning."

Chapter 5

Looking at the Biblical Text Through Students' Eyes

We have all experienced the fallacies of well-intentioned teachers who either fail to take into consideration the needs and backgrounds of their students or fail to uncover the essential meaning of the biblical text. Teachers often gravitate to one of two extremes in teaching the Bible. Either they try to teach their students exactly what they learned from the text for themselves; or, in an attempt to relate to students' needs, they stray from the original intent of the text. Both extremes fail to do justice to the nature of Scripture and the nature of the student. Teachers must exegete accurately both Scripture and the student. Every attempt must be made to help students learn the main point of the text in a way that makes sense to them developmentally and contextually. The greater the differences in age, culture, developmental level, and socioeconomic level between teacher and student, the more crucial it is to think through how to contextualize the Big Idea to the students' needs.

Studying Your Students

While the first step in preparing a biblical lesson should be to study the text thoroughly to find out what it says and means and how it applies in its historical context, the next step is to study the student. I am not suggesting a full demographic research project, psychoanalysis, or formal student interviews before every class but rather appropriate reflection and research into students' learning style, developmental level, cultural background, home life, education, and maturity. While the best way to gain this level of understanding about students is to interact with them in informal situations over a long period of time, this may not always be possible. Many times teachers do not have the luxury of getting to know students personally before teaching them. In such cases another option for teachers might be to gain some knowledge about the specific students from other teachers, students, and the media. Another readily available source for understanding student needs is through reading and research.

Richards and Bredfeldt, in their book *Creative Bible Teaching*, present five excellent tables summarizing the developmental characteristics of students at various age levels.[1] By becoming aware of the unique spiritual and developmental needs of preschool children, elementary school children, youth, and adults, teachers can more effectively gear their lessons to those needs. By understanding students' developmental needs in physical, emotional, cognitive, social, and moral areas of their lives, teachers will be more apt to engage them in learning.

Recent research relating to brain development is another source of insights on students' needs. Brain research related to children and youth has reinforced the need for teachers to become more aware of the interconnectedness of students' thinking, feeling, deciding, and acting. The implications of this research suggest that physical, emotional, and social stimulation within the learning environment have a direct effect on the growth of brain cells and cognitive development.[2] In Robert Sylwester's two books, *The Child's Brain: The Need for Nurture*[3] and *The Adolescent Brain: Reaching for Autonomy*,[4] he explains how biological insights about the nature of the brain show the distinctive needs of children and adolescents. As the distinctive book titles state, the major differences between children and youth are that while children need intentional nurturing, youth need autonomy in order to grow and develop. Brain research

---

[1] Larry Richards and Gary J. Bredfeldt, *Creative Bible Teaching* (Chicago: Moody, 1998), 100–104.

[2] Eric Jensen, *Enriching the Brain: How to Maximize Every Learner's Potential*, 1st ed., The Jossey-Bass Education Series (San Francisco: Jossey-Bass, 2006), 47–84.

[3] Robert Sylwester, *A Child's Brain: The Need for Nurture* (Thousand Oaks, CA: Corwin, 2010).

[4] Robert Sylwester, *The Adolescent Brain: Reaching for Autonomy* (Thousand Oaks, CA: Corwin, 2007).

continues to provide us with more and more insights into how the brain functions and what it needs to grow and develop.

Along with examining research and writings on student needs, another option for discovering the unique needs of students might be to observe them in a variety of informal situations. As perceptive teachers observe students outside the classroom, they are able to pick up insights about how they behave, interact, learn, express themselves, communicate, and think. By continually observing others under the guidance of the Holy Spirit, teachers can gain valuable clues to the emotional, intellectual, volitional, and behavioral needs and issues of their students. These insights become the building blocks of contextualizing the lesson to the lives of students.

Recently I witnessed a vivid example of "contextualization" while attending chapel at Crown College where I teach. Grace Fabian, a Wycliffe Bible translator who spent more than 50 years translating the New Testament, told a story of a breakthrough she had in communicating the gospel to an unreached people group in Papua, New Guinea. For a while she struggled with how to translate 2 Cor 2:14 in a way that would convey the depth of excitement in that text. The concept that God "always leads us in triumphant procession in Christ and through us spreads everywhere the fragrance of the knowledge of him" (NIV) seemed difficult for her and her husband to communicate in the tribal language. A breakthrough came when one of the tribesmen explained what normally happened when his tribe won a battle over a neighboring tribe. As he explained it, the winning tribe paraded the captives back to their village in much the same way soldiers did in biblical times. When they got to their village, they had a symbolic victory dance in which the warriors laid the captives on their backs and put their feet on the necks of their captives while they lifted their loincloths and ceremoniously "mooned" the captives. While this illustration may not appear in your Bible, it did find a prominent place in their Bible. Grace went on to explain in chapel how this picture graphically portrayed to the tribe the decisiveness of the victory of Christ over Satan and his demons. The tribe finally could understand the excitement and joy of living in a constant state of victory over the evil forces of the enemy.

This illustration shows us how important it is not just to restate biblical terminology without thinking through how the recipients of the message will understand it. Rather than simply restating the principles and Exegetical Big Idea of the text as we understand them, we must look at how we could rephrase them to communicate them more effectively to our students.

Reflecting on the Biblical Text from the Perspective of the Students

In order to connect with students, teachers need to put themselves in the role of their students as they reflect on the biblical text. Teachers need to hypothesize what the students might be thinking, feeling, experiencing, struggling with, frustrated with, happy about, or anticipating while they are reading the text. This stage of the preparation process is "incarnational"—just as Jesus put Himself voluntarily in our shoes, so we must put ourselves in the shoes of those we are teaching.

As important as the objective nature of God's Word is as our ultimate authority and truth, we must strive to connect the timeless principles in God's Word to the needs of our students. As Richards and Bredfeldt affirm:

> The ultimate objective in teaching the Bible is not Bible knowledge, though that is very important; it is *applied* Bible knowledge in the student's everyday life. We have said earlier that Bible content is crucial because of its inspired and revelatory nature. But we must remember, we teach people, not lessons. So we must begin with people.[5]

A helpful way to order this process of connecting to the needs of students is by using the categories—cognitive, affective, volitional, and behavioral—as filters through which to visualize their distinctive needs as you analyze the text. It demands that the teacher look at the text through the students' eyes and their experiences in each of these categories. What would the students be thinking about when reading the story or hearing the words or sentences? What would they be feeling? What would be natural questions that would come to them? What would they struggle with relating to the text? What would be difficult for them to put into practice from the story? What might they not understand? What would be frustrating for them to understand from their perspective? What would not make sense? By wrestling with these questions from the students' perspective, the teacher will be more apt to relate the Big Idea of the text to students' needs.

The Option of Breaking the Big Idea into Bite-Size Pieces

Sometimes teachers focus on one of the minor principles from a text rather than the Exegetical Big Idea in order to meet students' needs at a deeper level.

---

[5] Richards and Bredfeldt, *Creative Bible Teaching*, 94.

This is especially true in teaching through a series related to the same passage or a similar topic. Sometimes, when either preaching or teaching, I start with an overall Big Idea of a passage in my initial lesson and then break it down in subsequent lessons, focusing on subprinciples related to the Big Idea. In these situations I will focus on one or more minor principles from the text and develop the lesson using structure similar to what I would use for a lesson built on the Big Idea. When teaching on a minor principle from a biblical text, we always must be careful to examine it in its historical and cultural context within the framework of the Exegetical Big Idea. Principles taken from a smaller segment of a biblical passage must fit under the Exegetical Big Idea of the larger context.

An example of such a series might be an "armor of God" series from Eph 6:10–20. A Big Idea for such a series might be the statement, "If we are to stand firm against Satan's attacks, we must put on God's armor." This would be applicable for a preaching series, a VBS week of meetings, a youth retreat, or a men's retreat. If I were designing such a series around this Big Idea, I might suggest several principles that could be the focus of single lessons in a series. If I were leading a series of lessons for junior high students, I might start each principle with the statement, "In order to stand firm against the enemy, we must . . ." Then for each lesson I might use statements to complete the principles such as: "Draw on Christ for strength." "Take advantage of all of God's resources." "Realize who our enemy is." "Understand the battlefield." "Practice the discipline of standing firm." "Wrap our lives in truth." "Protect our hearts with righteousness." "Be always prepared to share the gospel." "Protect ourselves from Satan's arrows through faith." "Protect our minds with assurance of Christ's salvation." "Offensively arm ourselves with the Word of God." And, "Constantly pray for ourselves and other soldiers." While a youth pastor could try to teach this lesson in one session under one Big Idea, it could be much more in depth and effective if it were spread out over 13 lessons starting with the Big Idea and using the 12 principles suggested above. Spreading the lesson over several sessions would give the teacher a better chance of meeting more students' deeper needs related to dealing with the enemy.

In using a topical series rather than a series from one biblical text, teachers must be careful not to take principles out of context just to fit into their lesson theme. For example, it would be inaccurate to use Gal 5:1 NIV, "It is for freedom that Christ has set us free," to teach young people that they should not follow the moral guidelines of their elders. The main reason that this would be inaccurate is that the Big Idea for the text as a whole is that Christians should not slip into either the slavery of legalism or the slavery of sin since Christ has made us free by grace through faith. The text is not dealing with how young people should respond to guidelines given by their elders. While such a principle may sound applicable to most students struggling with submission to their elders, it violates the intent of the biblical text. It is wiser to teach topical lessons as principles within the larger context of a biblical book or story than to extract biblical ideas that fit present situations.

As an example, in teaching high school students about dealing with sexual temptation, it would be better to build a series of lessons from the whole life story of Joseph rather than to focus on his temptation with Potiphar's wife. The principle of how Joseph overcame the temptation in this situation was the result of a pattern of commitments Joseph had learned through a lot of mistakes and practice over time. It is difficult to understand how Joseph was able to say no to such a temptation without seeing his instinctive response within the context of his life story. To summarize Joseph's secret as simply "turning and running" seems to trivialize the deep-seated commitments that are the foundations of a life of integrity. Heart-deep teaching demands an approach to teaching that looks deeper into both Scripture and the heart of the students.

Contextualizing the Exegetical Big Idea in a Teaching Big Idea

The teacher needs to think through how the Exegetical Big Idea and other principles would be applicable in the lives of the students. The teacher should take into consideration their age, developmental level, maturity, and life context. Based on the needs and characteristics of the students, teachers may modify the wording of the Big Idea to make it relate more directly to those students with whom they are working. Richards and Bredfeldt explain this differentiation between the "exegetical idea" and the "pedagogical or teaching idea" as simply restating or revising the Exegetical Big Idea so that it makes sense to the age group or people group being taught.[6]

The secret of applying an Exegetical Big Idea to the lives of students is having a deep understanding of the needs and issues in their lives. This necessitates knowing students well enough to identify what they are thinking, feeling, struggling with, concerned about, and doing. The teacher must wrestle with the issues, concerns, frustrations, dilemmas, and dreams of students from their perspective.

---

[6] Ibid., 133.

Yet even in relating the Exegetical Big Idea or a principle to younger students, there is no need to dumb down the lesson. Rather, the key is to relate the main point to concrete issues and dilemmas of children. All but the youngest children can understand cause and effect, consequences, and reasons for doing things. As they navigate through the complex world of "big people," it is essential that they learn to see how God relates to all of life. Since the essence of good principle is to connect theology with practice, writing a relevant teaching or pedagogical Big Idea can steer the lesson to guide all but the youngest children to discover the purpose and meaning behind their actions. By stating a Teaching Big Idea in a form that communicates a clear principle, students can be stretched to discover the reasons for what they are learning. Childhood then becomes a rudimentary training ground for establishing a well-thought-through biblical lifestyle. Rather than simply learning what they need to believe and do, they will learn to discover the reasons.

If I were teaching from Phil 4:4–7, I might choose an Exegetical Big Idea such as: "When we take the time to rejoice in the Lord and pray rather than worry, God's peace protects us." This Exegetical Big Idea could be easily adapted for many age groups as a contextualized Teaching Big Idea. For young children it could be stated as, "When we pray to Jesus and refuse to worry, God will give us His peace." Even when designing this lesson focus for young children, I want them to discover the valuable connections between theology and the different dimensions of their lives. I want them to reflect on how their actions and attitude affect their emotions toward God. Getting students to explore the connections between the first part of the Big Idea and the second part is crucial. Both children and adults should discover from this text that their inner peace from God depends on their attitude and communication with Him.

An appropriate Teaching Big Idea from the same passage for a group of businessmen might be: "All the planning and calculating we do to prevent a crisis should never take the place of prayer." The way this Teaching Big Idea is stated for adult businessmen is contextualized to their specific struggles and tendencies. By acknowledging the essential intent of the biblical author related to emotions, thinking, volition, and doing, we are more apt to bring about the work the Holy Spirit desires to accomplish in the students' lives. If we can visualize the Holy Spirit's intentions in the lives of our students in the way we state our Teaching Big Idea, we will set the stage for heart change.

Often teachers tend to gloss over some of these most important deeper issues in both the text and students' lives under the illusion that we need to keep it simple. From my exposure to children, teens, and adults, both from churched and unchurched backgrounds, people are more than capable of reflecting on a much deeper level about spiritual principles if they can make a meaningful connection to something within their immediate experience. When the Teaching Big Idea is closely connected to the biblical text, it instills a valuable connection between God's Word and life. The key is that the lesson must not only be biblically sound but also experientially connected to the students' needs and issues in life. This is true for every age group. God's Word is not just meant to be known intellectually, as important as that is; it is also meant to be assimilated into every aspect of a person and expressed in behavior. In order for this to happen, the teacher must visualize the needs, issues, concerns, and desires of students as he formulates the Teaching Big Idea for the lesson.

Developing a Content Outline

Once the Teaching Big Idea is established and contextualized to the students' needs, the next step is to construct a content outline related to the Big Idea and based on the structure of the analytical outline. This provides the students with the structure to discover the details and Teaching Big Idea from the scriptural passage. For example, if the Teaching Big Idea for a group of children is stated as, "When we rejoice in Jesus, stay close to Him, and refuse to worry, God will give us His peace," from Phil 4:4–7, the content outline might be:

How Do We Get God's Peace?

1. Rejoice in Jesus.
2. Stay close to Jesus.
3. Pray to Jesus.
4. Thank Jesus.
5. Refuse to worry.

This content outline comes directly from the analytical outline of the biblical text. Its form is simplified to be relevant to children, yet it is true to the original meaning of the text. This outline will then be used to establish lesson goals and structure. The structure of the content outline depends on the passage of Scripture studied and the Teaching Big Idea. It should be clear, accurate, and applicable to the students' lives.

Structuring a content outline begins with stating a clear introductory title for it. This comes directly from the Teaching Big Idea as a whole or from either the *subject* or the *complement* within the Teaching Big Idea. The *subject* relates to the main topic of the sentence, while the *complement* relates to the "descriptor" of the subject.[7] For instance, if the Teaching Big Idea is, "In order to be forgiven by God, we must forgive those who have hurt us," then the subject would be "God's forgiveness," while the complement would be, "We must forgive others." The title of the content outline could be taken from either the subject or the complement of that statement. If it was taken from the subject, it could be stated as, "What We Must Do to Be Forgiven by God." If it was taken from the complement, it could be stated as, "The Consequences of Refusing to Forgive Those Who Hurt Us." If the title was taken from the Teaching Big Idea as a whole, it could be stated as, "The Keys to Forgiveness." If the title is clearly related to both the Teaching Big Idea and the details in the analytical outline, then it will naturally lead the teacher and student into the text to discover the truth of Scripture related to the Big Idea. The wording of the content outline should follow through to complete or respond to the title statement.

These are examples to show a few ways titles for content outlines could be designed in relation to the Teaching Big Idea.

A Teaching Big Idea from 2 Pet 1:3–11 might be, "Because God has blessed us with everything we need to live a godly life, we must make every effort we can to grow more like Him." A content outline title based on the subject might be: "Our response to God's blessings." This approach would focus on the things mentioned in the text that true Christians need to work diligently on based on what God has given them. A content outline based on the complement might be, "What motivates the true Christian to work at spiritual growth?" This approach to the lesson would focus on the blessings God has given Christians so that they could be all He wants them to be. Yet another title could focus on both the subject and the complement of the Teaching Big Idea, such as "God's Part and Our Part in Spiritual Growth." As you can see by these illustrations, a good title naturally leads both the teacher and the student toward the main purpose of the lesson as stated in the Teaching Big Idea.

Developing a clear content outline seems to be one of the most difficult parts of lesson preparation for teachers. Common errors include not following the structure in the analytical outline, not relating it to the Teaching Big Idea, not following a parallel grammatical format, not identifying the significant detail in the passage, and making it too complicated. In this next section we discuss ways of designing a simplified content outline that avoids these errors.

---

[7] Haddon W. Robinson, *Biblical Preaching: The Development and Delivery of Expository Messages* (Grand Rapids: Baker, 1980), 31–48.

The key to developing a content outline based on the analytical outline is first to identify its structure. By carefully examining the key words, verbs, repetitions, parallel statements, lists, commands, reasons, consequences, transitions, and qualifiers in the text, the basic structure of the text will usually become obvious. The content outline should rise naturally from the text rather than be forced on the text. For example, in the content outline I developed for teaching children Phil 4:4–7, I picked the four main commands in the text and the results of obeying the commands as the major points of the content outline. A child could easily find these points in the text and understand the consequences of obeying the four commands. Knowing, understanding, and obeying these four commands are central to experiencing God's peace in a difficult situation. The structure of the text clearly identifies these four commands and their consequences as the central points.

The content outline must also relate directly to the Teaching Big Idea. In this case the content outline provides the details of what we must do to experience the peace of God in difficult situations. If the Teaching Big Idea is stated accurately, based on the analytical outline, then the content outline should naturally fit under the Teaching Big Idea. The Teaching Big Idea should provide a general principle and the major details of the text.

For example, if I were teaching the Philippians passage to children, the Teaching Big Idea might be, "When we pray to Jesus and refuse to worry, God will give us His peace." Here the two sections of the content outline focus on the two parts of the Teaching Big Idea. The subject, or the first part, deals with what we do, and the complement, or second part, deals with what God does. The content outline simply adds the details found in the biblical passage. For younger children I would include less detail, while for older children I would include more. For instance, for children ages four or five, I might use a content outline based on a Teaching Big Idea such as:

"When we feel scared, we need to 'jump into Jesus' arms.'"

> Content Outline
> Title: What It Means to "Jump into Jesus' Arms":
> > Rejoice in Jesus.
> > Talk to Jesus.
> > Thank Jesus.
> > Forget your worries.
> What Will Happen When We Jump into Jesus' Arms?
> > Peace

While this outline is simple, it includes the timeless principle from the text, that when we are worried about something, the best way to deal with it is to seek our refuge, joy, and security in Jesus. In some profound way I think the picture generated in the minds of young children of "jumping into Jesus' arms" hits the point of the text even better than words.

The depth of such a lesson comes not only in accurately understanding the depth of the scriptural passage but also in appreciating the deep way such a lesson might penetrate the hearts of the children. Even as I reflect on this passage related to young children who may be facing big concerns, I get excited. Already I am visualizing children I have known and worked with who need to experience the miraculous power of God in their lives related to the truth of this text. They don't just need to hear the words from the Big Idea or the content outline. They need to feel the warmth, wisdom, security, and peace of the arms of Jesus. By the time I get to this part of a lesson, I am bursting with creativity, passion, and insights for getting my students to experience the truth of the lesson. This passion, based on a thorough study of both the biblical text and the students, sparks the creativity in the next stage of lesson preparation.

Chapter Summary

When I read the text from the students' perspective and ask the Holy Spirit to illuminate my perception, He brings illustrations, connectives, parallels, stories, and applications to my mind to clarify and illuminate the discovery process. As ideas come to mind while I meditate on the text, I jot them down. This is usually the most insightful part of my preparation for teaching.

Once when I was guiding a team of children's teachers through this process, teaching the story of the lepers who were healed (Luke 17:11–19), I asked my student teachers how we could get the children to feel the emotions that the lepers may have had while being healed. One of them suggested that we wrap the kids in toilet paper (representing rags covering the sores) while they played the role of lepers begging Jesus to heal them. We decided that this learning activity would be an ideal way to get the children to identify with the range of emotions the lepers might have faced. The value of this learning activity was not primarily in the fact that it was engaging and interactive but that being wrapped in toilet paper provided a natural connection to something "very nasty" for children. As we acted out this whole story with about 50 children, we realized the brilliance of this simple teaching idea. I have found that some of my best ideas for teaching come out of this early stage of preparation when I wrestle with the text from the perspective of my students.

In this chapter we have discussed how to dig deeper into the Word on behalf of your students.

1. Study the needs and characteristics of your students.
2. Reflect and meditate on the text from the perspective of the students.
3. Adapt the Exegetical Big Idea to your students' needs in a Teaching Big Idea.
4. Establish a content outline based on the Teaching Big Idea, accompanied by an appropriate title.

In order to touch the hearts of students, teachers must intentionally look at the text through students' eyes in regard to each of the four aspects of the heart: mind, emotions, will, and behavior. By systematically and routinely reflecting on the implications of the text in each of these areas of the person, the teacher is much more apt to tap into the essential heart yearnings of students. While the yearnings of the heart are as varied as the students in the class, thoughtful reflection in preparation will allow the Holy Spirit optimum opportunity to lead teachers to focus on the most pertinent issues. As teachers ask the Holy Spirit for enlightenment to help illuminate Scripture to permeate the hearts of students, God will supernaturally give insight.

Questions and Applications

1. State two subjects of our exegesis and briefly explain the importance of each.

2. Why might it be helpful when teaching to divide a large passage of Scripture into several sections?

3. What is the difference between an Exegetical Big Idea and a Teaching Big Idea? When is it especially necessary to make this distinction?

4. What is involved in reflecting on the Exegetical Big Idea from the perspective of your students?

5. Based on your study of Eph 1:1–14, complete the four steps from this chapter to help you look at the biblical text from the perspective of your students.

- Study your students.
- Meditate on the text from the perspective of your students.
- Establish a contextualized Teaching Big Idea.
- Establish a content outline with an appropriate title.

Chapter 6

Setting Goals to Encourage Deeper Student Learning

Establishing a Lesson Purpose and Setting Goals to Help Students Learn at Deeper Levels

In this chapter we discuss how to design a purpose statement and goals to help the learner move deeper into the biblical text and deeper toward internalization of the principles in the text to bring about changed behavior. While each lesson may focus on only a few steps in this journey, these steps will fit in a larger plan of spiritual formation following the taxonomies discussed in chap. 3. Based on a careful study of both the text and the student, the teacher can map out the purposes and goals for the students' learning and growth.

While most published curricula are based on stated goals, few encourage students to progress toward deeper learning in cognitive, affective, volitional, and behavioral areas. While curricula identify goals in at least three areas, often including knowing, feeling, and doing, they seldom compel students to move deeper in those areas of learning. Learning often becomes trivialized to tokenistic evidences of desired outcomes while failing to initiate significant changes in thinking, feeling, choosing, or behaving. In an attempt to catalog documented evidence of learning, teachers may try to get the students to say, repeat, do, or express prepackaged responses to learning activities without allowing them the time or creativity to wrestle with their own expressions of learning or discovery. Stated goals then become programmable learning outcomes that students follow with little sense of autonomy or reflection. This approach to goal-setting limits heart-deep learning by failing to engage students to initiate their own objectives related to their lives. Regardless of how teachers state their lesson goals, they must allow students the freedom and flexibility to take as much responsibility for their learning as possible. While teachers need to have a clear understanding of the purpose for the lesson based on the Big Idea, they should allow flexibility for the students to reflect on and establish specific objectives based on their own needs and burdens.

Establishing the Purpose Statement for Learners Based on the Big Idea

Recently I heard a sermon that illustrates the importance of having a clear Big Idea and teaching purpose. While the presentation was biblically and theologically sound, it lost its potential impact in the lives of the audience because of the lack of a clear Big Idea and purpose. People seemed to struggle to stay focused because the tangents, illustrations, and major points went in different directions. It was not as if the tangents were insignificant. Many were interesting, insightful, and important. It was just that the listener had a difficult time knowing where the preacher was heading. There seemed to be no central theme, Big Idea, or purpose. Fortunately, near the end of the sermon, the preacher began to express what he was passionate about and what he wanted the learner to know and do. Yet he wasted a lot of time getting there. By focusing on too many other themes, he detracted from the main purpose of his sermon.

When a preacher or teacher builds a Bible lesson on a compelling Big Idea with a clear, relevant purpose, the participants are much more apt to respond. To establish the overall purpose of a lesson, the teacher starts with the Big Idea and puts it into a purpose statement related to what the teacher wants the learner to learn. For example, in teaching a lesson for young adults, we could choose a Big Idea from Phil 4:4–9 such as: "Even in the midst of horrible circumstances, we can pray with thanksgiving because God is close by us and in control." For this Big Idea I might use a purpose such as, "The participants will thank God even in difficult times because He is both close and in control." The focus of the lesson is that young adults learn to practice thanking God in the midst of difficulties and challenges. The word "because" suggests a reason or a rationale for thanking God based on at least two specific details in the text. For the young adults to accomplish the purpose of this lesson, they will be stretched emotionally, cognitively, volitionally, and behaviorally. The overall purpose of the lesson is for them to progress to deeper levels of learning to accomplish the stated purpose. The purpose is integrative, involving all of the domains.

Emotionally, the participants will need to acknowledge and reflect on the struggles and frustrations in their lives. Cognitively they will need to search the Scriptures and identify and understand the rationale of why we should thank God in tough times. Volitionally, participants will have to wrestle with that tough decision of thanking God in the midst of a difficult circumstance. Practically they will have to obey and continue to obey by praying and thanking God no matter what their circumstances. If the purpose of this lesson were to be accomplished in the lives of the participants, their hearts would change and influence their behavior.

Stating Heart-Deep Learning Goals

After establishing a "teaching purpose" based on the Big Idea and contextualized to the age and other variables of the students, the next step is to think through the various outcomes the Holy Spirit might want to accomplish in the lives of the students. Heart-deep learning goals have four distinct characteristics. First, the goals follow the natural taxonomies of deeper level learning in each of the four domains. Second, they focus on the Big Idea of the biblical text. Third, they become more and more integrative with the other domains as they move deeper. Fourth, learning goals orient both the teacher and the student toward reflecting and applying the Big Idea to students' lives. The goals are both integrative and practical in that they focus on interacting with all the domains toward the end of effecting character and behavioral change.

The best way to stay focused on your overall lesson purpose is to state the teaching purpose at the top of a page and then brainstorm all the things your students will possibly need to learn to accomplish that purpose, based on your original analysis of the text. Categorize what you want students to learn under each of the four domains: cognitive, affective, volitional, and behavioral. By reviewing the taxonomies for each of the domains, it is helpful to visualize the potential depth of learning in which students could engage within each of the domains. In order to keep the lesson student centered, I have found it helpful to state the purposes, goals, and objectives in a similar format, completing the sentence: "The purpose of this lesson is that students will . . ." This format emphasizes what you want the student to learn rather than what you will teach. The statement of each learning goal should begin with a verb and include an object to the verb. (Example: A goal of the lesson is that students will *list the three commands in the passage*.)

The following chart gives examples of verbs that could be used to state goals in each of the domains following the taxonomies discussed in chap. 3.

The most productive way to establish heart-deep goals is to begin by brainstorming potential goals for the lesson in each of the four domains. Then, following the taxonomies stated in the chart above, I move from simple to deeper levels of learning. After listing all the possible goals related to the "teaching-learning purpose," I narrow the number of goals down to one to five in each domain. The chart on the next page gives an example of the results of the goals I came up with using this approach.

While it is helpful to list these goals separately within the four domains, the domains flow together as the goals go deeper. As the goals progress toward the center of a person, they become more and more integrated. The last goals tend to integrate thinking, feeling, willing, and doing. Thus the last goals in each domain tend to be more heart-deep.

If students were to move toward the goals stated in this lesson, they would be more apt to thank God when praying to Him the next time they faced difficulties. This would be true of almost any age group. Although teachers of different age groups might choose different learning experiences, the outcomes of the lessons would follow a similar set of purposes and goals.

Learning goals become the foundation for structuring the learning experiences making up the lesson. Often by the time goals are established, ideas have already germinated about how to help students learn them. The most difficult and time-consuming part of lesson preparation is done by the time I establish a good purpose statement and goals based on a thorough reflection on the biblical text. When I begin my preparation early in the week before teaching, I find myself thinking about my teaching goals all week. Driving the car, walking my dog, or canoeing all become opportunities the Lord uses to bring to my mind creative teaching ideas related to the lesson. When I sit down to finalize my learning experiences for the lesson, they come naturally. For that reason I encourage teachers to begin their preparation and establish their goals for teaching as early as they can.

Verbs for Stating Goals in Different Domains

	Cognitive Domain	Affective Domain	Volitional	Behavioral/Psychomotor Skills
• *Knowledge*	Identify, recall, recite, recognize, name, state, reproduce, list, memorize, know, trace, become aware of, become familiar with, discover	• Become aware • Perceive • Focus attention on • Attend to • Respond positively to • Take the initiative to • Structure it as a part of life • Integrate it into lifestyle	• Become aware that it is uncontrolled • Admit, acknowledge, confess • Choose, decide, commit to, repent, determine to, plan to • Gain control, make progress, show improvement • Develop a positive attitude, be convinced of, be sensitive to, be enthusiastic about, develop a desire to, sympathize with • Become more and more instinctive • Become integrated into character	• Become aware of, become prepared for/to • Practice skill with another person • Become more confident, proficient, consistent • Perform at a high level of confidence, proficiency, or consistency • Perform related tasks based on previously used skills • Create new performances
• *Understanding*	Comprehend, reflect upon, apply, connect, analyze, compare, contrast, examine, discern, synthesize, classify, select, evaluate, choose, separate			
• *Wisdom*	Integrate truth into life			

CHART 1

Text: Phil 4:1-9

Big Idea	*Even in the midst of horrible circumstances, we can pray with thanksgiving because God is close by us and in control.*		
Purpose of Lesson	The purpose of this lesson is that the participants will thank God even in difficult times because He is both close and in control.		
Potential Lesson Goals *(The goals of this lesson are that students will)*	**Cognitive**	**Affective**	**Volitional**	**Behavioral**

Cognitive	**Affective**	**Volitional**	**Behavioral**
• Understand the difficulties the believers in Philippi were experiencing. • Identify the four specific commands Paul gives his people in verses 4–7. • Discover why we should thank Him even when things are difficult. • Realize what we are to thank God for when we pray in difficult situations. • Realize the benefits of developing a joyful, thankful heart during difficult times.	• Admit how we usually feel about God when we face difficulties. • Become aware of reasons to thank God even in difficult times. • Integrate thankfulness as a natural reaction to challenges.	• Choose to thank God every time we ask God for something. • Make thankfulness our instinctive response to difficulties.	• Become more disciplined in thanking God when we ask God for help. • Develop an attitude of thanksgiving when asking God for requests.

CHART 2

Questions and Applications

1. State in your own words the four characteristics of effective goals.

2. Why is it so important to state good goals?

3. What are the dangers of being too pointed in stating your goals?

4. Based on your previous preparation from Eph 1:1–14, write out a purpose and a list of all the potential goals you would like your students to learn, following the directions in this chapter. Categorize your goals under each of the domains, and list them in order from simple to deep.

Chapter 7

Understanding How People Learn

The Danger in Starting with Methods

The key to designing effective learning experiences is not to read a book on techniques to come up with a list of choices to make your lesson interesting. It is not to take verbatim the methodological suggestions from a prepared curriculum. And it is not merely to borrow a creative approach demonstrated at a training event you recently attended. Weimer, in her book explaining the nature of learner-centered teaching, explains the danger in haphazard methods of selecting learning approaches:

> When the criteria for selecting a technique are "neat idea," "I like it," and "this would work," then instructional practice evolves into a hodgepodge of isolated, unrelated techniques. Individually, they all are good ideas, but taken together, they do not reflect a set of internally consistent assumptions, nor are they a collection that advances an overall approach to teaching or one that exemplifies a certain philosophy of education.[1]

---

[1] Maryellen Weimer, *Learner-Centered Teaching: Five Key Changes to Practice*, 1st ed., The Jossey-Bass Higher and Adult Education Series (San Francisco: Jossey-Bass, 2002), 186.

While designing effective learning experiences may include being on the lookout for innovative, creative techniques and strategies, I have found that a more fundamental process involves asking the question, "What will the class participants need to experience and wrestle with to accomplish the goals I have established from the biblical text?" Many times this has less to do with techniques than with common sense. In fact, the most innovative and exciting learning activities may even take away from what you want your students to learn.

I can remember an experience someone very close to me went through as a junior higher in a parachurch club activity. The experience was designed, I'm sure, to help the kids feel close relationally to one another and to release some of their pent-up sexual energy. The activity involved pairing up with someone of the opposite sex and rolling together across the floor in a race to the other side of the room. Not only did my son feel awkward pairing up with a girl he did not even know, but also the experience of rolling together with a girl who was heavier than he fell short of accomplishing the goals of that activity. The experience not only terminated his involvement with the club but had other long-term effects. We must be careful not to choose fun or creative methods from a hat. Rather, we must become more skilled at asking commonsense questions about how our students learn at their developmental level. Rather than review characteristics of the various developmental levels, it might be more helpful to remember how we learned things at different ages. The natural ways we learned things may provide us with a better foundation for choosing effective learning experiences in our classes and programs.

We begin this chapter by discussing how we learn, looking primarily at the ordinary ways we have learned things throughout our lives. Next we will examine what some researchers say about how people learn, grow, and develop. We then examine the nature of learning experiences and how good learning experiences influence growth. Finally we examine learning-style differences in light of current brain research. I hope the insights in this chapter will be instrumental in helping teachers come up with creative ways to design effective learning experiences in the next chapter.

How We Learn

When I think back to some of the most significant things I have learned in life and how I learned them, I realize they did not happen while I was just sitting around. Most, if not all, of the significant things I have learned came while I was active. Whether they were spiritual or not, they all involved me doing something with my mind, body, senses, will, intuition, emotions, or imagination. Take, for example, how I learned to snow ski as a 12-year-old.

Where I grew up in London, Ontario, we lived near a ski slope. When my best friend got a pair of skis for Christmas, I was talked into buying a used pair so that I could go with him. For ten dollars I bought a pair of long, blue skis with bear-trap harnesses. No one taught us. We learned on our own. Yet we helped each other through the trials. I eventually learned to ski by experimenting, trying, falling, reflecting on my failures, listening, watching, practicing, and dreaming. As I got older, I learned by teaching others, practicing more vigorously, reading, imagining, and competing. As a college student I became a ski instructor.

Or take the example of how I learned to show respect for elders. When I was in grade school, my buddy dared me to throw a snowball at a passing car. Little did I know that the principal was driving the car. The means by which I learned that lesson of respecting elders came twice, once in the principal's office that morning and once again when I got home that afternoon. That was truly a lesson I learned through experience of a rather intense nature. Throughout my life I continued to learn that lesson about respecting elders by observing, listening, making mistakes, being disciplined, reading, watching movies and videos, and reflecting. I suffered the consequences for lack of respect and enjoyed the rewards of respecting elders. Learning, regardless of the context, happens through experience.

In reflecting on how I learned various lessons in life, I saw that this usually happened through engagement, interaction, and activity. In the cognitive domain this happens through thinking, wrestling, reflecting, questioning, hypothesizing, affirming, memorizing, speculating, imagining, and repeating. In the affective domain, learning happens through valuing, appreciating, enjoying, tasting, experiencing, evaluating, perceiving, observing, responding, feeling, and touching. In the volitional domain, learning happens by choosing, obeying, suffering consequences, trying things out, making mistakes, practicing, feeling remorse, and experiencing failure. In the behavioral or psychomotor domain, learning happens by trying, initiating, practicing, stretching, exceeding limitations, overcoming barriers, persevering, struggling, and repeating. All the verb forms used to describe real learning can be stated in verb participles ending in "ing." Every learning experience based in real life involves active participation and interaction within all the domains of the person. Just as learning to snow ski involves engaging muscles as well as courage, so writing an article involves active thinking as well as discipline.

Learning is by nature active, interactive, and engaging. Even listening involves activity of the mind. Participants must discipline their thoughts, focus their attention, direct their gaze, and control their body language. Good listening skills involve all of these behaviors and activities. Learning happens most effectively through active engagement of every aspect of the person. The more engaged and active a person is in the learning process, the greater the potential for learning to take place.

In designing learning experiences to accomplish goals, the teacher must put himself in the place of the students and ask how that person would most naturally learn the goals of a lesson. The learning experience chosen for each goal should be based on the development level, the maturity level, and the learning context of the learner. Teachers must also be sensitive to their own strengths and weaknesses to make sure they design learning experiences that they have both the skills and aptitude to implement effectively.

While the most appropriate way of communicating information may sometimes be teacher centered such as lecturing—presenting, preaching, telling, or exhorting—the best way to help people change is to involve them holistically in the learning experience. Each lesson needs to involve a variety of learning activities to accomplish the lesson goals and engage the learner. Since the goal of discipleship or spiritual formation is transformation of the person into Christlikeness, we must engage people more holistically in learning experiences that actually accomplish our goals.

If the ultimate purpose of the disciple of Jesus Christ were to know about God and His Word, the job of the teacher would be easier. Yet as Jesus reminds us in Matt 28:20 NIV, discipleship involves "teaching them to obey everything" that He commanded them. Jesus' command was not a return to the legalism that had become a part of Hebrew culture but a return to God's original plan from the garden of Eden in which humankind would fellowship with Him, love Him, and follow Him intimately and experientially. This is what Blackaby and King highlighted in their book *Experiencing God.* People come to know God through their experience with God.[2] Likewise, teaching people of all ages to obey Christ's Word from the heart involves engaging the whole person in the learning experience. It demands attention to the content of the Word as represented by the Big Idea as well as the process of helping the learner to experience the goals inherent in the text.

Sometimes pictures make complicated things more clear. Midway through my teaching career, at a local ice cream store near Taylor University, I scribbled the following diagram on a napkin. I was trying to visualize the dynamics of

---

[2] Henry T. Blackaby and Claude V. King, *Experiencing God: How to Live the Full Adventure of Knowing and Doing the Will of God* (Nashville: B& H, 1994), 8.

Kite Diagram

The Growth of Obedient Faith

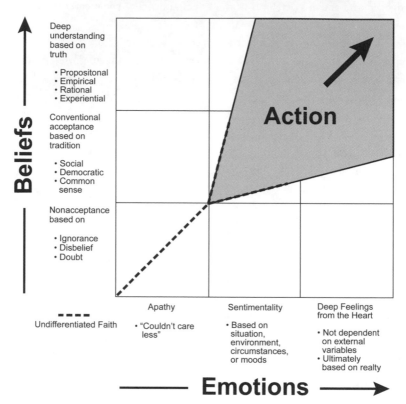

how people learn and grow in their faith in Jesus Christ, integrating both social science research and scriptural principles.

The diagram describes the growth of obedient faith, which, as we discussed earlier, is the only faith that saves. Obedient faith in Jesus Christ is the only faith that leads to abundant and eternal life. The dynamic of how this faith is learned can be explained by the interaction of one's cognitive beliefs, emotions, will, and actions. The interaction among the various domains can be explained by the three-dimensional nature of the diagram.

The vertical axis represents the development of cognitive beliefs related to saving faith in Christ. The three levels represent major steps in the developmental process of growth and maturation of belief. The first cognitive level, labeled "nonacceptance," describes a negative, apathetic, or neutral understanding of the gospel message similar to Fowler's *Primal or Undifferentiated Faith*[3] or Kohlberg's *preconventional morality*.[4] This could be based on several factors such as age, developmental level, exposure or lack of exposure to the authentic message, disbelief, or doubt. It is different from Fowler's category *Primal Faith*, in that it could also describe an older person who for some reason was apathetic or antagonistic to the gospel message. The second cognitive level, labeled "conventional," is similar to Kohlberg's second level of moral development in that one's cognitive beliefs stem mostly from the person's immediate family, community, or closest friends. At this stage a person's beliefs reflect those of the persons they spend the most intimate time with.[5] In this step of development, people tend to reflect the cognitive understanding of their parents, family, church, or close friends. The third level of cognitive belief reflects my conviction that biblical Christian faith is based on a solid presupposition that is rationally, empirically, and experientially valid. Philosopher J. P. Moreland backs up the validity of such a strong basis of knowledge in support of our faith in Jesus Christ in his recent books *Confident Faith*[6] and *Kingdom Triangle*.[7] Contrary to other developmental researchers who do not believe that the Christian faith is based on propositional truth, I am convinced that the highest level of faith development reflects a deep understanding of biblically based knowledge that can be supported empirically, historically, rationally, and experientially. This highest level of cognitive belief does not reflect the ambiguity seen in many other theories of faith and moral development.[8] Rather it reflects a confidence and steadfastness based in the facts and principles of Scripture. Yet there is a certain humility that characterizes this highest level of cognitive development reflected in the Christian's ability to listen and empathize with those with differing beliefs. A person who truly reflects an understanding of the knowledge

---

[3] James W. Fowler, *Stages of Faith: The Psychology of Human Development and the Quest for Meaning*, 1st ed. (San Francisco: Harper & Row, 1981), 119–21.

[4] Lawrence Kohlberg, *The Philosophy of Moral Development: Moral Stages and the Idea of Justice*, 1st ed., Essays on Moral Development (San Francisco: Harper & Row, 1981), 17.

[5] Ibid., 18.

[6] James Porter Moreland and Klaus Dieter Issler, *In Search of a Confident Faith: Overcoming Barriers to Trusting in God* (Downers Grove, IL; Nottingham, England: InterVarsity, 2008).

[7] James Porter Moreland, *Kingdom Triangle: Recover the Christian Mind, Renovate the Soul, Restore the Spirit's Power* (Grand Rapids: Zondervan, 2007).

[8] Perry G. Downs, *Teaching for Spiritual Growth* (Grand Rapids: Zondervan, 1994), 102–4, 18–19. In these two sections Downs critiques Kohlberg and Fowler's views from an evangelical perspective.

of Jesus Christ will follow biblical principles in how they communicate with and relate to those who may believe differently.

The horizontal axis represents the development of the emotional aspects of a person's faith. I have identified three stages a person moves through related to their emotions. The first is a stage of apathy; the second, sentimentality; and the third, deep feelings from the heart.

The first stage of *apathy* could also be characterized as *neutrality*. In this stage a person expresses no desire for things of God or even an attitude of apathy to things of God. This could be due to the fact that, as a young child, the person had no significant older person in his life to attract him to the things of God. In some situations older people may have even discouraged or hardened him against coming closer to God or Jesus. Whatever the case, a person in this stage has little or no desire to approach God. The next stage, of sentimentality, closely resembles the conventional stage of cognitive belief. In this stage a person feels good about God usually because of the situation, environment, or mood he is in. His faith is based primarily on his immediate feelings of acceptance, warmth, excitement, pleasure, community, affirmation, or peace. This is a normal stage that many people go through in their faith journey toward higher levels of emotional maturity.

As I think back to my childhood and teen years, I realize that my feelings about my faith were based on how I felt about my Sunday school class, my club activities, my church experience, and my youth group. It was not that I did not have a relationship with Jesus; it was that my feelings about Jesus were directly dependent on how I felt about the Christian-related groups of which I was a part. As normal as this stage is in the development of children and teens, it is not a good place to stagnate as an adult. If a person does not progress beyond this point, it can lead to apathy and complacency.

The third stage related to the emotional aspects of faith development is characterized by *deep feelings from the heart*. At this stage a person displays a deep commitment and passion to follow Jesus Christ regardless of changing feelings and circumstances. This level of emotional development parallels the deep emotions reflected in Phil 4:4–9 (NIV), where Paul challenges the believers in Philippi to "rejoice in the Lord always," discipline their minds to focus on the truth, and put into practice the things he has taught and modeled before them. Paul promises that when they live out these three spiritual life principles they will experience both the peace of God and the God of peace. This passage exemplifies the central theme of the Kite Diagram, showing integration of the mind, emotions, and behavior in spiritual formation. Obedient action based on the integration of thinking, feeling, and choosing becomes both the result and the catalyst for continued integration and deeper learning toward Christlikeness.

Parents and teachers alike often focus more on the kind of behavior they want from their children or students than the kind of learning environment they provide for them. The first principle the Kite Diagram reinforces is what many educators believe—that the best way to influence peoples' behavior is to bring them up in an intellectually challenging and emotionally supportive environment. As young people are nurtured in an environment that is both cognitively stimulating and emotionally warm, they naturally are drawn toward the belief and value system of their parents and other nurturers. Yet children, teens, and adult seekers need a warm, inviting group of people to help them feel secure and to assimilate them into a faith tradition. Such an environment needs to be not only warm and inviting but also rich in the biblical knowledge that provides the foundation for Christian faith.

George Barna, in his book *Transforming Children into Spiritual Champions*, explains how his research shows that "few Christian adults make their moral, physical, emotional, and intellectual choices on the basis of sound reasoning from Scripture."[9] While most Christians say that they believe the Bible, Barna goes on to show that most of them do not have a foundational understanding of biblical facts or doctrine. He concludes that homes and churches need to provide a stronger instructional environment in the foundations of biblical knowledge to bring children, youth, and adult seekers to a firm conventional belief in Jesus and His Word. A nurturing environment for young believers must provide both warm security and solid teaching.

Yet in order to mature beyond the conventional stage of belief and the sentimental stage of emotional understanding, people must be challenged. Cognitively, this means people must be encouraged to think for themselves rather than just parrot the beliefs of those they respect. In order to move toward a deep understanding based on solid truth, people must be engaged in wrestling, questioning, researching, testing, discussing, and brainstorming. Only then will people be able to clarify truth for themselves based on solid proof, backed up by Scripture, reason, and experience. While some Christians may hesitate to challenge their children and teens to ask difficult questions about their faith, it is essential in building a solid, mature belief system. The same principle is true about emotional development. Parents, teachers, and spiritual leaders must challenge children and students to get out of the nest emotionally

---

[9] George Barna, *Transforming Children into Spiritual Champions*, Seminar Ed. (Ventura, CA: Issachar Resources, 2003), 55.

if they are to develop into emotionally healthy people with a passion to serve the Lord even in tough times. Just as an eagle pushes its offspring out of the nest to learn to fly, so we must help our children and students to live successfully outside the cocoon of home and youth group. In order to be mature, Christians need to learn how to live victoriously in the security of Christ's love, even in disappointment and suffering.

Another principle found in the Kite Diagram is that action is not only the result of the integration of emotional and intellectual support and challenge but also the catalyst to the integration of thinking and feeling in the development of mature faith. When we obey and act on what we know to be true, even if the motivation is external, the action itself can help us understand and develop our desire to ingrain it in our hearts at a deeper level. Just as a wind surfer's kite moves the surfer through the waves as it fills with wind, so the Christ follower's active step of obedience moves him farther along the journey of obedient faith.

A clear example of this comes from the way I learned to enjoy ministering to nursing home residents. When I was a young teenager, my mother made me play my violin at the nursing home each month with the youth group. As much as I hated going in the beginning, the more I realized how much the old folks appreciated the attention, the more I enjoyed it. Over my adult life I have made it a regular practice to play my violin and minister in a nursing home. It brings me deep joy that is beyond comprehension. My fiddle lessons seem to relate to other contexts of life as well. The beginning steps of obedience in just about any area are the most difficult. Yet in the act of obedience, the Holy Spirit seems to fill the believer in a fresh way to enable him to experience both the joy and the confidence to keep on obeying. Peter's words in Acts 5:32 (NIV) seem to reinforce this principle, that the Holy Spirit is "given to those who obey him." When we act in obedience to the truth, it could be said that the Holy Spirit fills our kite and supernaturally takes us to higher levels of deeper faith. Even if our initial acts of obedience are externally motivated, the more we practice what is right, the more that behavior becomes internalized within each aspect of our hearts. The more we practice it, the more it becomes a habitual part of our nature.

The Kite Diagram can provide a helpful way of visualizing the integration of the different aspects of the heart in the development of mature faith in Jesus Christ. As the Holy Spirit acts as the supernatural catalyst for growth in our minds and emotions, He expresses the intentions of our hearts in the fruit of our actions. Purposeful activity and practice seem to be keys to heart-deep learning.

Understanding Learning Experiences

Learning activities are the ways and means effective teachers use to help students not only hear the Word but experience it. By incorporating multidimensional learning activities, involving as many domains as possible relating to the learning goals, good teachers engage their students in accomplishing their goals. Kurt Lewin writes that learning must actively integrate thinking, feeling, and doing within a learning experience. While people learn through their senses, experience itself is not enough for purposeful learning. Processes of thinking, feeling, and doing must be activated at the heart of the person.[10]

David Kolb, building on this and other educational concepts, went on to describe a four-step process by which people learn. The process begins with *concrete experience* in which the learner is involved in an experience related to the goal of the lesson. In the next stage, *reflective observation*, the learner thinks through his observations about the experience. Next, in the *abstract conceptualization* stage, he attempts to think through his observations to come up with generalizations or principles related to his experience. Last, in the *active experimentation* stage, he puts into action those generalizations or principles based on his reflections of his experience. Kolb suggests that this cycle of learning integrates all of the aspects of the person in learning by focusing not just on the experience but on thinking about it, reflecting about it, sharing feelings about it, and determining to act on what he learned. This cycle of learning has become a model for many lesson plans implementing a more holistic approach to learning.[11] Kolb's four steps of a learning experience provide a good conceptual model for the approach that I will be suggesting in this book. This approach was first popularized in the evangelical church in Larry Richards's "Hook, Book, Look, Took Method," which appeared in the first edition of *Creative Bible Teaching.*[12] Kolb's four steps of a learning experience also provided the fundamental framework for much of the writing in the area of learning styles.[13]

The key elements in Kolb's Learning Cycle include engaging the learner in concrete experience, interacting and reflecting on that experience, pulling

---

[10] Kurt Lewin, *Field Theory in Social Science: Selected Theoretical Papers*, 1st ed. (New York: Harper, 1951).

[11] David A. Kolb, *Experiential Learning: Experience as the Source of Learning and Development* (Englewood Cliffs, NJ: Prentice-Hall, 1984), 42.

[12] Larry Richards, *Creative Bible Teaching* (Chicago: Moody, 1973).

[13] Marlene D. LeFever, *Learning Styles: Reaching Everyone God Gave You to Teach* (Colorado Springs: David C. Cook, 1995).

those observations together into generalizations, and then designing and implementing an active response to the principles learned. The distinctive focus of such learning activities is that the learner is always engaged in the experience. Engaging learning activities should be used whenever possible to accomplish the goals of heart-deep teaching.

Jane Vella, in her book *Taking Learning to Task*, reaffirms this fundamental principle of learning that "learners learn when they are actively engaged in the content." When content is taught using effective learning experiences that engage the learners, students not only enjoy the experience but also learn and internalize the content at a deeper level.[14]

A lot of research is opening doors to a wide spectrum of resources to design effective learning experiences. Rather than use research findings as a "bag of tricks" to help us find the easiest and quickest path to learning, we need to use research to provide us with wisdom and insight into how to build more effective strategies to help people learn.

Respecting Learning Style Differences

Brain research since the 1980s has blossomed into a complex web of interdisciplinary theories that have impacted the field of teaching and learning. While the studies themselves can seem complex, the implications are simple. Teachers must create environments that help students connect to learning goals. Since connections are multidimensional, the teacher must create environments that provide a wide variety of avenues to invite the learner to enter the learning environment. Eric Jensen explains that while this approach may seem complex, it is a natural characteristic of the way the brain functions.

> The brain simultaneously operates on many levels of consciousness, processing all at once a world of colors, movements, emotions, shapes, smells, sounds, tastes, feelings, and more. It assembles patterns, composes meaning, and sorts daily life experiences from an extraordinary number of clues. It is so efficient at processing information that nothing in the living or man-made world comes close to matching human learning potential. Knowing this, perhaps, it is easier to conceive how this amazing multiprocessor called our brain is undernourished, if not starved, in the typical classroom. Many educators unknowingly inhibit the brain's learning ability by teaching in an ultralinear, structured, and

―――――――――――
    [14] Jane Kathryn Vella, *Taking Learning to Task: Creative Strategies for Teaching Adults*, 1st ed., The Jossey-Bass Higher and Adult Education Series (San Francisco: Jossey-Bass, 2000), 7.

predictable fashion. The result is bored or frustrated learners who then perpetuate the underachievement cycle.[15]

To stimulate "heart-deep learning," teachers must engage the learner in multidimensional approaches to learning involving a wide variety of strategies, methods, and experiences to help the student connect with the intended goals of the lesson. Heart-deep teaching involves providing the learner as many learning experiences as possible. Jensen provides an excellent summary of the "various factors, characteristics, and examples of relevant activities" measured by the various categories of learning style inventories. These categories are differentiated according to the things they assess. The four categories Jensen identifies are: context variables, input preferences, processing formats, and response filters. These learning style preferences represent the various avenues people may take to approach any given learning environment. Being aware of these differences can help the teacher provide a variety of choices for students to engage actively in learning.

Context Variables

The first category of learning preferences, called context variables, relates to how students feel about their immediate context.[16] This includes the influence of the social environment of the class, relationships, difficulty of the material, the temperature, and the atmosphere. Within this category are four subsections: field dependency vs. field independence; flexible vs. structured environment; independent, dependent, or interdependent; and relationship vs. content driven.

The first category under context variables relates to field dependency vs. field independence. Learners who are field dependent tend to prefer close social relationships, field trips, and natural learning contexts. They tend to want to learn by doing, exploring, interacting, and touching. They are usually influenced more by what they experience than by what they connect with abstractly. Learners who are field independent, on the other hand, tend to appreciate the typical classroom more with its books, computers, ideas, and concepts. They enjoy reading, studying, and reflecting. They prefer to learn without being too dependent on the environment around them.

The second category under context variables relates to whether learners prefer a flexible or a structured environment. Those who prefer a flexible environment tend to enjoy a lot of creativity and variety in the classroom while

---

[15] Eric Jensen, *Brain-Based Learning and Teaching* (Del Mar, CA: Turning Point, 1995), 43.

[16] Ibid., 138.

those who prefer structure in their learning environment appreciate outlines, guidelines, rules, and procedures.

The third category under context variables relates to whether students like to work independently, dependently, or interdependently. Independent learners prefer to study alone without distractions. They can often be found studying alone in the library or another room, or in a quiet place. Dependent learners, on the other hand, enjoy working in groups or teams and with friends. They tend to learn as they interact and socialize. They can be seen and heard just about anywhere people gather or interact. Interdependent learners tend to enjoy both working alone and working in groups, depending on the situation. The distinctive of these people is that they enjoy helping others learn and put a high value on the success of the group.

The fourth category under context variables relates to whether students are primarily motivated by relationships or the content. For those who are relationship driven, a good relationship with the teacher is imperative to learn effectively. For students who are content driven, learning is not dependent on a relationship with the teacher but rather on their desire to learn the content.

Input Preferences

The second category of learning preferences identified by Jensen relates to the preferred sensory form of input, whether it is olfactory (smell), gustatory (taste, eating), visual, auditory, or kinesthetic (bodily movement). While all people learn through sensory input, some naturally prefer one form over another. People tend to be drawn toward their preferences. Under this category of learning preferences, we will examine visual, auditory, and kinesthetic forms of input. Input relates to the type of sensory stimulation coming into the learner.

The first input preference is visual, which is divided into two categories, external and internal. External visual learners prefer to see rather than hear. They prefer handouts and written instructions rather than verbal ones. They appreciate smart boards, PowerPoint, pictures, and illustrations. They appreciate structure, clarity, and organization. Visual internal learners, on the other hand, appreciate building visual pictures of things in order to understand them. They tend to dream and imagine outcomes before progressing toward them. While the first type of visual learner appreciates external pictures and visuals, the second type prefers to create pictures in the learning process.

The second input preference is auditory, and it is similarly divided into external and internal categories. Auditory external styles of learners prefer auditory input over visual. They learn by interacting with others. They tend to be good communicators, storytellers, preachers, and teachers. Their preferred style of learning is by talking and listening. While auditory internal learners also prefer auditory over visual, that dialogue is primarily internal in the form of reflection, daydreaming, and speculating. They prefer times in class to reflect, ponder, and imagine as they engage in inner dialogue related to the ideas presented in class.

The third input preference is kinesthetic, and it is similarly divided up into both an external, tactile category and an internal category. Kinesthetic tactile learners prefer getting involved in the action of a learning experience. They want to feel, touch, manipulate, test, and try just about everything. They would much rather do something than just read about it or hear someone explain it. They tend to be active learners. The kinesthetic internal learner, on the other hand, prefers to feel something internally before getting involved. He wants to be "touched" at an emotional level before engaging in a learning activity or a response. Such learners may tend to shy away from too much external activity but be drawn toward things that move them at a deep level within.

Processing Formats

The third category of learning preferences identified by Jensen is labeled "processing formats." This category of learning style analyzes how the learner manipulates data perceived by the senses. It relates primarily to the hemispheric dominance. While the left-brain hemisphere focuses on speech, language, and calculations, the right-brain hemisphere focuses on senses and pattern recognition. Under this category are four style orientations relating to how learners tend to process input from their senses: contextual global, sequential and detailed linear, conceptual, and concrete.

Right-brain global learners are referenced under the term *contextual global*. These learners look at the big picture before the details. They focus on themes, images, pictures, passions, and overviews first. They tend to desire intuitive meanings and values they bring to the table themselves rather than be told. They like to speculate about potential visions rather than be given the right answer.

Sequential detailed/linear learners, in contrast, prefer a clear, detailed, specific plan for learning. They are usually considered left-brain learners emphasizing sequential, articulate, and structured learning experiences. They think in logical patterns, preferring to have the details spelled out for them rather than having to think of things on their own.

Conceptual (abstract) learners prefer the world of ideas focusing on books, words, reading, writing, and computers. They enjoy discussing and hypothesizing theories and concepts. They don't like to be told what to think but would rather wrestle with problems, ideas, and theories.

Concrete (objects and feelings) learners prefer the world of touching, manipulating, holding, and doing. They enjoy physical activity and active learning. Often drawn to the practical trades or "hands-on" professions, they enjoy being directly involved in doing things. They tend to be practical and skilled.

Response Filters

The fourth category of learning preferences is based on how people naturally respond after they have processed the information from their environment. Their intuitive response is usually based on factors such as time, assessment of risk, referencing points, or personality traits. The categories under *response filters* include three pairs of styles representing ways learners tend to respond after they have processed the information: The first is *external referenced vs. internal referenced*; the second is *matcher vs. mismatcher*; and the third is *impulsive experimental vs. analytical experimental*.

Externally referenced learners respond to life's choices based on what others think. They tend to be context-dependent, giving careful attention to what those in their external environment think they should do in a given situation. *Internally referenced* learners, in contrast, respond to life's choices based primarily on their personal values, regardless of what others think. They tend to make decisions independently.

Matchers tend to respond to choices by looking for similar patterns, consistencies, and confirmations. They tend to repeat things and look for consistent applications. They seem to have a propensity to conform to established standards and procedures. *Mismatchers*, on the contrary, respond to choices by looking at inconsistencies or opposites. They prefer variety and change and often play devil's advocate. They test and bend the rules, always trying to experiment with new ways of doing things. They seem to rebel against the conventional way of doing things in favor of novel responses.

Impulsive experimental learners respond most of the time by trying it out or just "doing it." Rather than think it through, this type of learner would impulsively test it out first. *Analytical experimental* learners, on the other hand, respond to choices by thinking, reflecting, pondering, and considering all the alternatives before deciding on an action. They tend to look at the past and future rather than act impulsively. While both styles enjoy responding in a specific way, the impulsive learners will tend to do so without thinking much while the analytical learners will take their time and think through their alternatives.

A brief review of the various styles of learning related to each of these learning preferences shows that no one style is either best or most conducive to successful learning outcomes. Each style has its own strengths and weaknesses. The point most researchers make is that teachers must be sensitive to the distinctive learning style preferences of each of their learners to maximize the potential of learning within any given class. While students may find it easier to learn within their natural style preferences, teaching exclusively within a person's preferred learning style is not advantageous to learning. Students need to learn within a wide variety of learning styles to be successful in real-life learning-situations. The best application of learning style research for teachers is to provide a wide variety of learning approaches and to give the students as many choices as possible. By choosing a broad variety of learning experiences to attract a wide spectrum of learning styles, teachers can maximize the learning potential in a class.

In order to master the art of teaching creatively using a variety of learning experiences, teachers must become aware of their own biases relating to their learning and teaching style preferences. By objectively acknowledging one's own natural style, a teacher is more apt intentionally to design alternative approaches based on the learning preferences of others.

My tendency is to be more right-brained in my teaching style. I like to paint big pictures, focus on passion and emotion, emphasize intuition and discovery, share personal stories and illustrations, and encourage creativity and innovation. As a result, I tend to downplay structure, organization, detail, precision, and formalities. If I were just to teach in my natural teaching/learning style without giving attention to learners who tend to be more left-brained learners, I would frustrate many of my students. Over years of teaching, I am learning the value of developing skill in designing learning experiences to involve a greater variety of learners. While most of us might tend to think that our style of learning is the best, the reality is that God has made us all different. By being sensitive to the different learning styles of students in our classes, we will be more apt to engage our learners in heart-deep learning.

The application of this research on learning styles could be as simple as reviewing the variety of styles of learning before planning the learning experiences for a lesson. This would remind teachers of their natural teaching style biases, prompting them to be careful not to overemphasize them with students.

By intentionally engaging a variety of learning styles in each lesson, the teacher could design a holistic learning experience that would appeal to as many class members as possible.[17]

Yet the teacher must realize that the learning experiences are always secondary to the goals of the lesson and should never become ends in themselves. In other words, learning experiences should always be subject to the lesson goals from the biblical text under the overall lesson purpose. Learning experiences should help the students move progressively deeper through the levels of cognitive, affective, volitional, and behavioral learning toward the overall purpose and goals of the lesson.

Questions and Applications

1. Make a list of 10 of the most significant things you have learned in life. Beside each thing you have learned, identify how you learned it with a verb ending in "ing" (example: practicing, failing, getting up again and again, listening).

2. What are three specific principles you have found helpful in the Kite Diagram?

3. How might you use Kolb's Learning Cycle to help plan a series of learning experiences?

4. Make a list of your distinctive learning-style characteristics based on Jensen's categories.

5. How would you summarize the way you like to teach based on your learning preferences?

6. What will you need to do to discipline yourself to do in your teaching in order to relate to learners different than you?

---

[17] Eric Jensen, *Brain-Based Learning: The New Paradigm of Teaching*, 2nd ed. (Thousand Oaks, CA: Corwin, 2008), 137–46.

Chapter 8

Designing Learning Experiences that Encourage Heart-Deep Learning

I have found that novelty and spontaneity can spark deep levels of learning in the most surprising situations. Once when preaching, I asked one of my ministry volunteers to participate in an on-the-spot interview related to a point I was making from the biblical text. His informal comments did more to take the congregation to a deeper emotional commitment than anything I said. Implementing creative learning strategies to a class can radically change the involvement of learners in heart-deep learning. By learning to take risks and be creative, a teacher can unleash a whole new dimension of learning to the classroom. After spending most of her life training teachers to be creative, Marlene LeFever stated that "a creative teacher is willing to break out of the mold and risk failure because he or she believes God can use a new idea."[1]

In her book *Creative Teaching Methods*, LeFever suggests the following categories of learning experiences to help teachers engage students in more effective learning: drama, role-play, mime, simulation, story, discussion, case study, creative writing and speaking, art, music, and web-based learning. In this section we will explore how teachers can use these types of activities to

---

[1] Marlene D. LeFever, *Creative Teaching Methods* (Elgin, IL: David C. Cook, 1985), 13.

engage students in deeper experiences of learning. We will also discuss how we can use small groups, questions, and a creative strategy I have often used to help students research issues related to their moral development.

Drama

Drama not only engages the actors in the presentation but also provides a more realistic picture for the audience. I have used drama with all age groups to help people connect on a deeper level with the characters in a biblical story or identify with situations from real life. I can still remember *The Lion, the Witch and the Wardrobe*, a drama presentation our young adult group produced in a church where I served as youth pastor. The scene involving the Turkish delight has stuck in my mind, reminding me of the danger of the enemy's addictions.

In a ministry I directed in Indiana with at-risk children, we used drama almost every week to capture the interest of kids who were unchurched. During these dramas of Bible stories, home situations, scenes of temptation, school conflicts, and crisis experiences of kids, the eyes of children were focused on the action upfront. Drama is one of the best ways to engage people of all age groups in a biblical theme. Sometimes I wonder why pastors do not use drama more often during the Sunday service to present the sermon theme to the whole congregation.

Role-Play

Role-play is similar to drama in that it involves acting yet different in that it tends to be more sporadic and situational. I use it with all age groups because it takes little planning and is highly engaging. It is especially useful in the beginning of a lesson to help the participants visualize their natural tendencies related to a given topic. For instance, when teaching a lesson to teens on controlling the tongue, a great way to start the lesson is to get the teens to divide up in groups of four and come up with a skit depicting the problems they have encountered with gossip in their schools. This not only engages the students in the theme, but it begins to convict them of their tendencies to gossip. It can also be used near the end of a lesson to help the students role-play or practice what they have learned. I found that role-play was effective with unchurched children and youth especially since it allowed them to relate biblical principles directly to their unique situations. I used role-play regularly as a learning experience in a class on parent-teen relationships. I would get parents and teens to reverse roles and act out typical situations relating to conflicts with such things as dating standards, house rules, use of the car, and going to church. Role-play in these learning situations helped parents and teens experience how each other felt when experiencing frustration. In many cases it led to recognition of fault, sincere confession, and attitude change. It was often the spark that ignited a change in heart.

Mime

Mime, while practiced all over the world as an art form, can also be used in an informal, practical form to communicate without words through movement and expression. A good friend who studied mime under Marcel Marceau, one of the world's greatest instructors, expressed the belief that mime could be both professional and common. After she presented a spectacular mime demonstration of a Bible story for our Kids Club, she stayed to teach the children how to express themselves creatively through mime. After the children learned the basic skills, we gave them several opportunities to use mime to express their feelings and those of the characters from biblical stories. By encouraging people to express feelings through movement, expressions, gestures, and actions, mime can be a vehicle through which the actors can process their feelings and help others express theirs. Mime is an effective way to tap into the active, artistic, emotive, and creative side of people. Mime, like any other creative learning activity, can spark movement within the heart related to the goal of the lesson.

Simulation

Simulation games attempt to give participants a simple experience of a real-life situation. They get participants to imagine themselves in a dilemma faced with the realistic challenges of that situation. By making it a game, students avoid the risks involved in real-life situations yet deal with similar obstacles. Since many simulation games take more time than most learning experiences, they are often relevant as learning activities for camps, retreats, and parties.

I developed a simulation game for a retreat focused on helping teens identify the masks they wear to cover up who they are on the inside. While the overall purpose of the lesson was for students to grow stronger in their identity in Christ, the simulation game focused on getting them to express their masks and to discern the real people behind the masks. To set up the playing field, each person constructed a mask on the outside of a big paper bag. The masks depicted the way they came across to others to camouflage the way they really felt about themselves. The goal of the game was to talk to at least three people and learn something more about the real person inside. This was done in order to help people overcome obstacles to sharing their real struggles. The key to this learning experience was in the small-group discussion that followed. For many of the participants, this experience early in the retreat helped them open up to others and experience the love of Christ from other group members in a way they had never done before. It softened their hearts and caused them to let down their defenses.

While simulation games and activities can be designed for almost any biblically based goal, they take time and energy. Yet I have found that some of the best experiences I have used were designed by teams rather than one person. As a children's club director, youth pastor, camp director, pastor, and retreat planner, I have had much greater success when I had my leadership team members help plan such learning activities together than when I planned them myself.

Story

Stories light up the mind. They captivate the imagination, engage the emotions, stimulate thinking, and provide springboards for action. I have never forgotten the story of the martyrdom of Jim Elliot that I heard when I was a teenager. The passion and drama of his life spurred me on to commit my life to Christ and full-time ministry as a college student. The stories of David, Joseph, Moses, Daniel, and Paul imprinted on flannel graph seem to be the fabric of my childhood.

As a good storyteller shares an adventure, listeners of all ages picture themselves in the characters rehearsing emotions, thoughts, and dreams. Stories are intensely interactive. They spawn activity deep within hearts of all ages.

Stories can be used to activate the working of the Holy Spirit at a heart level in many contexts. As a preaching pastor for over nine years, I have always told a story to the children in the worship service based on the Big Idea of the sermon. The story always involves Spunky and Dunky (two little monkeys) and Buddy Bear (a big bear who saved them from poachers in Africa and adopted them into his family). While the theme of the story is always based on the Big Idea of the biblical text of the sermon, it takes place within the immediate drama of "The Adventures of Spunky and Dunky and Buddy Bear." Whether the monkeys get lost, disobey, get into trouble with animal neighbors, or get caught in a thunderstorm, both the kids and the adults in the audience clearly identify with their situation. The Spunky and Dunky story becomes a springboard for an adventure that progresses into the sermon. Many times church members both young and old shake my hand as they leave the service, expressing how much they learned from Buddy Bear.

Teachers can share stories with students or students can share stories with the rest of the class. Stories work well in the introduction and conclusion of a lesson. In the beginning they can introduce a dilemma, illustrate a common struggle, set the stage for what is to come, or demonstrate the question that will be answered in the Big Idea. Near the end of a lesson, good stories can be told to encapsulate the Big Idea, reinforce the major point, or imprint the consequences of failing to follow the Big Idea. Throughout the lesson they can be used at any point as transitions between segments, illustrations for points, or interludes to gain students' attention.

Stories became the foundational teaching method for our Kids Club in Indiana. Whether they were Bible stories, real-life illustrations, testimonies, or examples from the lives of the leaders or kids, we used brief stories as the main way of teaching doctrine and principles from the Bible. Since our kids had short attention spans, we constantly used short, dramatic, engaging stories every week to involve them in learning the goals from our lesson. If you were to watch our storytellers in action at our Monday night meetings, you would see them captivating the kids in the adventure of serving Jesus through telling stories with lots of drama, expression, movement, pathos, hand motions, voice inflection, eye contact, and passion. While storytelling was a significant part of every club meeting, it was always balanced with more interactive learning activities to keep the kids moving.

Discussion

People learn though expressing their thoughts and wrestling with ideas rather than simply listening. This is true for people of all ages, children through adults. It is even true of my 98-year-old mother-in-law who has lived with us for 12 years. While her eyesight is fading and she cannot hear well, she loves to talk if we take the time to ask her good questions. Last night at dinner, just for fun, I asked her why she let me date her daughter. You would think I had opened a long-lost treasure. She had so much fun rattling off both the amusing and deeply serious stories from the past.

Children today miss the attentive listening ear of older teens and adults. Moms are working more and dads are out of the home much of the time. Kids are spending more and more time connecting with music, screens, and gadgets. Little time is left to have meaningful conversations with older people. As much as kids today crave activity and stimulations, I am surprised at how much they still desire and enjoy meaningful conversation with adults. At Kids Club, each week we planned at least 20 minutes in small groups made up of two to five kids and one adult leader. During this time the adults would ask questions, stimulate discussion, generate response to the Big Idea, and listen attentively to the children. Needless to say, this was consistently identified by the kids as one of the most important parts of the club. What is surprising is that this discussion time ranked right up there with games as the thing they enjoyed the most.

Small groups are not just children who enjoy talking with one another and older adults. Youth and adults also enjoy sharing meaningful discussion in small groups. Whether the small groups are ongoing or informally designed to discuss specific parts of a lesson, they can be valuable opportunities for participants to move deeper in learning, discovering, and applying the Big Idea and principles to their lives. Some of the most valuable discussion groups for me have been intergenerational, in which two or more generations are learning and discussing biblical principles. In one church I served, we designed a churchwide weekend retreat focusing on growing together as the family of God. During this experience all of the learning activities were interactional and discussion based with at least three generations making up each learning group. In this context learning activities integrating discussion became catalysts to generate intergenerational learning.

Even the elderly enjoy purposeful discussion related to learning from God's Word. In a rural church that I served as pastor, many of the younger adults were complaining that the older members did not want to be part of the new small groups we had started. The word got out that they did not enjoy sharing on a deeper level in small groups. After talking to several of the older adults, I decided to initiate a series in the summer just for the older members studying various psalms. We decided to meet on Tuesday mornings from 10:00 until 11:30 and then go to a restaurant for lunch. I started the study by asking people from the group about their favorite hymns and slowly getting them to share what made those hymns so special to them. As we sang hymns while I accompanied them on the violin, the group became more and more vulnerable. Soon these elderly adults who had the reputation of not wanting to open up personally were sharing on a personal and deep level. As we progressed to the inductive Bible study, participants continued to share personal and deep thoughts related to the principles we were discovering from the psalm. Over the eight weeks of that series, the group of about 25 older adults continued to discuss and share, much like intimate friends. Singing, sharing, discussing, and eating together sparked a level of intimacy and depth that they had seldom experienced before as a group. I can remember meeting a couple of the ladies from that group at the grocery store several years later. After each giving me a big hug, they reminisced about how much they enjoyed that summer studying the psalms together.

I am convinced that depth in learning God's Word is often directly related to how much people interact on a personal level as they discover, wrestle, and apply principles from the text to their lives.

Case Study

Case studies are situations taken from real life in which people are faced with decisions dealing with gray moral or ethical issues. Usually the stories are read or told up front, and the participants are asked to decide what they would do based on biblical principles. The best case studies are those that can have different outcomes depending on the variables involved. A good case study may have several alternative solutions and take wisdom and discernment to decide. While Scripture has many clearly stated moral and ethical principles that must be obeyed regardless of situational variables, Scripture may be ambiguous in other areas. For example, while we should not gossip about other people, the following case study is a little more challenging.

> As a Christian mother, you found out that a friend of your 17-year-old daughter who attends your church is a practicing lesbian. The difficulty is that she has been spending much more time lately with your daughter. While your daughter is very bright, she is a rather new Christian with few Christian friends. Since your husband left the marriage several years ago for a younger woman, you are anxious about what to do in this situation.

The best case studies are those that relate to several, somewhat conflicting biblical principles. In this case many relevant biblical issues seem to conflict: trusting God in difficulties, separation from evil, hating evil, influencing the lives of those caught in sin, loving the sinner, being nonjudgmental, not being influenced by evil, staying clear of all temptation, bringing up your children to love the Lord, obeying and respecting parents, church discipline, and others.

This would be an excellent case study for a class of teens, parents, newly married couples, intergenerational participants, or young adults. The discussion could be related to any of the themes stated above. The key to using a case study is not to get the students to come up with the "right" answer but to wrestle with the ethical and moral issues related to the situation. This case study could be used at the beginning of a class as a springboard to get students primed to study a passage of Scripture dealing with any of the issues mentioned. After wrestling with such an engaging case study, students would be even more eager to search Scripture for wisdom to resolve their ambiguity.

Following a careful reading of the case study, participants are usually asked one or more questions to get them to think through the issues and alternative ways of dealing with the situation. Questions that could be used are:

- What are some of the things going through the mind of the mother as she wrestles with what to do?
- What would you do as the mother and why?
- What are the options for the mother, and what is the rationale for each?
- What would be the potential consequences of each option in the lives of each of the characters?
- What are some of the issues the mother would need to consider to make a wise decision about how to deal with this situation?
- What biblical principles might shed light on this situation?
- What makes this a difficult decision for the mother?

Another illustration of using the case study method for such a purpose is found in the following example based on 1 Cor 10:23–11:1. While the theme of this passage is the believer's freedom in Christ, the Big Idea could be stated as, "Christians are free to do anything within the bounds of Scripture as long as it does not cause others to stumble."

An effective way to engage high school students to want to get solid answers from the Word related to this principle would be to start with a per-plexing case study like this:

> You are a member of a leadership team from a local church that is designing an outreach event to students at your local high school for Halloween. The group has picked Halloween as the theme of the event because your school community has a long tradition of celebrating Halloween as an opportunity to go wild. Your team wants to use the theme to attract students and to present the gospel. While you are initially excited about the event as an opportunity to see some of your friends get exposed to Jesus, the more the plan takes shape, the more you are having second thoughts. It seems as if most of the team is

mainly concerned about exaggerating the experiential impact of ghosts, evil, horror, the Devil, witchcraft, and the occult rather than unveiling the rich blessings of living for Jesus. You are concerned that the event may have more of a negative impact on the students than a positive one. You are also concerned that the event may draw many of your nominal Christian friends deeper into the dark side. You are deeply concerned. What should you do based on scriptural principles?

Following the reading and reflecting on the case study, students would split into small groups to brainstorm and discuss what they might do based on their understanding of how Scripture relates to this situation. After a designated time, a representative from each group would be asked to present its conclusions to the whole group. Group conclusions would be summarized by the leader with minimal comment or assessment. By this time students are usually frustrated by the apparent ambiguity expressed by their peers. This frustration, curiosity, and ambiguity provide the opportunity for the leader to direct the students to 1 Cor 10:23–11:1 to search for a principle to help them navigate this case study dilemma.

Once again, how a teacher uses this type of learning experience depends on the goal of the class and the purpose of the learning experience. Methods must follow goals. Case studies by definition are designed to encourage higher level thinking. They may be used to help participants become aware of the complexity of certain issues, to wrestle with ideas, to view issues from different perspectives, to become more tolerant of different views, to become more open, to develop deeper convictions, to think through the consequences, or to become aware of their own biases. Yet case studies can be dangerous if they are used as an end in themselves or a way of finding truth. They are used best when introducing an inductive Bible study or applying truth that has been found from a comprehensive study of God's Word as described in chap. 4. Case studies should always be supplemental learning experiences to expand, develop, or apply truth objectively verified from God's Word.

While case studies take time to produce and to implement, they are both engaging and interactive for students. They certainly accelerate the journey toward heart-deep learning.

Creative Writing and Speaking

While some students learn best by memorizing a clearly organized plan of action related to a subject, others want to speculate, dream, imagine, or hypothesize plans related to a dilemma on their own. Creative, right-brain thinkers often want to express themselves either vocally or in writing first. If they are forced to take something that is given to them and memorize it, they usually will do that to please the teacher or to jump through a hoop, but they will not learn it deeply. It will seldom affect their thinking, feeling, choices, and actions. It will simply be stored somewhere in the brain to be regurgitated later.

Silberman, in his book *Active Learning*, suggests using creative writing and speaking exercises to promote reflection and depth in learning. He suggests asking students to write out and then read a "present-tense action account of an experience they have had (as if it were happening in the here and now)." Possible kinds of experiences might include recent problems, events, activities, or challenges. By instructing students to write in the present tense and express how they are feeling in that situation, the students will be more apt to become personally involved in the learning experience. Rather than having all students share their written accounts, Silberman suggests either asking a limited number of volunteers to share or asking students to share with one another in pairs.[2]

Creative writing or speaking can be used as a learning experience in many parts of a lesson to stimulate or engage some learners. Either can be used at the beginning of a class to get students to initiate a situation or dilemma that is relevant to them. If I were initiating a lesson dealing with chronic exaggeration, I might start the lesson by telling a brief story about a time that I used exaggeration to cover up my own insecurity. Then I might ask my students to get into small groups to design a story they would write, tell orally, or act out to demonstrate the roots and consequences of struggling with bragging. By giving the students a choice of how they could accomplish the task, I would appeal to different styles of learning. Yet they would all have to learn to work together to integrate their strengths and weaknesses as a group to accomplish the task.

Art and Music

Art and music provide integrative ways to invigorate the mind, stimulate creative juices, and motivate people of all ages to learn. Learning experiences involving spatial, musical, and bodily kinesthetic intelligences not only give variety to the classroom but also stimulate and activate different parts of the brain to think at a deeper, more engaged level. The brain functions in an integrated unit intimately connected by an elaborate communications system.[3]

---

[2] Melvin L. Silberman, *Active Learning: 101 Strategies to Teach Any Subject* (Boston: Allyn and Bacon, 1996), 124–25.

[3] "Trillions of bits of information are stored in chained protein molecules called *peptides*, which circulate through the brain (and body), transmitting their knowledge to available

Research on the brain has shown that factors such as movement, artistic, and musical expression have a pronounced influence on this communication system within the brain. When appropriate learning activities involving music, art, and movement are integrated into a lesson, they have the potential of activating various parts of the brain to learn at deeper levels.[4]

Building musical and artistic learning activities into your lessons can be as simple as getting students to express their ideas in drawings, pictures, stick figures, songs, rap music, or mime. It could involve setting the tone of a more reflective lesson with appropriate music or getting a class to express the emotions of a verse of Scripture. Often I get my students to express a particular emotion or response to something we are learning as a group by asking them to stand up and act it out while standing in place. For example, I might ask a class of children to express how they would use their hands to tell Jesus they want to be closer to Him and know Him at a deeper level. I could even ask them in small groups to make up a short song with motions and then have each group act it out. The kids would have no trouble expressing to their parents on the way home what they learned in church. While such an activity might take a half hour or more, it would be well worth the time if the children go home with an imbedded, personalized strategy for how to ask Jesus to come closer to them.

The point of using music or art is not simply to keep the children busy. The purpose is to get the students to think through the purpose and goals of the lesson at a deeper, more integrated level. Movement, artistic and musical expression can stimulate the parts of the brain to focus on the learning goals of the lesson.

Web-Based Research

Technology has changed the way the current generation learns. While books and face-to-face interaction characterized learning of previous generations, the present generation is becoming more and more accustomed to learning through electronic media. While this change in learning context has its critics, we must learn how to take advantage of its benefits as well as avoid its pitfalls.

Technology will continue to give us more ways to gain multimedia exposure to all forms of information and processes. These resources can be immensely

---

receptor sites on each and every cell in the Body." The functioning of this communications system is activated by the "complex interactions between genes and our environment, and are modulated by countless biochemicals." Eric Jensen, *Brain-Based Learning and Teaching* (Del Mar, CA: Turning Point, 1995), 17.

[4] Eric Jensen, *Brain-Based Learning: The New Paradigm of Teaching*, 2nd ed. (Thousand Oaks, CA: Corwin Press, 2008), 17.

valuable to help the teacher and learner teach and learn at deeper levels if used wisely. Interactional learning can enhance students' exposure to multimodal learning experiences including sight, audio, music, rhythms, and touch. Such experiences can simultaneously stimulate mind, emotion, will, and behavior. When used in a way that accomplishes meaningful goals and objectives consistent with the Big Idea of a text and the needs of students, these tools can be valuable assets in helping the learner respond to God's Word at a deeper heart level.

For example, in response to a lesson on proclaiming the gospel to this generation, high school students could design an evangelistic video for YouTube, a web page, or a blog. Students of almost any age group could be given a research assignment on the web on almost any relevant topic. Students could use almost any of the popular social network sites to communicate and keep themselves accountable during the week. Students and the teacher could use the Internet to keep in touch with each other for both information and communication. Classes or groups could use websites and blogs to share ideas, information, publicity, and questions. There is no limit to the creative ways technology can be used to challenge deeper level communication and learning.

Yet technology also has inherent dangers. One of the greatest dangers is that it can become an entertaining placebo that keeps children or teenagers occupied. Because the medium itself is so captivating and stimulating, it can become an end in itself. Just as television, videos, and CDs have been used to babysit children, so the technological innovations of the future will be used. Regardless of the increasingly interactive nature of learning technologies in education, nothing will be able to replace the depth and intimacy, warmth, and reality of a face-to-face relationship between teachers and students.

Questioning

While questioning is almost always related to discussion, I have listed it separately because it can be integrated into almost every teaching setting as a specific methodology with or without discussion. Often in sermons or lectures I use rhetorical questions just to get people to think or to wrestle with an idea. Jesus, in His teaching ministry, often used questions in this way. As Roy Zuck states, "Jesus asked clear, direct, purposeful questions that made his teaching stimulating, spirited, and soul-searching. His queries aroused interest, provided thought, requested information, elicited response, clarified issues, applied truth, and silenced critics."[5] Just as Jesus used questions to stir up hard hearts, we can use them to challenge or shake up people into thinking about

---

[5] Roy B. Zuck, *Teaching as Jesus Taught* (Grand Rapids: Baker, 1995), 236.

things they seldom would ponder on their own. Such questions are useful at the beginning of a session to get people to think or look deeper into an issue.

Well-designed questions can encourage people to dig deeper in each of the domains: cognitive, emotional, volitional, and behavioral. By posing questions from various domains during a lesson, the teacher can help students think through issues more holistically by seeing the interconnections between their thinking, feeling, deciding, and acting. Such questions move students toward more heart-deep learning. To move students deeper, questions from these domains should be phrased using verbs that progressively move deeper through the appropriate taxonomies discussed earlier. In an inductive small-group Bible study for young adults based on Eph 6:10–20, a series of inductive questions moving deeper yet progressing through all the domains might look like this:

- Why do you think we need help in overcoming temptation?
- What strategies to fight temptation have you found to work best, up until this point in your Christian walk?
- What are some reasons we continue to need God's supernatural help in temptation?
- What seems to be the overall solution stated in the text for overcoming temptation, if you were to pick the major point of the text?
- What are the pieces of the armor, and what do you think they represent?
- Which pieces of armor do you think you need most and why?
- What would happen if you went to battle without the proper armor?
- What are some experiences you have had in which you faced temptation without wearing some of these pieces of armor?
- What do you sense the Lord is leading you to do as a result of studying this text?
- How can we carry what we have learned tonight into our lives this next week?
- How can we pray for one another right now in light of what we have learned from this text?

The key to writing good questions is the same as any other learning experience. Preparation must begin with the purpose of the lesson and the intentional goals stating what you want students to learn. Questions should then flow out of your goals in each of the domains.

When designing questions for small-group Bible studies, I have followed these seven principles to keep the group moving actively in the right direction.

First, encourage the participants to explore the alternatives to the Big Idea. Get them to wrestle with what it would be like to live or believe the opposite of the Big Idea. By getting the participants to visualize, discuss, speculate, or imagine what life would be like under the antithesis of the Big Idea, it can motivate them to discover the value of the Big Idea. If the Big Idea of a Bible study were, "In order to become close to God, we must discipline ourselves to take time alone with Him every day," then a potential introductory question might be, "What happens in a close relationship with someone we love when we neglect spending quality time with them? Can anyone think of a recent example?"

Second, carefully word the main question to help participants discover the Big Idea of the text. All other questions related to understanding and application should fit under the main question.

Third, when you ask observation questions from the text, get participants to tell you where in the text they found the answer. This will keep the focus of the group on the text rather than allowing participants to base comments on speculation or opinion. If the answers are not accurate, rephrase the question and ask for input from other group members. Always show respect for participants while guiding the whole group to verify accuracy of the answers given.

Fourth, before discussing the application of the principles discovered in the text, get group members to summarize the main things they learned from the text. This helps clarify the Big Idea and the major principles from the text and establish the focus of what they are striving to apply to their lives.

Fifth, once the principles are established and understood, move to deeper levels of application, response, and implementation into life.

Sixth, refrain from asking questions that can have simplistic or yes/no answers. By focusing on clear yet reflective questions, the group will move more quickly to deeper levels. Small groups often flounder in apathy because the answers to the questions are so simple nobody wants to respond.

Seventh, never answer your own questions. It is much better to rephrase the question or repeat it with different words than to answer a question yourself. Silence, while it may seem awkward, can be an opportune time of reflection and meditation as participants wrestle with issues or internal questions. It is better to wait out silence than to break it with a simplistic answer.

Well-phrased questions can be valuable tools to help students dig deeper into the biblical text with their minds, emotions, and wills. They stimulate learners to use all their faculties creatively to discover, investigate, analyze, and explore. If questions are stated in ways that allow freedom of thought and expression, they can be effectively used to engage all ages. While learners from various ages and stages of development respond naturally to questions at their present level of perception, good questions can stimulate them to dig deeper to higher levels of thinking, feeling, decision-making, and behavior. Good questions, therefore, are often the best ways to engage people of all ages toward deeper levels of learning. In reflecting on Jesus' use of questions in His teaching, Zuck concludes: "Questions provide one of the most important means by which teachers can involve students of all ages in the teaching-learning process."[6]

Small Groups

The wise use of small groups in teaching can provide variety to larger classes, build relational connections, and appeal to students who learn through verbalizing thoughts and feelings. If used too much, however, small groups can frustrate students who are more linear and content focused. Having clear goals for each small-group activity is imperative.

When teaching large groups of children, teens, or adults, it is helpful to split into small groups either on a regular or occasional basis to give students time to interact, reflect, wrestle with questions, or respond. At the Kids Club I directed, we broke into small groups after the large-group presentation every week to help the kids discover the Big Idea of the biblical story or text and then to discuss its implications for their lives. Often the children were involved in a learning activity in the small group to think through how they would put the Big Idea into practice. The learning activities varied from drama, to writing, to art, to strategizing plans. This approach also works well with teens and adults. The key to using small groups within a large-group teaching environment is to communicate goals for the groups clearly and succinctly.

Earlier in my teaching career I wrote the following testimony reflecting my deeply rooted conviction about the educational value of small-group ministry.

> When I think of small group, my mind takes me back to my college years—me and four of my buddies sitting on the floor of our dorm room talking about girls, God's will, the future, and the Bible. Although we were not sophisticated, we were sincere. That relaxed

---

[6] Ibid., 235.

approach has stayed with me ever since. The small group has given me a method of discovering God's wisdom from his Word within the context of a caring group.

Through various ministries, the method has stuck. As a youth pastor I gathered around me a group of teens who committed themselves to get together for Bible study and prayer. My primary strategy as a college resident hall director was to provide opportunities for all my students to be involved in a small accountability group each week. In other contexts as a pastor, I have invited unchurched teens and adults into my home for Bible study and found them surprisingly open to God's Word.[7]

Almost 10 years later I wrote about my continued conviction of the value of small groups in the context of intergenerational learning, in a chapter for *New Directions for Small-Group Ministry*.

Some of the most innovative uses of small groups in my ministry have come from intergenerational small groups involving at least two different generations of people in Bible study. I have organized and led Bible studies mixing parents and teens, four generations together, different whole families learning together, and Bible studies within family units. Such learning environments allow rich opportunities for learning from different ages and places in life's journey. Due to the variety of ages included in an intergenerational Bible-based learning experience, meaningful activities related to the lesson goals are essential. Purposeful activity provides a way for persons of all ages to work together. Children, teenagers, and adults alike will build stronger insights from practical, hands-on learning experiences.[8]

As you can see, my appreciation of the value of small groups has continued to expand to include new ways of using them to bring people together to learn at deeper levels. Incorporating people from various age groups in a small-group experience enriches the conversation and the depth of learning. By hearing, experiencing, and reflecting on different perspectives across the age span, participants can see issues from a variety of points of view.

---

[7] Jim Plueddemann and Carol Plueddemann, *Pilgrims in Progress: Growing Through Groups* (Wheaton, IL: Harold Shaw Publishers, 1990), 62.

[8] Gary C. Newton, "Small Groups in an Intergenerational Context," in Paul Borthwick et al., *New Directions for Small-Group Ministry* (Loveland, CO: Vital Ministry, 1999), 57–70.

Researching Personal Moral and Ethical Dilemmas from a Biblical Reference Point

Young people today in many ways are more similar than different from those of past generations. By nature young people learn best through experience and testing things on their own. This is true of all people regardless of culture. While some cultures condition young people to mimic the beliefs, behaviors, and attitudes of adults, deep learning happens only when young people internalize values and behaviors through cognitively processing them on their own. However, if Christian educators simply leave children and youth to wrestle with ethical and moral issues on their own, they will find that the natural impulses of young people will lead them into behaviors and directions that are not wise. This is in part because the frontal part of the adolescent brain—which controls judgment, planning, and decisions—develops at a slower rate than the lobe that controls senses and movement. Adolescents need understanding, support, and structure in controlling their impulses. They need to learn to develop the use of logic, wisdom, and common sense. Studies have shown that the more thoughtful, logical, insightful part of the adolescent brain can be stimulated by building mental connections between impulsive actions and thoughtful reflection. By training the adolescent brain to think more logically and rationally, young people can be stimulated to think through their impulses and to exercise self-control.

I am convinced that one of the goals of discipling young people between the ages of 11 and 25 should be to train them to gain more and more skill at thinking through their impulses, desires, and passions from a biblical perspective. Yet such discipleship will not permanently affect the hearts of young people unless they are actively involved in the process of learning. It is not simply a matter of telling them how to think, preaching at them, or giving them external boundaries. Mental muscles, like physical muscles, grow through expressing, discovering, wrestling, exploring, testing, and questioning. One of the most effective ways to influence students' moral and ethical behavior is by actively involving them in problem-solving and moral dilemmas that involve both their emotional and rational mental functions.[9]

Once students are connected to an issue emotionally, they are usually more motivated to deal with it. For example, while children or teens may not naturally be concerned about studying elderly people in a nursing home, a well-planned immersion experience in a nursing home could radically change their

---

[9] Jensen, *Brain-Based Learning*, 91.

attitude. Once young people develop emotional connections of empathy and friendship with older people, they become more interested in learning about them. The emotional and cognitive domains must be intimately connected for a person to become engaged in a learning experience.

Therefore, if teachers can connect with students' emotions, they will be more apt to draw students into the learning experience. I believe one of the best ways to help young people dig into the Word is to get them to experience the joy of discovering practical biblical solutions to their everyday problems. By starting with the issues they are connected to emotionally, they are more apt to persevere in the adventure of discovering applicable and objective truth in Scripture. One of the best ways to train young people to develop lifelong habits of ethical and moral decision-making is by engaging them in personal discovery of moral and ethical principles based on a systematic study of God's Word. While many young people are not initially excited about studying and researching the Bible, their attitude changes when they realize they are dealing with pertinent issues in their personal lives. As soon as children, youth, or adults are aware of serious needs in their lives and express some desire for help, they are ready to try this learning approach. While some might say this approach is too difficult for children, I have used it consistently in my ministry with at-risk children from unchurched backgrounds. Sometimes such children seem even more motivated to a problem-solving approach because they depend on problem-solving more in their everyday lives than children who have more given to them. Since they discover answers for themselves through this approach, students tend to follow through in putting into practice the principles they discover.

I developed this teaching strategy early in my ministry as a youth pastor after reading Nicholas Wolterstorff's book *Educating for Responsible Action*.[10] While I initially used it to help teens and adults think through moral and ethical issues, I later adapted it in a simpler format for children. It combines a sensitive, student-centered discovery approach with the firm belief that God's Word contains every principle needed to live a godly life in a pagan world.

This learning activity can relate to almost any issue or topic. Its goal is to help students describe and define an issue or problem in their lives and discover and follow through toward a biblically based solution.

Step 1. This approach begins with issues and dilemmas that students decide they want to deal with, either by themselves or in groups. Sometimes I

---

[10] Nicholas Wolterstorff and Christian Schools International, *Educating for Responsible Action* (Grand Rapids: CSI Publications: Eerdmans, 1980).

have asked students to pick an ethical or moral area of struggle in their lives that they have not resolved. I ask them to write their struggles down anonymously; then, after compiling a comprehensive list, I give a copy to each participant. Some of the issues that almost always come up are:

Addictive or compulsive behaviors: smoking, drinking, eating disorders, drugs, Internet

Sexual issues: masturbation, dating, sexual standards, oral sex, sex before marriage, homosexuality, rape, incest, abuse, pornography

Family issues: forgiving parents or others who caused abuse, divorce, sibling rivalry, parental favoritism

Spiritual issues: accepting God's forgiveness, the unpardonable sin, losing one's salvation, fear of hell, distrust of God, baptism of the Holy Spirit, sanctification, recurring sin, guilt, sins from the past

Self-esteem issues: hating oneself, failure, comparing oneself with others, body image, personality problems

Relationships: no friends, loneliness, rejection, unforgiveness, gossip, hatred, distrust of authority figures, critical spirit

Ethical issues: movies, Internet, music, books, occult, swearing or inappropriate language

Step 2. Students either individually or in small groups pick an issue to deal with. They state the nature of the issue in their lives as succinctly as possible, and the goal they want to accomplish related to the issue. I usually explain the different categories of goals in each of the domains and encourage them to set realistic yet deep goals. I encourage them to decide whether they want to work on this by themselves or in a small group dealing with similar issues. I usually separate people by gender.

Step 3. Students identify two or three subordinate issues related to the major issue that could be researched from Scripture. An example might be a student who is dealing with a pattern of constantly exaggerating. Secondary issues related to the main issue of constantly bragging might be low self-esteem, feeling inadequate before God, or jealousy of other people. Related issues are usually best discovered within a closely interacting small group in which participants know and trust one another. This process helps students to develop deeper thinking skills of analysis, discernment, and problem-solving.

Step 4. After students have identified the major and secondary issues, they are instructed on how to research the issues using a Bible dictionary, concordance, or word study resource, in either hard copy or online. Their research goal is to identify axioms or principles related to the issues based on the biblical references, stories, or theological concepts. I usually have students take note of the key scriptural passages related to each issue and the principles derived from those. I have them write out the principles in the form delineated in chap. 3. Each principle should involve a reason, consequence or rationale, and an action. For example, if I were researching the problem of constantly exaggerating, I might choose a principle from the story of Joseph such as, "Making ourselves look better than we really are often puts us in situations lower than we wish to be." This step teaches students higher level Bible study skills involving research, analysis, summary, integration, and consolidation.

Step 5. Students think through how each of the identified principles could apply to their situation. The students' goal in analyzing the results and applications of the principles is to pick three or four principles that seem most relevant and helpful to their situation. The rationale behind this approach is that since the students have initiated the discovery process, they will be more apt to follow through to put the principles they discover into action in their lives.

Step 6. Students develop a potential action plan to deal with their issues based on their chosen principles. The plan involves an outline of the steps they will take to resolve the issues based on the principles they identified from Scripture. By this time students will likely have decided to put this plan into action.

Step 7. Students make a commitment to the teacher or small group to begin to put the plan into action. It is best if students set up something like a contract with their goals and ways of documenting the accomplishment of their goals. Students should be as specific as possible about times, dates, people, deadlines, schedules, and accountability partners.

While such a learning experience may be best accomplished in a retreat or camp setting, I have also found it effective in a class, small group, or one-on-one setting. It may take additional classes or sessions to accomplish it well. While this learning activity seems most applicable to those who are teens or older, I have used a simplified inductive approach with children ages eight through 12. The skills learned are especially relevant for students struggling with learning how to discover their own direction in a world that is both seductive and deceptive. This methodology balances self-initiated discovery and research with an objective source of biblical truth. It is built on the principle of learning that when people discover things on their own, they imprint them deeper into their hearts. This implies that students will be more apt to practice what they have wrestled with on their own. While just telling them the issues and principles might be a quicker way to "teach" students, it is not necessarily the best way to help them internalize truth at a deeper level.

There are many other ways to involve students in problem-solving. Often it is as simple as getting students to discuss issues in their lives related to the theme of a lesson. Then, rather than simply telling the students the biblical answer or your opinion, you get them to discuss the issues more in depth and guide them in discovering biblical answers themselves. This approach trains the student to develop higher-level skills of analysis, synthesis, and application. Problem-solving stimulates the brain to function in many ways. "Problem solving is to the brain what aerobic exercise is to the body. It creates a virtual explosion of activity, causing synapses to form, neurotransmitters to activate, and blood flow to increase. A brain that is worked out with mental weights remains younger, smarter, and more creative longer in life."[11] Using problem-solving as a learning activity engages the student in deeper-level learning.

Responsibility-Building Strategies: Questions, Reflection and Feedback, and Accountability

If the goal of our teaching is deeper-level learning, it is wise to include learning activities to assess what we are expecting our students to learn. Even better than that, we should include learning experiences to help our students become aware and reflective about what they are learning. Often termed as a "metacognitive" approach to teaching and learning, this strategy of active learning purposes to train students gradually to take on more and more of the responsibility for their own learning and assessment of their learning objectives. Bransford explains that "teaching practices congruent with a metacognitive approach to learning include those that focus on sense-making, self-assessment, and reflection on what worked and what needs improving." As students are guided through learning activities that help them set goals, evaluate what they are accomplishing, reflect on the process of what they are learning, give and accept feedback, and initiate accountability measures for their learning, they will become more mature learners. "The emerging science of learning underscores the importance of rethinking what is taught, how it is taught, and how learning is assessed."[12]

Designing learning activities related to helping students take more responsibility for their own learning starts with giving them more autonomy in setting

---

[11] Jensen, *Brain-Based Learning*, 147.

[12] John Bransford, National Research Council (U.S.) Committee on Developments in the Science of Learning and National Research Council (U.S.) Committee on Learning Research and Educational Practice, *How People Learn: Brain, Mind, Experience, and School*, expanded ed. (Washington, DC: National Academy Press, 2000), 12–13.

goals for the class or activity within the overall curricular purposes. Helping them become more aware of what they know, what they don't know, and what they need to know can be the first step in this process. This can begin with helping students to explain what they already know about the topic discussed. Often a simple, open-ended question at the beginning of a class can help students to share freely about what they know and don't know about a topic.

For example, when teaching a lesson to young adults related to overcoming temptation, the teacher could begin with asking: "What are some of the ways you have found effective in dealing with temptation in your own experience?" By finding out what students already know at the beginning of a class, a teacher can avoid boring them by repeating what they already know. Students' initial input can provide a foundation and a springboard for building the lesson. By acknowledging students' valuable contributions, the teacher can encourage the class to take more responsibility for their own learning.

After getting the students to share what they know, it is helpful to find out the limitations of their knowledge. Case studies or problem-solving activities are good ways to discover the limitations of students' knowledge and wisdom. When such learning experiences are used to explore students' breadth of knowledge and understanding, they provide opportunities for students to set their own goals and objectives for what they need to learn. By getting students to identify what they want and need to learn related to their own situations and experiences, they are much more apt to be motivated to accomplish their learning objectives.

This is true even when teaching children. Often they know much more than teachers presume about a subject. When the teacher gets children actively involved as both teachers and learners at the beginning of the class, they become much more actively engaged.

During one experience teaching a large group of children between the ages of eight and twelve from unchurched backgrounds—one of the first lessons of our new season, with lots of new children—our leadership team started with a small-group learning activity in which the children drew pictures of everything they knew about who Jesus was and what He did. Although most of these children had not regularly attended church or Sunday school, we were amazed with what they drew. Their spontaneous pictures showed a depth we could have never imagined including: crosses, nails, Trinity triangles, Bibles, God images lifted high, and Jesus walking on water, healing blind men, hugging sheep, carrying lambs, talking to little children, feeding crowds with fishes, and wearing a big smile. What a great way to start a series on Jesus! We had so many springboards for illustrating the details of our lessons that year. The fact that the ideas came from the children made them coteachers with us in the learning experiences of that year. When students are given an opportunity to share what they know and express freely what they do not know, they become much more responsible for their learning. As they become more comfortable in assessing their own goals and objectives, they become more actively engaged in learning at a deeper level.

Students of all ages grow more responsible as learners when they are held accountable for goals they are involved in setting. It is important that they have input on both their goals and their assessments. By deciding themselves what they want to learn and accomplish, students are more motivated to reach their goals. When students set goals, it is wise to help them establish ways of keeping them accountable to achieve the goals. While the means of accomplishing this depend on the ages of the students and context of the class, some suggestions include using the phone, Internet, face-to-face encounters, texting, and letters. By organizing and implementing both formal and informal accountability networks, teachers can encourage optimum accomplishment of students' goals and objectives.

Connecting Learning Experiences to Lesson Goals

After identifying some of the types of learning activities that could be used to teach a lesson, the teacher's next step is to connect appropriate learning activities with goals. Establishing learning experiences for a lesson can be as simple as asking yourself the most effective way your students could learn each goal.

Using the lesson from Phil 4:4–7, the following learning activities represent learning experience options that a teacher might initially propose when designing the lesson for children. They are organized around the four domains representing the different aspects of the person.

Domain: Cognitive

Goal: Understand how worrying about something affects the children.

POTENTIAL LEARNING ACTIVITIES

Watch and reflect on skits representing the effects of worry in kids' lives.
Identify in small groups the worries they face and write them on the board.
Discuss in small groups how they feel when they worry a lot.
Cut pictures from magazines about situations that might cause them to worry and display them on a poster.
Watch a short video of a real situation that might cause kids to worry.

Design and play a simulation game in which kids will experience and debrief an experience of worry.

Answer a question about how they try to stop worrying.

Goal: Realize why they don't need to worry as Christians.

POTENTIAL LEARNING ACTIVITIES

Answer the question about why they don't need to worry based on the passage.

Hear and interact with the testimony of a Christian who was successful in dealing with a difficult situation because of God's provision.

Act out the answer from the text as to why they don't have to worry (the Lord is close by them).

Brainstorm why Christians don't have to worry as much as those who do not know Jesus.

Goal: Identify what they need to do instead of worrying about something.

POTENTIAL LEARNING ACTIVITIES

Identify the alternatives to worry suggested in the text.

Identify what the text says should accompany our prayer to God from v. 6.

Ask them to explain how and why they would thank God for something in the midst of a difficult situation.

Give them a case study for their reaction in which a boy has been turned down as a pitcher on a Little League team.

Goal: Identify the consequences of praying and thanking God instead of worrying.

POTENTIAL LEARNING ACTIVITIES

Ask them what the text says are the results if we pray and give thanks.

Ask them to think of a Bible story that illustrates what happens when people pray and thank God instead of worrying.

Domain: Affective

Goal: Admit what worries them most in life.

POTENTIAL LEARNING ACTIVITIES

Ask them to share in small groups about things that worry them most.

Ask them to draw pictures of things they worry about a lot.

List or draw pictures of all the things kids mention that they worry about.
Have children cut pictures out of magazines and build a collage representing what they tend to worry about most.

Goal: Appreciate the difference it makes to know that God is always near.

POTENTIAL LEARNING ACTIVITIES

Give them an illustration of a time when the presence of a trusted parent or friend helped you feel more at peace in a scary situation.

Ask the children to share stories of people who made them feel more at peace when they were in danger or difficulty.

Bring in an older teen or adult to share a brief story of how God's presence comforted them in a difficult time.

Present a skit showing a child going through a difficult time with Jesus represented as holding the child up in His strong arms throughout the experience.

Goal: Experience peace that comes through talking to God about a difficult situation.

POTENTIAL LEARNING ACTIVITIES

Have the children pray for one another about the specific things that worry them.

At the end of a prayer time, have all the children hold hands in a circle and offer a prayer of blessing and peace upon them in the name of Jesus, thanking Him for being so close and comforting.

After sharing worries and praying for the worries of children in the small group, ask them how the experience made them feel.

Domain: Volitional

Goal: Choose to talk to God and thank Him instead of worrying about a specific issue.

POTENTIAL LEARNING ACTIVITIES

Ask the children what God is challenging them to do based on what they learned from the scriptural passage studied.

Have the children form small groups and discuss what God may be telling them to do related to the passage.

Domain: Behavioral

Goal: Become more disciplined in praying to God with thanksgiving when worries first surface.

POTENTIAL LEARNING ACTIVITIES

> Get the children to set specific goals for what, when, and how they will pray the next week.
>
> Write down goals on a reminder card posted on a mirror or dresser.
>
> Follow up the next week with a question related to what, when, and how the children prayed about their worries during the week.
>
> Challenge the children to pray for one other child's specific worry the next week.

After brainstorming all the learning activities that could be used to help the children accomplish the goals, the next step is prayerfully to choose the most effective learning activities and sequence them in an order that would provide variety, continuity, and clarity to accomplish the purpose of the lesson. While it may be a temptation for some more analytical teachers to design their lessons according to the structure of the statement of goals, dealing with one domain at a time, I think it is wiser to integrate the domains at each step in the lesson. Goals from the various domains should be woven together in a seamless journey toward cognitive, affective, volitional, and behavioral depth. Every attempt should be made to integrate the goals from the various domains as students wrestle with the meaning, implications, and applications of the Big Idea to their lives. A more organic way to sequence the learning experiences based on how we naturally accommodate and assimilate new ideas will be discussed in the next chapter.

Questions and Applications

1. Using the goals and objectives you developed from Eph 1:1–14, make an extensive list of the learning experiences from this chapter you could use to accomplish each of the goals. Try to be as creative and interactional as you can. State the appropriate learning experiences under each goal.

2. When you have completed your list, underline the learning experiences that seem most appropriate for your class and age group.

PART IV

STRUCTURING
THE LESSON

While it may be helpful in planning a lesson to use the term *steps*, it usually does not happen in steps. The learning process usually happens much more organically in natural patterns and waves. Sometimes there are crises of learning, falls, mistakes, and lags in learning. Sometimes learning appears more like a journey with many ups and downs, vistas and valleys, breakdowns and moments of "eureka!" Yet there is a predictable pattern of how we assimilate new ideas and accommodate them into our way of living. I appreciate David Kolb's study of the dynamics of the cycle of experiential learning because it seems to describe accurately the often-nebulous pattern of how people naturally learn through their experiences in almost every area of life. It is especially relevant to the area of spiritual formation and the learning of scriptural principles.

Kolb describes a natural cycle of how we learn experientially, sequentially using four processes that describe what takes place inside the person. The sequence begins with a *concrete experience* of something that connects with the learner on an affective level. In the next stage, *reflective observation*, the learner watches and reflects on his experience. Next, in the *abstract conceptualization* stage, the learner begins to make sense out of his observations and reflections by organizing them into conceptual categories or principles. Then, in the *active experimental* stage, the learner puts these newly found principles or concepts into practice in real life. And so the cycle continues as the learner continues to perfect his practice through reflection, analysis, and improvisation.[1] While I think this process of learning is more accurately described as a process rather than a series of steps, organizing it in steps is helpful to describe the different categories of learning experiences when designing a lesson.

Bernice McCarthy has used Kolb's cycle of learning to create a popular curriculum design model called the "4MAT System," which not only follows the natural rhythm of how people learn but also appeals to various students' learning styles.[2] Her adaptation of Kolb's Cycle of Learning focuses on engaging the various types of learning styles into the lesson. As you can see by her diagram below, McCarthy's teaching cycle engages all learners including imaginative, analytic, commonsense, and dynamic.

While the structure of the learning activities may vary, I follow an organizational pattern involving four steps, similar to Kolb and McCarthy's model, that is especially appropriate to teaching the Bible. While I am uncomfortable

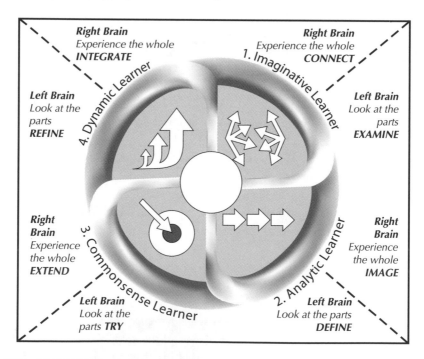

---

[1] David A. Kolb, *Experiential Learning: Experience as the Source of Learning and Development* (Englewood Cliffs, NJ: Prentice-Hall, 1984), 42.

[2] Bernice McCarthy and Dennis McCarthy, *Teaching Around the 4MAT Cycle: Designing Instruction for Diverse Learners with Diverse Learning Styles* (Thousand Oaks, CA: Corwin Press, 2006).

using "steps" to describe an organic pattern of how we tend to learn best, I will use the terminology of "steps" to help those who need a clear structure to understand and remember the process. The four steps or stages in the teaching process involve: first, priming students' heart pumps; second, getting students to dig deeper into the Word; third, stimulating heart talk; and fourth, encouraging heart change. By following the natural cycle of learning intrinsic in Kolb's model of how people learn experientially, the teacher integrates the types of learners in the class according to their learning preferences. By following the cycle, the teacher actively involves the learner in processing information at increasingly deeper levels of engagement.

The ordering of learning activities is built on the natural sequencing of the learning goals from simple to deep, following the pattern of the learning cycle moving from direct experience engaging students' emotions, to observation and reflection, to analysis and conceptualization, to application, and finally to creative planning and problem-solving. Throughout this cycle the goal of the teacher is to encourage students to dig deeper into their hearts and Scripture to discover and apply truth to transform their lives progressively into the likeness of the character of Christ.

Starting with the learners' experience related to a particular theme, the teacher helps them explore a question or problem from their perspective. Based on the solutions they postulate and the questions they still have, the teacher uses their lingering questions as a springboard for discovery of the biblical text. The teacher then guides the learners to find answers from the biblical text by searching for the Big Idea and supporting principles. As learners begin to understand the Big Idea and principles of the text, they are challenged to identify applications to their daily life. Once they understand how to apply the principles to life, they are challenged to go even deeper by wrestling with what the Holy Spirit wants them to change in their lives. They are then challenged to make specific goals to live out the Big Idea and principles. Using a variety of interactive and experiential methods throughout each stage of the cycle of learning, the teacher strives to ignite every part of the learner to pursue truth at the deepest possible level. As the teacher partners with the Holy Spirit, He opens the heart of the learner to transformation.

The purpose statement, the list of goals, and the list of potential learning experiences provide the foundation from which to design the structure of the lesson. In the next four chapters, we will look at how to choose and sequence the learning experiences into a lesson that helps students learn at a deeper heart level, engaging all areas of the person with the principles from God's Word. Each chapter will focus on one of the four steps in designing transformational lessons. Each chapter will clarify how the teacher designs effective learning experiences to move students to deeper levels of knowledge, understanding, application, and transformation related to the lesson purpose and goals.

Chapter 9

Priming Students' Heart Pumps

When I was a child, I spent summers at our cottage in Ontario. Without indoor bath facilities or running water, we had to use a nearby outhouse and walk a quarter mile for drinking water. I learned rules at a young age about these two facilities that I never really understood until later in life. After using the outhouse, I was to pour something called "lime" into the hole, and before using the water pump I had to take the cup of water beside the pump and pour it down the spout beside the spigot. What I later learned was that the lime was used to cover something up and the water was used to get something going. While I will not comment on the effect of the lime in the outhouse, I will expound on the water in the pump. The water primed the pump by lubricating the suction valve to create a vacuum to draw the water up through the spigot. Priming the pump was necessary to get the water moving.

I picture in my mind an old movie in which a thirsty traveler in the desert of Egypt came to an oasis with a solitary spigot rising from the sand. Beside it was a small bottle of water and a note that said, "Your only hope is not to drink this water but to pour it down the spout to get a bounteous supply of water." However, instead of heeding the advice, he impulsively drank the water to sooth his parched tongue. By failing to prime the pump, he forfeited the opportunity to draw on the rich water resources deep within the earth. We too can make this mistake if we fail at the beginning of our lessons to get students' "juices" moving to become receptive to the living water of truth from God's Word.

This chapter deals with both the *why* and the *how* of designing learning experiences to prime students' heart pumps. In the first section of the chapter we will identify eight purposes for priming students, and in the second section of the chapter we will discuss how to do this effectively. Various strategies and learning experiences can be used to engage students in wrestling with issues related to the Big Idea of the text. An approach called "milking the backside of the Big Idea" will be explained as one strategy to help students become personally and deeply engaged in the issues, questions, and needs related to the Big Idea. Using the "backside of the Big Idea" as a springboard for student reflection, this chapter will give suggestions on how to get students to explore their thoughts and feelings related to the biblical theme. Other options for learning activities to "prime students' heart pumps" will be explained.

Purpose of Priming the Pump

Priming the heart pumps of students could mean many things based on the analogy from the cottage. Synonyms come to my mind such as: jump-starting, stimulating, sparking, softening, encouraging, or lubricating. Whatever the functional value of the term, it is used in this educational context to prepare the hearts of students to learn, go deeper, or reflect on the topic. If the dry valves in a pump are not primed, it does not matter how hard we pump; no water will be drawn up the spigot. In a similar way, if students' hearts remain hard, cold, or dry, they seldom respond to even the most relevant methods or content. When the valves in the students' hearts are properly lubricated, they are more apt to respond to God's voice.

Richards and Bredfeldt refer to this opening stage of lesson development as the "hook." They suggest that a good introduction gets students' attention, "surfaces a need," and "sets a goal."[1] While I have integrated these purposes to my understanding of *priming the pump*, I focus more directly on preparing the hearts of students to learn the specific purpose of the lesson. By focusing on stimulating the innermost part of the student to learn the purpose from the beginning of the lesson, the teacher is more apt to accomplish that goal.

The introduction is perhaps the most significant part of the lesson. For this reason I have identified eight purposes of the "Priming the Pump" stage. Any of them could provide the direction for what the teacher wants to accomplish. The richer the priming experience, the more potential there is to draw water from the well of God's Word into the depths of the heart of the person. The

---

[1] Larry Richards and Gary J. Bredfeldt, *Creative Bible Teaching* (Chicago: Moody Press, 1998), 154–56.

purposes of the priming experience include creating an appropriate learning climate, getting students' attention, surfacing a need, establishing a goal, finding out where they are, softening their hearts, stimulating them to learn, and providing a springboard into the Word.

The first purpose of the priming stage is to create an appropriate climate for learning. In most learning situations this means a warm and accepting atmosphere in which each person is recognized and affirmed. The physical environment could be designed through background music, decorations, lighting, or the configuration of the chairs. The teacher could create a warm and affirming emotional environment by getting to class early and talking informally with students. Often by telling a humorous story, playing a fun game, or asking an engaging question, teachers can help students make the transition between everyday concerns and the lesson. It is important for teachers to be intentional about details of the climate they want to establish. For example, if a teacher of junior high boys was leading a lesson on taking risks for Christ, it might be appropriate to post pictures of high-risk adventures around the class. As the students entered the class and were captivated by scenes of parachuting, rock climbing, white-water canoeing, cliff-diving, and skateboarding, they would be one step closer to thinking about the fears and benefits of high-risk activities. Teachers should intentionally plan the class environment related to the purpose of the lesson.

The second purpose of the priming stage of the lesson is to get the attention of the students. Regardless of the students' ages, they come to Bible study, small group, Sunday school class, or youth group with a wide variety of emotions, concerns, activities, worries, and issues on their minds. It is important to captivate their attention early in the lesson to turn their hearts in the direction of what the Lord wants them to learn from Scripture. The most effective opening learning experiences captivate students' emotions and minds and get them to focus on the theme of the lesson.

The third purpose of the priming stage is to bring to the surface the needs of students. This purpose focuses on giving them opportunity to share, express, act out, visualize, or state their needs. As students share their concerns, needs, and questions related to the theme of the lesson, they become more engaged. If they sense the teacher and other students hear what they are saying, they're more apt to be transparent. In such a climate students are more likely to share true needs at a deeper level. By establishing a tone of concern, empathy, and sensitivity, the teacher sets the stage for deep learning. By designing learning experiences that give students the opportunity to share feelings at the beginning of a lesson, teachers can often jump-start the process of heart-deep teaching and learning. Teachers, however, must refrain at this point from giving answers or solutions to the needs brought up by students. While it may satisfy the teacher that he has met the students' needs, it fails to allow students to develop the skills to learn the answers on their own. It is better not to give answers but to listen carefully as students share the depth and breadth of their needs related to a specific theme, issue, or question.

The fourth purpose of the priming stage is to establish a goal for the lesson. While the goal has been set in the teacher's mind long before this point, a purpose of the opening stage of the lesson is to establish the goal in the hearts of the students. Rather than simply state the goal for the students at this time, it is often wise to let the goal emerge from the students themselves as they engage in a learning experience or activity. If the initial learning experience is designed well, the students will be able to state the goal for the lesson in their own words without the teacher telling them. For example, if I were teaching teens about overcoming temptation, I might start by splitting them into small groups and getting them to come up with skits depicting common temptations that they face. Following the skits, I could ask them what major questions they had, related to what they observed. It would be simple to rephrase their responses into a purpose statement related to the Big Idea of the lesson. By designing a learning experience that naturally leads students into stating the purpose of the lesson themselves, teachers are able to instill the purpose of the lesson into students' hearts. Within the early learning experiences of a lesson, students should become aware of the goal.

The fifth purpose of the priming stage is to get students to express where they are and what they know. It is often necessary in teaching students new material to find out what they already know. This keeps the teacher from repeating content, and it also lets the teacher know the students' level of understanding. By giving students a chance to articulate what they know about a theme, subject, or concept before new material is taught, the students are more apt to connect what they already know with the new material. Research compiled by the National Research Council, summarized in a book titled *How People Learn*, emphasizes the importance of taking the time to help students process what they bring to the learning experience before introducing new material.

> Students come to the classroom with preconceptions about how the world works. If their initial understanding is not engaged, they may fail to grasp the new concepts and information that are taught, or they may learn them for purposes of a test but revert to their preconceptions outside the classroom.[2]

---

[2] John Bransford, National Research Council (U.S.) Committee on Developments in the Science of Learning and National Research Council (U.S.) Committee on Learning

The researchers explain that it is important for teachers to draw out the understandings and perceptions of reality that people of all ages bring to a learning situation. This involves getting students to express what they are thinking and feeling related to the issue or topic of a lesson. Based on what the students say, teachers can assess the depth and breadth of their knowledge and adjust teaching strategies appropriately. They can also use the illustrations and comments from students as platforms on which to build their new ideas. Students are affirmed as teachers use students' ideas in their presentations of new material.

The sixth purpose for the priming stage of the lesson is to soften the hearts of students. When a learning experience is chosen for this purpose, it is designed to open up a student's heart, mind, and will to the Big Idea in the lesson, making the student more willing to change behavior. Although somewhat crude, this step could be compared to marinating meat to make it tender. As the mallet and the herbs are applied to the meat, it becomes softer in texture and richer in taste. Likewise, as the learner immerses himself in the learning experience, he becomes more open and enriched. Other examples of "softening the heart" might be seen in coaching a reluctant swimmer to enter cold water or coaxing a timid child to ride a bicycle for the first time. In both cases the instructor gently encourages and guides the learner mentally, emotionally, and volitionally to move physically. In a similar way the priming stage of a Bible lesson should soften the learner's mind to be open to take in new ideas and concepts, soften the learner's emotions to desire to learn new things, and soften the learner's will to become more open to change in behavior.

The seventh purpose for the priming stage of the lesson is to stimulate or motivate the student to want to learn the Big Idea. When this purpose is used in a priming experience, its goal is to influence directly the student to seek the Big Idea from the biblical text in response to the issue, problem, or dilemma introduced. An introductory experience that would fit this purpose might include a movie clip of a situation illustrating what happens when someone moves in the opposite direction to the instruction given in the biblical text. For example, a lesson for young adults might begin with a series of short videos produced by some of the group members, giving testimonies of several young adults who chose to live together before getting married. Rather than use only the clips that reinforced the values of the lesson, it might be even more challenging to include all those interviewed. The ambiguity of such an introduc-

---

Research and Educational Practice, *How People Learn: Brain, Mind, Experience, and School,* expanded ed. (Washington, DC: National Academy Press, 2000), 14–15.

tion would certainly stimulate the participants to want to dig deeper into the issue of living together before marriage. If the introduction simply promoted the benefits of following the biblical instruction, the participants might not be nearly as motivated to dig into Scripture or wrestle with their own feelings of ambiguity related to the topic.

The eighth purpose for the priming stage of the lesson is to be a springboard for the learner into the Word. After a stimulating introduction to a lesson, there is too often a sense of letdown as soon as the teacher announces that it is time for class members to open their Bibles. A major purpose of the introductory part of a lesson is to create anticipation and excitement for students to dig into the Word. To do this well, the introduction cannot dump the Big Idea on the students. If teachers tell the students the main point of the lesson in the introduction, many learners will immediately check out because they feel they have nothing else to learn. The goal of priming the pump is to create a sense of anticipation, curiosity, adventure, or ambiguity so students want resolution from God's Word. The goal of the introduction is to get students motivated and excited about digging into God's Word to discover and wrestle with principles that will help them make sense out of the problems, dilemmas, and issues they face.

Contrary to the way most Bible lessons begin, an effective lesson introduction should go far beyond a simple attention getter, a corny game, or an illustration of the Big Idea. The introduction should engage and prime the learners' heart pumps to want to discover the Big Idea and principles related to the theme of the lesson. Create an appropriate learning climate, get students' attention, surface a need, establish a goal, find out where they are, soften their hearts, stimulate them to learn, and provide a springboard into the Word. The goal of this part of the lesson will be to stir up students' passion for truth and prime their hearts at the deepest possible level to want to find answers for life's questions in God's Word.

Once teachers understand the purpose and value of the first stage of the lesson, it becomes easier for them to choose appropriate learning experiences to get students engaged with issues related to the Big Idea of the biblical passage. The second part of this chapter will discuss "how" questions related to using effective learning experiences to prime the pump.

How to Prime the Pump

Once a person understands the reasons for priming the pump, the next logical question is *how* to prime the pump. Just as there are effective and ineffective ways of priming a water pump, so there are effective and ineffective ways of priming learners' heart pumps. In this section we discuss how to engage learners actively in the first part of a lesson.

This can be done directly or indirectly. The most common approach is through illustrations, skits, drama, stories, object lessons, videos, music, or direct experience focusing on the purpose or Big Idea. Let us examine a typical example of this direct approach using a lesson taught to junior high students based on the Big Idea: "In order to resist Satan's temptations, we must wear the armor of God." A direct approach might involve a student dressing up in the armor from Eph 6:10–18 to simulate a battle overcoming the Devil. Such an introduction would introduce students to the biblical text and the elements of overcoming the enemy. This approach has been effectively used in many contexts such as preaching and teaching large groups, camps, and VBS. It gives students a visual image, a symbol, and a reference point. In the direct approach the teacher usually uses a "hook" to introduce the theme. Certain types of learners enjoy this approach because it gives them a picture of where teachers are heading and what they want students to learn. Often teachers using this direct approach tell students what the main point of the lesson is up front, how to understand it better, and how to apply it to their lives.

Yet as popular as this direct approach has been, there are situations where a more indirect, inductive approach may stimulate deeper, student-motivated learning. If teachers want to encourage students to reflect at a deeper level later in the lesson, then students would need to have an opportunity in the introductory stage to reflect and share personally. Sometimes giving them the Big Idea at the beginning of the lesson, even in the form of a good demonstration, object lesson, or example, may focus their thinking too quickly on what the teacher wants to teach rather than what they may be wrestling with related to the theme of the lesson. Could there be a better way to get students to express what they are thinking, feeling, or doing related to a topic before dumping the "right" answer on them? Rather than beginning with a direct approach or the "front side" of the Big Idea, what would it be like to start with the "backside"?

Milking the Backside of the Big Idea

One of my favorite ways of priming students' heart pumps to learn is by "milking the backside of the Big Idea," something I mentioned earlier.

Try to think of a time when no matter how hard your parent, teacher, or friend tried to get you to believe or do something, you thought or did just the opposite. Now think of a different strategy that person could have used that might have worked better. The response I have most often gotten from people is that a more nondirective or interactive approach might have worked better. This is especially true when a person has a hard or calloused heart related to a belief or behavior. In such cases a person sometimes needs to drop his defenses and reflect on the reasons for or consequences of his beliefs or behaviors rather than be told directly or preached at. If a person begins to soften his heart by opening his mind, emotions, and will just a little, he will be more apt to become open to the Holy Spirit speaking through the Word later in the lesson. The teacher's goal in this approach is to get the students to reach deeper within themselves to articulate what they are thinking, feeling, committed to, or frustrated with, in an attempt to get them to set their own goals related to the Big Idea of the lesson text.

In my first full-time ministry position in Lancaster County, Pennsylvania, I had the opportunity to witness milking in many contexts from rustic Amish farms to sophisticated modern operations. Whether it was done by hand or machine, the process was the same. In my mind this is a perfect picture of the role of the teacher in cooperation with the Holy Spirit in the teaching-learning process. With a clear picture of the purpose of the lesson, the teacher gently draws out the ambiguities, questions, frustrations, needs, and concerns of the student. In doing so, the teacher methodically and systematically "milks" the backside of the Big Idea. To put it another way, the teacher gets the students to explore the deeper issues related to their intellectual, emotional, volitional, and behavioral questions about the Big Idea. Before becoming exposed to the Big Idea, they are primed for heart-deep learning by digging deeper into the antithesis or "backside" of the Big Idea.

Let us look at an example from a lesson for young adults based on a Big Idea from 1 Cor 6:14: "We need to be careful whom we pick as close friends since the closer we get to people, the more they can influence us." An antithesis of the Big Idea might be, "Since we are such relational people, we need to try to get as close as we can to everyone we can." As you can see, this "backside" statement is debatable. It would tend to reflect the natural way many young adults would think about social relationships. They tend to be open to relationships wherever they may be found. Because of the controversial nature of the statement, it would be a great way to get young adults engaged in thinking, reflecting, wrestling, and debating about the conflicting thoughts and feelings within them related to building friendships. The teacher's role in this context would be to find the most effective way to get people to wrestle through the "backside of the Big Idea." Several methods come to my mind: pairing them up with other people they do not know well to discuss whether they agree with the statement and why, splitting a larger group up into groups of four to come up with a skit illustrating the principle, asking the group to share stories of friendships that turned out both good and bad, or sharing a case study related to a new Christian who had just moved to another city to take a job and was struggling with where to go to find a friend. The purpose of these learning experiences is not to tell the learners the Big Idea but to get them to reflect on the deeper issues in their hearts related to the Big Idea of the lesson. By focusing on the "backside of the Big Idea," students would be more apt to wrestle openly with the real issues in their lives.

In the introductory priming activity, the teacher encourages students to reflect personally and collectively about the implications of doing the opposite of the Big Idea. The goal would be to get them to explore, express, identify, or reveal an unmet need, question, or concern related to the "backside of the Big Idea." A wide variety of learning activities could be used to get them to reflect on the antithesis of the Big Idea, including provocative questions, direct experiences, case studies, role-plays, dilemmas, discussion, or debate.

While being cautious not to disclose the Big Idea during this first stage in the lesson, teachers should be careful to provide enough structure to help students stay on track in exploring the wide range of emotions, thoughts, and actions related to the "backside." Yet the structure should allow the Holy Spirit to bring the truth from the students rather than telling them the Big Idea. Often when students hear the main point of the lesson from the teacher, they shut down searching or exploring further themselves. Or they may simply become apathetic if they think they have heard it before. For this reason I have learned to refrain from giving direct answers to students' comments, insights, illustrations, and questions in this "priming" stage of the lesson. Rather I encourage them to answer their own questions by reflecting at a deeper level cognitively, affectively, volitionally, and behaviorally. By motivating students to express their own reasons, consequences, results, issues, questions, or alternatives, they tend to take more responsibility for their own learning. Sometimes I may play the role of devil's advocate to get the students to think through the alternatives and the complexities of the Big Idea. By "milking the backside," I stretch the thinking, feeling, choosing, and doing capacities of the students in an attempt to help them reflect on a deeper level. Such reflection whets their interest to dig deeper into the biblical text to find their own answers and clarify other issues.

This approach to beginning a lesson is based on an assumption that most people respond best to something they first think through themselves. If students reflect first on the complexities, questions, ambiguities, and issues related to the "backside of the Big Idea," they are apt to build more of a desire to go deeper in exploring truth.

This approach is especially effective if the students are defensive or hardened to the direction the scriptural passage leads. For example, if we were trying to teach elementary school-age children to honor their parents, it might be best to start with a learning experience that would get the students to explore either the consequences of not honoring parents or the reasons they might not want to do so. By reflecting openly about these two possibilities, the children would likely be more open to consider what the Bible has to say. If the students acted out in small groups how they have gotten into trouble because they disobeyed their parents, they would tend to be more open to admit they have struggles in this area. On the other hand, if all the teacher did was tell them the reasons for honoring parents, they might not even wrestle with the ambiguities in their hearts related to this issue. Yet it seems easier to get children simply to memorize rote answers than to wrestle with the ambiguities hindering their learning. Getting them to do the latter often disarms their defenses and motivates them to be more willing to search for deeper answers from Scripture.

I have used this approach with young adults in helping them to explore their tendencies to talk too much rather than listen. In one situation I divided the class into groups of four to come up with a skit depicting how talking too much destroys the dynamics of a team completing a healthy project. The skits were hilarious but also convicting for all involved. The participants immediately shared the consequences from their own experiences of talking too much. The discussion that followed was a natural springboard into the scriptural passage that identified both the consequences of talking too much and the benefits of listening attentively.

This type of learning activity to teach children ages eight through twelve from Phil 4:4–8 could be suitable in accomplishing at least two goals for the lesson. (Note that you start with goals rather than methods.) The two goals for the children that might lead me to use this "backside approach" would be "to understand how worrying about something affects them" and "to admit what worries them the most in life." Focusing the children's attention on these two goals at the beginning of the lesson would set the tone and get them to think on a deeper level.

I might set up four skits in which participants act out dysfunctional yet typical ways people tend to respond to worries and concerns. I might start with skits that are somewhat humorous and then move to more serious ones. Scenarios could include: first, a child who worried about why nobody liked her and started making up exaggerated stories about herself; second, a boy who was so worried about whether a girl liked him that every time he got near her he accidentally did something stupid; third, a mother who was so worried about losing her job and running out of money that she started to act mean to her kids; and fourth, a boy who was so afraid when he saw his parents fighting so often that he started to get poor grades in school from lack of studying.

The purpose of these skits is to get the children to identify how the characters deal with their worries and to discuss how they tend to deal with worry. While the skits would happen in a large group, I would divide them afterward into small groups with leaders to discuss the reflection questions. If they are in a warm, supportive group, most children would love to discuss the reasons they worry and the ways they react to worry. By first "milking the backside of the Big Idea," the children would be primed to want to resolve their issues of worry. Under the guidance of a wise small-group leader, children could be encouraged to dig deeper into their thoughts, feelings, choices, and actions related to worrying in this introductory learning activity. Such an activity could last up to half an hour if the children are engaged. It could be a valuable experience for them to become aware of their needs; dig deeper into their thinking, feeling, and habits; and articulate their desires to want help in dealing with worries and experience more of God's peace. Rather than tell the children the biblical answer in this first learning experience, the teacher should prime the pump to get them to want to find the answer from Scripture in the next learning experience.

Transition to Bible Exploration

After children have wrestled with the "backside" of the Big Idea and discussed and identified the major issue or question related to the "antithesis of the Big Idea," the teacher should encourage them to state it clearly. Often I use a question such as: "What issues or questions come to your mind from the skits (or other learning activities)?" or, "What principles did you pick up from the skits?" or, "Why is it so difficult for us to do the right thing?" Then, depending on how I have stated the Big Idea, I restate and summarize the children's comments in a way that provides a springboard into the study of God's Word. Based on a lesson related to the Big Idea, "In order to have a godly influence on others, we must control our tongue by giving God more control of our heart," I might say something like: "While I think we all realize how difficult it is for us to control our speech, let us find out from God's Word what the key is to controlling what comes out of our mouths."

This transition statement summarizes the main things the students learned from the priming experience and introduces the main question as a springboard into discovery of the Big Idea. In this case the key to control what comes out of our mouths is "giving God more control of our heart."

If the priming experience is designed well, it should naturally lead the class to come up with the question or dilemma to be dealt with in the next part of the lesson. The teacher's role is to design a creative way for students to reflect on the "backside" of the Big Idea; give boundaries and structure for students' reflection; summarize their preliminary assumptions related to solving the problem, question, or dilemma; and transition them into discovering the answer or resolution of their questions or issues based on the Big Idea.

In this approach the teacher "milks" the backside of the Big Idea before getting the students to explore the Big Idea. By milking, the teacher draws out thoughts, feelings, desires, concerns, hesitancies, motivations, and questions related to the antithesis of the Big Idea. The teacher gets students to explore and critique the antithesis of the Big Idea to stimulate them cognitively, affectively, volitionally, and practically to become hungry and thirsty for truth in Scripture. This approach primes the students' heart pumps to draw in living water from the Word.

Questions and Applications

1. Explain how the pump illustration relates to the first step in the lesson.

2. State and briefly explain each of the eight purposes for "priming the pump."

3. Explain the author's rationale behind "milking the backside of the Big Idea."

4. When do you think this approach could be useful in beginning a lesson?

5. What are some other methods that could be used in "priming the pump"?

6. For each of the following Big Ideas, come up with a statement reflecting a corollary or a backside.

Example:

Big Idea: In order to be truly happy, we must give ourselves away.

Backside: The best way to be happy is to take care of ourselves first.

Big Idea: The best way to avoid falling into temptation is to run from it.

Backside: _____

Big Idea: We cut off the fuse of anger when we resolve it before going to bed.

Backside: _____

Big Idea: When we forgive our enemies, we prolong our life.

Backside: _____

Big Idea: God's will is found in simple obedience from the heart.

Backside: _____

7. Identify a learning activity for each of the above "Backsides."

Chapter 10

Getting Students to Dig Deeper into the Word

Too often the Bible teaching part of a youth group, Sunday school class, or Bible club ministry fails to engage and challenge students to dig deeply and reflectively into God's Word. In an attempt to make biblical themes relevant, teachers often fail to bring out the essential principle of the biblical text and help students apply it to their lives. While the lesson may be fun, interactive, and entertaining, it often fails to engage students in learning the essential truth of the biblical text. Often the result is that students graduate from their youth group experience with little understanding of basic Bible knowledge, minimal commitment to the authority of God's Word, or no training in how to discover biblical principles on their own. As they enter college or the adult world, they are ill equipped to wrestle with the temptations, worldviews, lifestyle questions, and dilemmas they will surely confront. George Barna's research on the religious beliefs of young people confirms that most youth who have grown up in evangelical churches and youth groups fail to have a strong enough foundational understanding of the Bible and a biblical worldview to enable them to deal with the pressures of life.[1] In light of the growing biblical illiteracy in our culture, the tendency to dumb down the biblical content must be avoided at all costs.

---

[1] George Barna, *Transforming Children into Spiritual Champions* (Ventura, CA: Regal, 2003), 28–42.

Yet it is possible to teach the Bible to all age groups so that they discover and engage in the central principle of the text and learn how to apply it to their lives. As they develop, children, youth, and adults can learn the grand narrative of God's relationship with humankind. They can understand the contexts, geography, history, and cultures of the people groups represented in the Bible. They can learn to appreciate the need for laws, principles, and grace to guide and motivate them to follow Jesus closely. They can learn to experience the love of God through Jesus Christ deep in their hearts. In order for students to learn the Bible in such depth, teachers must do more than dump biblical content on learners. Teachers must engage learners experientially in the pursuit and application of biblical truth.

"Getting Students to Dig Deeper into the Word" deals with guiding students to discover truth from the biblical text. This chapter is based on the assumption that people of all ages learn at a deeper level when they take the responsibility themselves for learning. Teachers will be encouraged to use more student-centered teaching approaches such as discovering, investigating, problem-solving, storytelling, acting out passages, questioning, active listening, group assignments, and researching. Teachers will learn how to provide structure for such learning experiences to ensure that students will find the necessary details and principles from the biblical text. Special attention will be given to strategies to help students discover and articulate the Big Idea in their own words. Yet as important as it is to get students involved experientially, that should never be an excuse for neglecting cognitive depth. Rather, experiential learning should be used alongside inductive, reflective, and speculative exercises to stimulate all aspects of the person in the learning process. By integrating active learning methods with systematic Bible study principles, teachers will avoid the error of biblical superficiality.

Deeper Learning Necessitates Reflection, Interaction, and Experiential Engagement

One observation I made after teaching for several years in a conservative, evangelical seminary is that preachers love to preach. They love to preach so much that many of them have a difficult time not preaching. While we certainly need excellent preachers and teachers who are able to proclaim the gospel clearly and authoritatively, are there not other effective ways to help people learn God's Word? In this chapter we explore some alternative ways to help people learn than to preach, proclaim, or tell. While there may be contexts where it is necessary and wise to teach or preach deductively, the focus of the approach in this book is on inductive teaching.

While Jesus taught and preached authoritatively, He also used many interactive and inductive methods. His methods depended on the context, His goals, and the condition of the hearts of those He was teaching. He used a great variety of teaching approaches to help His followers know and practice truth, including: "lecturing, discussions, questions, answers to questions, brief statements, conversations or dialogues, stories or parables, disputes, demonstrations, quotations, maxims, challenges, rebukes, comments, riddles, arguments, and even silence."[2]

Even though Jesus embodied truth, He did not always pick directive telling or preaching as the only or even most effective way of getting His followers to learn. Just because Bible-believing Christians hold to authoritative truth, it does not mean they should primarily teach by "telling."

As we mentioned in chap. 4, the term "epistemology" deals primarily with two concerns: the nature of truth and how we know truth. Just because Christians believe in absolute, authoritative truth does not mean people learn truth only through objective, directive ways. It is not inconsistent to believe that while the nature of truth is absolute, people learn through a variety of ways, both subjective and objective. Educational research related to learning and the chemistry of the brain has continued to reinforce the importance of experiential components of learning. When a person's environment is rich in healthy stimulation, "enrichment strengthens neural capacity." As a result, single cells grow, individual neurons grow, the central nervous system grows, and all brain and body systems grow and develop.[3] As learners interact and engage with ideas, objects, and people, learning takes place. When a cognitive learning experience actively involves the participants, they are more apt to apply the learning to make significant changes in their lives and other life situations. Experiential interaction and engagement with principles in God's Word serve as a catalyst for heart-deep learning.

The Need for Both a Strong Knowledge Base and Active Learning Strategies

Most of us have been part of a teaching experience in which we were completely lost because we did not have the basic knowledge, principles, or language to participate meaningfully. I can remember sitting in a computer training class

---

[2] Roy B. Zuck, *Teaching as Jesus Taught* (Grand Rapids: Baker Books, 1995), 165.

[3] Eric Jensen, *Enriching the Brain: How to Maximize Every Learner's Potential*, 1st ed., The Jossey-Bass Education Series (San Francisco: Jossey-Bass, 2006), 61–63.

trying to learn a new program that was supposed to make my life easier. Not only did the instructor go too fast, but the teacher used language that many in the class had never heard before. It was not that the students were stupid; it was that they had limited knowledge and understanding with which to connect words with actions. While most of us could repeat the steps in the process while the instructor guided us, some of us had no framework to incorporate the process into our minds. We lacked the preliminary knowledge, understandings, and skills to fit the instruction into our way of thinking and acting. This is true of most new learning situations. Students need to understand the basics before they can progress. In order to understand the basics, they need to have some initial motivation to learn. Once the pump is primed, students are ready to go deeper.

Teachers seem to gravitate to one of two extremes. They focus on either content or experience. Yet deeper learning involves the integration of solid content and both analytical and experiential learning. Deeper learning happens when developmentally appropriate content is absorbed through interactive, active, and experiential approaches. Basic knowledge and understandings are foundational to going deeper. Roy Zuck concludes, after analyzing Jesus' teaching strategies, that "attempts to teach thinking skills without a strong base of factual knowledge do not promote problem-solving ability or support transfer of new situations."[4] Teachers must build a platform of foundational facts and principles before students can build upon them to go deeper. On the other hand, just teaching facts, understandings, and concepts without interactive, experiential, and problem-solving learning experiences fails to help students understand how knowledge can be useful in life.[5] To find the details, principles, and interpretations of a text, we must start with objective Bible study and analytical research methods.

We have all experienced Bible studies in which participants primarily answer questions such as: "What do you think this says?" and "How do you feel about what he said?" and "How do you relate to what he says?" Many times Bible studies like this do not include any interaction with the historical or cultural context, grammatical details, word meanings, central purpose of the text, or literary context. Depth is defined by how deeply the participants dig into their own personal lives or how practical the discussion gets, rather than how accurately they uncover the intent of the text for their lives. In our culture it seems as if how we feel about the text is more important than what God wants

---

[4] Zuck, *Teaching as Jesus Taught*, 165.
[5] Ibid.

to accomplish in us through the text. In our approach to heart-deep teaching, we must help people discover as objectively as possible the facts, principles, and interpretation of the text, and then to experience the truth of God's Word in a way that transforms them from the inside out.

Such transformation only occurs when God's Word is respected as the truth and is examined in depth by both teacher and student in ways that are research based, interactive, active, and experiential.

Focusing on the Big Idea

While the first step of the lesson primes the pump for students to desire the living water from God's Word, the second step helps them find it. The transition statement after the first step of the lesson should be a springboard for the students into the Word to discover the answers to their questions, dilemmas, problems, or struggles. If the students' energy, excitement, or curiosity is flat after the first step, it will be difficult to get them excited about continuing their journey of discovery. On the other hand, if the students anticipate finding help, advice, answers, or insights from God's Word, they will more eagerly want to dig deeper into the Word in this step.

What drives students into the Word is the question from the first step of the lesson. If the question is paraphrased accurately from the students' experiences after the first step of the lesson, the biblical text can be introduced as the source for answers, solutions, help, or insights. While the words and terms used may vary depending on the age group of the class, it is important to use words that heighten students' anticipation for their adventure in the Word of God.

Although some teachers may be tempted to tell students at this point exactly what is coming next, I have found that this tends to smother the students' curiosity. While the analytical students prefer a clear outline of what is coming next, telling them too much too soon can rob them of the joy of discovery. By stating a clear question, the teacher can give students enough structure to focus their minds while not telling them the end of the story. Intrigue and suspense are great motivators. If the teacher has done the job well in the first step of the lesson, students should be motivated to dig into Scripture to find an answer in the next step.

The opening question in this step of the lesson will naturally lead into the content outline if the question is directly related to the content outline. One way of ensuring this connection is to take the question from either the subject or complement of the Big Idea. Let me explain with two examples from the passages we have been using.

The first comes from a lesson used for teaching a group of children ages 8–12.

Title: God's Worry Solution

Text: Philippians 4:6–7

Big Idea: When we pray to Jesus and refuse to worry, God will give us His peace.

Content Outline

What should we do when we feel like worrying about something?

1. Don't worry.
2. Pray.
3. Thank God.

What will happen when we do this?

God's peace will guard our hearts.

Lesson Purpose: The purpose of this lesson is that *the children will experience God's peace in the midst of difficulties because they asked for God's help and thanked Him instead of worrying.*

As you can see, the content outline provides the structure and content for the lesson. By answering the two stated questions, the students will discover the Big Idea. Although the students may pick up other facts and principles from the lesson, the main goal is that the students will experience God's peace in the midst of difficulty because they asked God's help instead of worrying about what was bothering them. If in the first step of the lesson the children wrestled with what they worried about and how worry affected their lives, they would be eager to learn how they could deal with worry from God's perspective and how God's way of handling worry could change their lives.

While a teacher could choose many ways to get students to discover the answer to the two questions in the content outline, the direction of this step in the lesson is clear. The teacher has several options for how to state transition questions to lead into the study of God's Word, depending on what the children focused on in the first step. Options might include: "So what do you think is the best way to deal with worry?" "What should we do when we are scared to death about something else?" and, "What does God expect us to do when we are so worried we can hardly think about anything?" Sometimes I will share an illustration at this point that heightens anticipation for an answer even higher.

The second example I will use is from the same passage but for children ages four or five. Such a lesson would have to be much simpler. Yet while most of them may not yet know how to read, we should never sacrifice biblical integrity for simplicity.

Title: Jumping into Jesus' Arms

Text: Philippians 4:4–7

Big Idea: When we are scared, we need to jump into Jesus' arms.

Content Outline

What it means to jump into Jesus' arms:
> Rejoice in Jesus.
> Talk to Jesus.
> Thank Jesus.

Forget your worries.

What will happen when we jump into Jesus' arms?
> Peace

In this learning situation I might begin by telling the children a story about an animal who was worried because he lost his mommy. During and after the story I would get the children to talk about times they were scared because they couldn't find their mom or dad. I would get them to express their feelings and even draw pictures of how they look when they are worried.

My transition statement into the Bible story could be taken directly from the subject of the Big Idea: "What should we do when we are scared?" The answer to my question would be found in the text in the expression "Jumping into Jesus' Arms," which is also the title for the lesson. The direction for the second step of the lesson would be clearly set. The main details in the text would answer the question in the content outline as to what it means to jump into Jesus' arms. The contextualized illustration would make it natural to use active learning experiences to help children identify with each of the points in the text and the Big Idea of the text. Rather than being dry and academic for the children, learning the Big Idea and other principles of the lesson would be deeply practical, emotional, instructional, and helpful.

Regardless of how creative a teaching experience is, it must still focus on the Big Idea of the text. While a lesson must target the needs of the student, this must always be done in relation to the Big Idea of the text studied. The lesson goals in each domain guide the student deeper into the learning experience, from simple to complex and from external to internal. I like to picture the process in the Heart-Deep Teaching Model introduced in chap. 3.

This diagram depics the center of the person as his heart, his innermost part of the person. Three ladders descend into the heart from different points around the circle. Each one represents one of the domains: cognitive, affective, and volitional. The rungs on each ladder represent the steps toward depth or the taxonomies explained in chap. 3. From the center of the heart extends another ladder with an arrow on the end. The arrow represents the action arising from the heart precipitated by the Holy Spirit's enabling influence in response to the integrated influence of the person's thinking, feeling, and choosing in response to God's Word. As the goals are accomplished at an increasingly deeper level following the taxonomies, the person becomes more apt to respond at a heart-deep level to obey the voice of the Holy Spirit and put God's Word into practice.

As the teacher, in cooperation with the Holy Spirit, encourages the students to accomplish the stated goals through specific, engaging learning activities, the students move sequentially deeper and deeper into the Word and apply it to the different aspects of their lives cognitively, affectively, and volitionally. The deeper they get, the more integrated the learning becomes in each of these domains. As the students discover and interact with the Big Idea, they respond to the prompting of the Holy Spirit in the various aspects of their being to commit themselves to obedience.

While this process may sound idealistic, its implementation involves sensitivity to the Holy Spirit, perception of the needs of students, reflection on the details of the biblical text, creative use of learning activities, and organizational skill in putting together a teaching plan.

Up to this point we have discussed several steps in lesson preparation. First, teachers complete an in-depth study and application of a scriptural passage. Second, the Big Idea is translated into a contextualized Teaching Big Idea to provide a focus for the lesson. Third, the Teaching Big Idea is put into the form of a purpose statement: "The purpose of this lesson is that the students will . . ." (integrated with the Teaching Big Idea). Fourth, a content outline is added to show the structure from the text of how the students can discover the Big Idea. Fifth, goals are listed under each of the domains to guide students to move deeper in heart-deep teaching.

The content outline provides the structure and main content for the lesson. By answering the two stated questions, the students will discover the Big Idea. Although the students may pick up other facts and principles from the lesson, the main goal is that the students will discover and apply the Big Idea to their lives.

A Summary of the Purposes of Step Two: Getting Students to Dig Deeper into the Word

As we have discussed so far in this chapter, the second step of the lesson has at least six purposes. The first purpose is to accomplish the stated content goals related to the simplified content outline built on the structure of the analytical outline. The second purpose is to help students discover and understand the Big Idea in reference to the problem, issue, or dilemma discussed in the first step of the lesson. The third purpose is to help students understand the relevant facts and concepts related to adequately understanding the Big Idea in its original context. This includes sharing with students significant clues to discovering the gold in the text. These clues might include significant structural details, key conjunctions or prepositions, hidden word meanings, or historical details. The fourth purpose is to help students move to deeper levels of cognitive depth, following the cognitive taxonomy moving from awareness, to understanding, to wisdom. The fifth purpose is to help students integrate cognitive learning with perception and depth in the emotional, volitional, and behavioral domains. The sixth purpose is to engage the learners as much as possible visually, actively, interactively, intrapersonally, reflectively, audibly, and experientially. By engaging students in discovering and wrestling with truth from the Word in a variety of ways, they are much more apt to integrate the principles from God's Word into their lives and respond to them in concrete ways.

Now that we have discussed the purpose of this step of digging into the Word at a deeper level, we will turn to the question of *how?* The best way to explain how to get students to dig deeper into the Word is to give an example of a lesson based on Eph 5:1–16 that could be taught in a youth group setting. The following represents my lesson preparation after a thorough personal study and application of the text. It includes an analytical outline, Big Idea, lesson purpose, content outline, and lesson goals.

Read the analytical outline reflectively, trying to identify the main principles in the passage.

Analytical Outline of Ephesians 5:1–16

Therefore
　　as dearly loved children
Be imitators of God and
Live a life of love
　　　　Just as Jesus loved us and gave himself up for us
　　　　　　　　as a fragrant offering and
　　　　　　　　sacrifice to God
　　　　But among you there must not be even a hint of sexual immorality
　　　　　　　　or of any kind of impurity or of greed
　　　　because these are improper for God's holy people

Nor should there be obscenity, foolish talk or coarse jesting
    which are out of place
    but rather thanksgiving
    for this you can be sure:

      no immoral, impure, or greedy person
      such a man is an idolater

      has any inheritance
        in the kingdom of Christ and of God
Let no one deceive you with empty words
    for because of *such things*
  God's wrath comes on those who are disobedient
Therefore
    do not be partakers with them
    For you were once darkness but now you are light in the Lord
Live as children of the light
    For the fruit of the light consists in all goodness, righteousness, and truth
And find out what pleases the Lord
    Have nothing to do with the deeds of darkness, but rather expose them
      For it is shameful even to mention what the disobedient do in secret
      But everything exposed by the light becomes visible
    For it is light that makes everything visible
     This is why it is said
       Wake up, O sleeper
       Rise from the dead
       And Christ will shine on you
Be careful then how you live
    Not as unwise but as wise
      Making the most of every opportunity
      Because the days are evil

Lesson Outline

Title: Flirting with the Dark Side

Text: Ephesians 5:1–16

Big Idea: In order to live as a fragrant offering to God within a decaying world, we must never participate in anything connected to the deeds of darkness.

Lesson Purpose: Students will live their lives reflecting the fragrance of Christ's love while refusing to participate in anything connected to the deeds of darkness.

Content Outline

How to live out the fragrance of Christ in a decaying world:

1. Imitate Christ's love to others within this evil world (v. 1).

2. Make a radical break from the deeds of darkness (vv. 2–14).
> sexual immorality
> any kind of impurity
> any kind of greed
> obscenity, foolish talk, or coarse jesting

Reasons why we should never flirt with the darkness:
> It is improper for Christians (v. 3).
> It is out of place for Christians (v. 4).
> Those who live in darkness will not inherit eternal life (v. 5).
> God's wrath will be unleashed on those who live (vv. 8–14).

3. Take advantage of opportunities to be a light in this evil world (vv. 15–16).

Lesson Goals

The goals of this lesson are that students will:

COGNITIVE

Understand the darkness within the culture in Ephesus.

Identify the major commands in the text.

Understand the reasons stated in the text why we should live in the light and refuse to participate in darkness.

Discern ways the enemy may be tempting them to participate in darkness.

Realize the dangers of flirting with the dark side.

Hypothesize what it means to live as a fragrant aroma.

AFFECTIVE

Become aware of the ways they have been flirting with the dark side.

Be convicted of dark lifestyle practices that need to change.

VOLITIONAL

Decide to turn from specific evil practices, behaviors, and involvements.

Commit themselves to live as an aroma of Christ's love in the stink of the world.

BEHAVIORAL

Become more consistent in staying away from sinful practices and involvements.

Plan strategically to make best use of the opportunities they have to be a
light in this dark world.

The most important place to begin in designing the sequence of steps of a
lesson is with the Big Idea and purpose statement. The purpose of the lesson is
"that students will live their lives reflecting the fragrance of Christ's love while
refusing to participate in anything connected to the deeds of darkness."

With this as my purpose, my first step or "priming the pump" experience
is designed to "milk the backside of the Big Idea," or get the students to see the
destruction that happens when Christians compromise their moral and ethical
standards by becoming too much a part of the evil of their culture. To accomplish this I might choose a music video such as *Slow Fade* sung by Casting
Crowns. This video shows dramatic scenes of a family threatened by a father
who is tempted by lust under the watchful eyes of his little girl. It ends with the
little girl singing the children's Sunday school chorus "O Be Careful Little Eyes
What You See." It vividly challenges the audience to evaluate the compromises
they are making with evil in light of their horrible consequences. Following
the video, after hearing some general reactions from students, I would split
them up into small groups for 15 minutes to think of ways their compromises
with evil may affect their lives or the lives of others around them. When they
get back into the large group, I ask the students to share some of the ideas that
came up in their discussions related to how their compromises may affect them
or influence others. I summarize their key ideas on the whiteboard.

As a transition I ask them to share their questions related to the issues
brought up by the video. I summarize their questions and state that the text we
have chosen to study focuses directly on dealing with these questions.

I usually follow these steps to design the "Digging Deeper into the Word"
part of the lesson. First, identify the goals you will focus on in this part of the
lesson. Second, choose learning activities for each goal. Third, sequence the
learning activities with appropriate transitions.

The first goal I would focus on in this lesson is the one related to helping
students understand the darkness of the culture in Ephesus. Before beginning
the Bible exploration activity, I would share insights about the cultural context
necessary for a proper understanding of the passage. It might also be appropriate to have students research these issues ahead of time and make a PowerPoint
presentation of some of the practices of the Ephesians related to temple wor-

ship, business, and sexual practices. This would help students identify even more closely with the challenges the early Christians faced.

As a general rule, I like to get students to search the Scriptures themselves to find the Big Idea or major principle of the story or text. This helps students respect the Bible as the trustworthy basis of their beliefs. In this situation I would have a good reader read the text expressively up front as students followed in their Bibles or on a PowerPoint presentation that breaks up the text into an analytical outline.

I would then ask students in the large group to identify the three major commands and what they mean related to vv. 1,2,15–16. I would record their answers on the board to serve as a reminder throughout the lesson.

Then I would divide them into small groups to discuss the following questions further:

1. What are the three major commands Paul gives to the Ephesians in the text?
2. What does it mean to live a life of love like Christ, as a fragrant offering (v. 1)?
3. What does it mean to make a radical break from the deeds of darkness (vv. 2–14)?
4. What are the reasons Paul gives why we should never flirt with darkness (vv. 2–14)?
5. What does it mean to take advantage of the opportunities we have to be light in this evil world (vv. 15–16)?
6. If we are to be the fragrance of Jesus Christ in the world, why must we make a clean break from participating in the evil of our culture?

I would conclude this step of the lesson by calling the small groups back into the large group to summarize what they came up with as the main thing they learned from the passage. I might have each group write its summary statement on the board or a PowerPoint slide.

The questions answered and discussed in the large and small groups would primarily focus on four goals stated under the cognitive domain:

The goals of the lesson are that students will:

1. Identify the major commands in the text.
2. Understand the reasons in the text why we should live in the light and refuse to participate in darkness.
3. Realize the dangers of flirting with the dark side.
4. Hypothesize what it means to live as a fragrant aroma.

By the end of this section of the lesson, the students should have discovered on their own the points in the content outline, the major principles, and the Big Idea of the text. They should have moved deeper though the levels of cognitive knowledge and understanding and begun to become aware of some of the ways they have been flirting with the dark side. The Holy Spirit is beginning to soften their wills and hearts to become more open to sharing some of the areas where they needed to confess and repent.

By the end of this second step of the lesson, students should be able to summarize the main point of the lesson or the Big Idea. They should see how the Big Idea was discovered through a careful analysis of the biblical text. Aided by the structure provided by questions from the teacher or small-group leader, students should have more confidence in studying the Bible to find practical help in solving issues in their Christian walk.

Since this step involves digging into the Word, by definition it is bound to be more analytical, cognitive, and left brained. For this reason it is important to integrate as many other dimensions of learning as possible to engage other types of learners in this process. Writing and drawing are two ways that students can express what they have learned during this step. Students could express themselves visually by mapping the structure of the main points of a text, drawing pictures of a concept, illustrating an idea, or outlining steps on paper or the whiteboard. While it may be helpful for visual learners if the teacher uses a whiteboard or PowerPoint for key points, overuse of visuals can turn learners into passive receptacles of knowledge. Whenever possible, learners need to discover the main principles themselves rather than learn them passively from the teacher.

PowerPoint can be used effectively to demonstrate contextual, historical, geographical, or archaeological details relating to the passage of Scripture studied. In the case of Ephesians, an interesting PowerPoint presentation could be made by either the teacher or the students to accentuate the reality of the evil influences in the Ephesian culture. Videos may be added to visualize details of the context of the biblical text.

If the passage involves a story or series of events, drama can be a good way to help students learn details. For younger children this may involve designing a script that follows the content outline of events in the Bible and having the children act out the events. Older children or youth could be given guidelines of how to discover the main points in a story and then have the freedom to design their own story line or dramatic description of the event. Giving students the opportunity to design their own drama based on details of a passage can help them engage in a biblical narrative in a new and profound way. Stories such as David and Goliath, Joseph and the pit, Daniel in the lions' den, or Peter walking on water can be recreated with new excitement when students are given the opportunity to write their own scripts. This not only gives students the opportunity to express themselves in creative ways but also motivates them to want to be accurate in how they act out the text.

In this chapter we have discussed step two of how to design a lesson that helps students dig deeper into the Word. We started by discussing the disappointing lack of Bible knowledge and understanding within our culture and the need for a renewed emphasis on deeper Bible study for all ages in the church. Next we explained how inductive learning stimulates deeper learning by engaging students at deeper levels. When students interact at an experiential level with the biblical content, they make more lasting connections of their minds, emotions, wills, and actions. Through discussion, interaction, and other methods of engagement with biblical content, students are more apt to internalize biblical principles. In the second part of the chapter, we examined three "Digging into the Word" teaching experiences for various age groups. We conclude by discussing some other methods that can be used in this step.

Questions and Applications

1. What are some evidences you have observed of shallow biblical teaching?

2. Describe the details involved in inductive methods of Bible study.

3. What are some values of inductive Bible study?

4. Why might people who believe in the authority of God's Word tend to be dogmatic regarding methods used to teach it?

5. According to the author, why is it important to teach God's authoritative Word using both objective and experiential approaches?

6. Summarize each of the six purposes for getting students to dig deeper into God's Word.

7. Pick a passage of Scripture and complete a thorough study of the text using the approach explained earlier in the book, and design a lesson plan for the "Digging into the Word" step following the guidelines in this chapter.

Chapter 11

Stimulating Student Heart Talk

This chapter focuses on strategies to challenge cognitive, emotional, and volitional reflection and application in students' hearts. With the students themselves discovering the Big Idea and other significant principles, they will be challenged to reflect creatively on implications of these principles for their lives. Students will be encouraged to share inhibitions, fears, hopes, hesitations, and attitudes they encounter in applying the Big Idea to their lives. Benefits and blessings of applying the Big Idea are also identified and discussed. In this section of the lesson, students are challenged to wrestle with the implications of the Big Idea to their lives at the deepest level possible. Depending on the age and development level of students, the teacher would seek to encourage and challenge them to think and respond at deeper levels through the journey to the heart discussed in chap. 3.

In the previous chapter we discussed ways to encourage students to dig into the Word to discover the main details of the text in relation to the Big Idea and other relevant principles. In this step we will suggest ways to help students process ideas and concepts identified from Scripture.

Jensen and Nickelsen use the term "processing" to describe what happens when learners take raw data or knowledge and wrestle with it to make it more useful in their lives. They use the illustration of how "processing turns oranges into orange juice, trees into lumber, and recycled plastic into new products.

Processing turns milk into cottage cheese, metal into a tool, and eggs into an omelet."[1] Processing is what goes on inside the learner that transforms information, principles, and concepts into personal, internalized values. By stimulating deeper-level processing skills, teachers engage more areas of the brain, including "emotions, movement, spatial, language, sound, memory, and thinking." This approach engages students through multiple intelligences and learning styles.[2]

In their book *Deeper Learning*, Jensen and Nickelsen identify seven values of processing that relate to all learning situations but especially study of the Bible.

1. Information has a better opportunity to become meaningful and therefore more memorable.

2. Processing allows time for students to think about what they are learning, pose questions for clarity, and discover answers to their questions. Questions lead to some of the most powerful learning experiences. A question not asked or answered is a lost opportunity for lasting learning.

3. Processing allows more opportunities to elaborate on the subject. Elaboration allows for stronger and fuller connections between the brain neurons. The chunks of information become more in depth, which allows more opportunities for connections in other subject areas and in application.

4. Processing allows for more viewpoints to be considered and used as sources of learning. Paradigms change because of processing opportunities, among other factors. Viewpoints are challenged during processing.

5. More emotion is attached to the content when there are opportunities for processing. Processing gives the students' minds time to connect the content with what they already know. Teachers can facilitate ways to bring emotion into the processing of content.

6. We are strengthening the working memory every time we give processing opportunities.

7. While the students are processing, the teacher's mind has an opportunity to reflect on how the lesson is going. This time can help the teacher make quick changes or rethink how something was taught. It is a time to make the necessary changes for success of all students.

---

[1] Eric Jensen and LeAnn Nickelsen, *Deeper Learning: 7 Powerful Strategies for In-Depth and Longer-Lasting Learning* (Thousand Oaks, CA: Corwin Press, 2008), 105–6.

[2] Ibid.

Not only will the students' brains benefit from processing, the teacher's will also.[3]

Processing is at the heart of the third step in the lesson-building process. As students interact with the principles, ideas, and concepts learned from the Word through interactive and multidimensional ways, the mental connectors in their minds begin to build more permanent communication links among the different domains. As students make connections between their thoughts and feelings, the Holy Spirit begins to soften their wills to bring about behavioral change. As these changes become integrated into the heart of the person, character is affected and transformation occurs. While some social scientists may not immediately appreciate the spiritual insights Christian educators gain from an awareness of the work of the Holy Spirit in this process of teaching and learning, His supernatural role is evident.

The Purposes of Step Three: Stimulating Student Heart Talk

The first purpose of this step is to accomplish the stated goals related to encouraging students to dig deeper into the implications of the Big Idea of the text to real-life situations. In planning out this step, it is best to designate which of the stated goals relate to discovering implications for life and then plan the strategies, methods, and learning activities for this step around those goals. The distinctive of this step is that it begins with a clear statement of the Big Idea summarized from students' discoveries in the prior step, and it goes even deeper.

The second purpose of this step is to encourage students to journey deeper toward the heart through each of the domains: cognitive, affective, volitional, and behavioral. To repeat an earlier illustration, it is as if the teacher "milks" or draws out the essence of the person in each of these domains. The teacher gently and systematically draws out the student to share and reflect on a deeper emotional, cognitive, and volitional level related to the Big Idea of the text.

The third purpose of this step is to encourage integration of the domains as students journey deeper toward the heart. As they process information and principles learned earlier, they associate, connect, assimilate, apply, elaborate, evaluate, meditate, hypothesize, and integrate ideas, principles, and concepts. This type of higher level or deeper level learning seeks interconnections for the different aspects of the person. It is not uncommon in this step for chil-

---

[3] Ibid., 107–8.

dren, youth, and adults to make insightful personal connections for ideas and emotions, decisions and actions, thinking and doing, emotions and behavior, doubts and dysfunctions.[4]

The fourth purpose of this step in the lesson is to stimulate as many dimensions of the person as possible. As students are meaningfully engaged related to a theme or Big Idea, they not only connect more with the theme in a variety of ways, but they integrate it within the various dimensions of their lives. Thus a major purpose of this step is to connect the student with the Big Idea of the text reflectively, interpersonally, intrapersonally, experientially, visually, audibly, and through meaningful activity. This should be one of the most engaging and stimulating steps of the lesson.

The fifth purpose of this step is to focus on real-life applications of the Big Idea to everyday lives. This section of the lesson should appeal to the commonsense learner who tends to be practical, hands-on, and active. It should help every student take away from the lesson something he can use to help him live more like Christ.

The fifth purpose of this step in the lesson directly relates to its title. The concept of "heart talk" is built around the idea that the deeper a person moves in the journey to the center of the heart, the more integrative learning becomes. Healthy interaction stimulates integration and transformation—interaction between student and student, student and teacher, and student and God, as well as "intra-interaction." Intra-interaction could be characterized as contemplation, reflection, meditation, and self-examination enabled by the Holy Spirit. It could be compared to a person having a dialogue with himself under the illumination of the Holy Spirit. While heart talk involves interaction at all of these levels, it seems that the deepest level is achieved when a person is allowing the Holy Spirit to examine the deepest hidden rooms in one's heart. When students, through the illumination of the Holy Spirit, uncover objective principles with God's Word and begin to apply them to their innermost beings, God supernaturally illuminates their hearts to conviction, repentance, transformation, and obedience. This is certainly the deepest outcome from this step of the lesson.

Methods Related to Stimulating Heart Talk

As we explained in chap. 8, a variety of methods and learning experiences can be chosen to accomplish the stated goals in any lesson. The key for this step is

---

[4] Ibid., 107.

to choose learning activities that stimulate students to reflect on the meanings, applications, and implications of the Big Idea to their lives both individually and corporately. Since meaningful activity and interaction stimulate such learning, it is wise to pick methods that are engaging and active.

A great way to help students come up with creative applications of a Big Idea is through drama, role-play, mime, or pantomime. These learning activities allow for creativity, emotional expression, humor, activity, and originality. I have used them effectively to teach all age groups except toddlers and infants. When dramatic learning experiences are done well, they can cause people to think, reflect, identify, relax, apply truth, become convicted, soften their hearts, or express repressed emotion.

Stories, case studies, debates, discussion, and questioning can also be used to stimulate students to go deeper in applying the Big Idea. It is best, however, not to overuse one method by repeating it in different steps. That is why I tend to choose a more active, interactive, and creative learning experience in the third step, especially if the previous step is more analytical.

Artistic expressions using music, writing, poetry, drawing, sculpture, collages, or crafts can also be used to express students' creative applications to ideas and principles learned from Scripture. When using such creative expressions, take time for students to interpret or translate their creations for the class. It is not enough simply to "do" an activity. Students must be given the opportunity to share what they have learned with the class to take advantage of the interactive dynamic of each participant's contribution.

Active, participative learning experiences can also be effective at this step. If the lesson were on treating others as more important than ourselves, it would be productive for students to pair up to practice asking the other person open-ended questions and listening to their responses. This could conclude by having the students debrief in a large group what they learned from the listening practice. Practicing skills together as a class not only is highly motivating, but it also enables the participants to experience the benefits of a newly learned behavior.

Whatever methods are chosen should move students deeper in applying the Big Idea and integrating the principles and concepts from the lesson at a deeper level in the heart.

In this next section of the chapter, we will examine some examples of how we can apply this lesson step in various contexts.

For our first example we will look at a lesson we discussed in chap. 5 for children ages four or five based on the following Teaching Big Idea and content outline based on Phil 4:4–7:

Teaching Big Idea: When we feel scared, we need to jump into Jesus' arms.

Content Outline

Title: What it means to jump into Jesus' arms:
>Rejoice in Jesus.
>Talk to Jesus.
>Thank Jesus.
>Forget your worries.
>What will happen when we jump into Jesus' arms?
>Peace

Since children this age usually do not read and have a limited vocabulary, learning must involve a lot of activity. In reviewing the purposes of this step of the lesson, we recall that the methods must help students, first, to apply the Big Idea and accomplish other application goals; second, to go deeper in the various domains; third, to integrate the domains; fourth, to engage actively in learning; and, fifth, to communicate with God at a heart-deep level.

The application step of the lesson is built on the content that students discovered in the previous step. In this lesson the children just heard a dramatic story from the Bible about how Paul felt God's peace even though he was in prison surrounded by people trying to hurt him. The children learned that when they feel scared they need to jump into Jesus' arms, just as Paul did. They also learned what it means to jump into Jesus' arms. They talked about what it means to rejoice in Jesus, talk to Jesus, thank Jesus, and forget about worries when we are in Jesus' arms. To help remember these four things, the children learned a catchy song with actions revolving around each of these points.

Based on the children's knowledge and understanding of the content goals in the second step, they were ready to apply these principles on a deeper level. Even though they are young children, they probably have lots of things that make them fearful. The goals related to this part of the lesson might include:

The goals of the lesson are that the children:

Practice jumping into Jesus' arms in real-life situations.

Practice rejoicing in Jesus, talking to Jesus, thanking Jesus, and forgetting about their worries when they are in Jesus' arms.

Experience the peace that comes from jumping into Jesus' arms.

A learning experience that might be appropriate for four- and five-year-old children would be to have a leader dress up to play the role of Jesus. Another leader could tell two or three short stories about a child who was fearful or worried. At a pinnacle in the story, the storyteller would get the kids to sing their song and instruct one of the children to jump into Jesus' arms as Jesus comforted and consoled him or her. Then the storyteller would coach the child through the four points of the content outline, getting the child to rejoice in Jesus, talk to Jesus, thank Jesus, and forget about the fear. The storyteller would repeat this sequence with a different short story and a different child, giving as many children as possible the opportunity to jump into Jesus' arms. After each story the child participant could be asked how he felt being held in Jesus' arms. The experience of peace and security would be highlighted as a result of being close to Jesus.

This learning experience would connect with children because it combines concrete activity, cognitive depth, emotional intimacy, and interaction. Biblical content is reinforced with music and actions, and the stories relate directly to the worries and fears that children normally face. Children would be deeply engaged in such a lesson. Alternative learning experiences for children could use stuffed animals or puppets. As children identify with the characters in a skit, drama, or puppet show, they naturally use their imaginations to visualize themselves in their place.

Our second example will relate to an intergenerational class of parents and their teenage children focusing on building better relationships through applying biblical principles. This lesson is based on a four-part series from Phil 2:2–5.

> Teaching Big Idea: If we are serious about our faith in Jesus Christ, we must seek to understand others rather than focus on ourselves (vv. 3–4).
>
> Purpose of the lesson: Parents and teens will practice understanding the perspective of the other person rather than simply focusing on their own concerns.

Goals Related to the "Encouraging Heart Talk" Step

The goals of the lesson are that participants will:
> Understand how communication patterns between parents and teens reflect the depth of our relationship with Jesus Christ.
>
> Realize their self-centered tendencies in communicating within the family.
>
> Identify how they could change the way they communicate.

Based on these goals taken from a longer list of goals relating to the complete lesson, I might suggest the following learning activity for the third step of the lesson relating to applying the Big Idea at a deeper level.

Role-Play: Parent-Teen Conflict

Purpose: To show how a typical parent-teen conflict develops from a lack of understanding and an inability of both persons to listen to each other.

Pick an adult to play the role of the teen and two teens to play the roles of the parents.

Hand out the following details to the participants a few minutes ahead of time.

Teen's role: It is a Monday night. You are going to ask your dad whether you can go to a party at your friend's house on Friday night. You know that it is a questionable activity so you are armed with your arguments. Your main points are that:

- Your best friend who is the son of an elder in the church is also going.
- You will have a chance to be a good testimony for the Lord.
- All the other sharp kids at school are going.
- There is no school the next day so it will be all right to stay up late.

Add any other arguments that come up but don't appear to listen to what your dad and mom say concerning their objections. Get hotter and hotter as the argument develops. Accuse your mom and dad of treating you like a kid, not understanding you, not trusting you, and being mother hens.

Parents' roles: It is a Monday night and your son is about to ask you whether he can go to a party at his friend's house on Friday night. Get him to tell you a little bit about the party. Push for details. Without listening to his responses, tell him why he can't go. Focus on these points:

- The parents probably won't be home.
- They have cable TV and DVDs—probably dirty movies.
- Girls are invited, and he's too young for that.
- He's supposed to be in bed by 11:00 p.m., and it won't be over till later.
- He's been acting more rebellious lately.
- He can't be trusted.
- He will grow up to be a reprobate.

Get hotter as the discussion progresses. Tell him he never listens. Cut down his character.

Before the role-play begins, tell the class to look for factors that contribute to a breakdown in communication that violates the principles discussed earlier from the biblical text.

At the conclusion of the role-play, lead a discussion of the factors lending to the communication breakdown. Some typical answers could be: too much emotion, lack of listening, lack of understanding, selfishness, anger, or lack of respect.

Try to summarize the discussion, centering on the lack of understanding of one another.

Ask them:

- Do you see any patterns in these skits that resemble how you sometimes talk in family conflicts?
- How could the participants have approached the situation differently as a parent? as a teen?
- What are some of the principles in the Scripture passage discussed earlier that were violated?
- How does the way we communicate with our parents or teens reflect the depth of our relationship with Jesus Christ?
- If we were to display the attitude that Jesus Christ displayed, how would we communicate with our parents or teens differently?

Write their suggestions on a flip chart. Give them clues by pointing back to the scriptural passage.

Some suggestions might include:

- Do nothing selfish.
- Look at the other person's point of view.
- Consider the other person's point of view better than your own.
- While presenting your interests, also try to restate the interests of the other person.
- Possess a humble attitude like Jesus.

Summarize the suggestions. Emphasize that both parents and teens will have to do more listening and less talking in order to understand one another better.

When I have taught this part of the lesson, both parents and teens have moved deeper in wrestling with their behavior, motivations, beliefs about Jesus, feelings toward their parents or teens, and the implications of the biblical text. Identifying with and acting out the feelings and behaviors of the other party have a dramatic effect in getting participants to come face-to-face with their own selfish tendencies.

The third example of a learning experience, the step in the lesson focusing on application and depth, is taken from a lesson from Eph 4:1–14 taught to high school students. This lesson was introduced in the previous chapter to illustrate the learning activity in the "Digging Deeper into the Word" step.

Lesson Outline

Title: Flirting with the Dark Side

Text: Ephesians 5:1–16

Big Idea: In order to live as a fragrant offering to God within a decaying world, we must never participate in anything connected to the deeds of darkness.

Lesson Purpose: The purpose of this lesson is that students will have lives reflecting the fragrance of Christ's love while refusing to participate in anything connected to the deeds of darkness.

Content Outline

How to live out the fragrance of Christ in a decaying world:
1. Imitate Christ's love to others within this evil world (v. 1).
2. Make a radical break from the deeds of darkness (vv. 2–14).
   - sexual immorality
   - any kind of impurity
   - any kind of greed
   - obscenity, foolish talk, or coarse jesting

Five reasons we should never flirt with the darkness:
   a. It is improper for Christians (v. 3).
   b. It is out of place for Christians (v. 4).
   c. Those who live in darkness will not inherit eternal life (v. 5).
   d. God's wrath will be unleashed on those who live in darkness (vv. 6–7).
   e. We are children of the light rather than darkness (vv. 8–14).
3. Take advantage of opportunities to be a light in this evil world (vv. 15–16).

Lesson Goals

The goals of this lesson are that students will:

COGNITIVE

Understand the darkness within the culture in Ephesus.

Identify the major commands in the text.

Understand the reasons stated in the text why we should live in the light and refuse to participate in darkness.

Discern specific ways the enemy may be tempting them to participate in
    darkness.
Realize the dangers of flirting with the dark side.
Hypothesize what it means to live as a fragrant aroma.

AFFECTIVE

Become aware of the ways they have been flirting with the dark side.
Be convicted of dark lifestyle practices that need to change.

VOLITIONAL

Decide to turn from specific evil practices, behaviors, and involvements.
Commit themselves to live as an aroma of Christ's love in the stink of the
    world.

BEHAVIORAL

Become more consistent in staying away from sinful practices and involve-
    ments.
Plan strategically how to make the best use of the opportunities they have
    to be a light in this dark world.

From the above list of goals for the whole lesson, I picked several that
would be appropriate to try to accomplish in this step focusing on going deeper
in the application of the Big Idea and biblical principles.

Goals for the Step—Stimulating Student Heart Talk

The purpose of this lesson is that students would:

Discern specific ways the enemy may be tempting them to participate
    in darkness.
Realize the dangers of flirting with the dark side.
Hypothesize what it means to live as a fragrant aroma.
Become aware of the ways they have been flirting with the dark side.
Based on these goals, the following learning activities could be designed
    to help high school students accomplish them.

Skits

Divide the students into groups of five. Instruct them to come up with a skit
that demonstrates the seductive nature of an area of their culture that they feel
is a real threat to Christian youth. Tell them that the goal is to show the dangers of Christians compromising with darkness as explained in the biblical text.

The skits should involve all the group members and last no more than three minutes. Give them 10 minutes to plan their skits. After 10 minutes, call the groups back together. Remind them of the purpose of the skits. To set the tone, tell them a short story from your life of how you messed up by compromising with the dark side.

Ask students to keep track of the subtle ways the enemy tries to seduce Christian youth in our culture. Ask them secondly to note the dangers of compromising with darkness. Write these two questions on the board to keep the students focused during the skits. After each skit, have the small group answer each of these two questions in the large group.

After the skits are finished, summarize the comments from the students related to the two questions and have a student write them on the board.

Divide students into small groups again and ask them to identify areas in their lifestyles where they may have been flirting with the dark side. Ask them to suggest what they would have to change in their lives to become a more fragrant offering in a stinky world. Ask each group to list specific changes they would have to make and to put their lists on the board. Call the groups together after the lists are on the board and summarize the students' suggestions.

A learning experience like this would not only get the students to wrestle with the application of the Big Idea but would move them much deeper in becoming convicted about areas of compromise. The collective support and reinforcement within the small groups and large group would have a significant role in encouraging students to be vulnerable and open to the Holy Spirit. Without the leader saying much, the students would encourage one another to be transparent and honest in dealing with addictions, behaviors, habits, and lifestyle issues related to the principles in the biblical text.

Summary

In many ways this step in the lesson is most crucial in the process of heart-deep teaching. This step is where teachers can use insight and creativity to partner with the Holy Spirit to design learning experiences that will motivate students to take the Big Idea and principles from God's Word seriously. While many teachers ask basic application questions during this step, heart-deep teachers use their understanding of how people learn and their understanding of the depth of the journey to the heart to design effective strategies to connect students' hearts with the deep riches of the gold in God's Word.

Questions and Applications

1. Explain the main distinctive of this step in heart-deep teaching and learning.

2. How does the term "processing" explain the dynamics of higher-level thinking skills used in this step of the lesson?

3. What are the values of processing in the teaching and learning process?

4. Explain the six purposes of this step of the lesson.

5. What are the categories of learning experiences listed by the author, and what specific methods are identified under each category?

6. For each of the three lesson examples given, describe the depth of learning the students are challenged to move toward in the learning experiences chosen.

7. Choose a biblical text and design a creative learning experience that would implement as many of the purposes of this lesson step as possible.

8. Why is this step so crucial to heart-deep teaching and learning?

Chapter 12

Encouraging Heart Change in Life

"Encouraging Heart Change in Life" explains the last but most likely to be ignored part of the lesson. Many teachers are satisfied if students merely identify a few general ways of applying the Big Idea. Yet the focus of this chapter is to go much deeper toward changing students' hearts, turning sitters into doers from the inside out. This step often marks the time and place when students decide to deal with issues, make changes, implement plans, and set higher standards based on what they discover and wrestle with from God's Word. This step in the teaching-learning process is often the seedbed in which students grow and blossom. When the soil in the classroom environment is characterized as a supportive, trusting, family community, it becomes a greenhouse for authentic discipleship. Trust and confidentiality are essential components of an environment that encourages such heart-deep change.

True learning expresses itself in life just as true belief reflects in lifestyle. It is not enough to develop learning experiences that train people to think differently, feel differently, choose differently, or act differently. Life change must come from a transformation of the heart, which includes all the dimensions of the person. Teachers must model such heart-deep learning before they can effectively teach others. Active learning experiences need to go hand in hand with reflective exercises to help students wrestle with the "whys" of various activities. Bible teaching and theological training should always be integrated cognitively, affectively, volitionally, and behaviorally. Godly thoughts, feelings, and decisions express themselves in godly behavior.

This chapter is divided into three sections. The first section will deal with traps that some teachers fall into in the last step of a lesson. The second section will discuss some legitimate goals for this step of the lesson, and the last section will explain the most effective methods or learning experiences to use to accomplish those goals, illustrated with practical examples.

Traps that Teachers May Fall into in the Last Step of a Bible Lesson

The first trap for some teachers at the conclusion of a lesson is to pressure students to make a commitment. While the teacher's motivation may stem from a sincere desire to see students respond to God's Word, it can often do more harm than good if it does not come from the heart of the student. Most of us have felt pressured by a preacher or teacher to do something to show that we have been convicted. Yet external pressure to respond is much different from internal conviction of the Holy Spirit in a student's innermost being. Often teachers can be pressured by lack of time, by a desire to demonstrate objective spiritual results, or simply by doing what the tradition of that denomination, camp, or organization normally does. When student responses are based on manipulation, external pressure, peer pressure, or superficial guilt, they can indoctrinate students against the genuine conviction of the Holy Spirit through the Word of God.

The second trap for some teachers comes by following curriculum suggestions too literally. While most curriculum writers suggest some kind of concluding challenge to respond to the lesson, often they do not give enough options to fit the needs of class situations. If teachers repeat the closing suggestions stated in the lesson material, they are bound not to connect with some students. Often in an attempt to relate to a wide variety of theological and cultural backgrounds, closing activities in published lessons are either too general or irrelevant. Any attempt to get the students to give a measurable response in such cases will be both trite and meaningless. Suggestions for children often include superficial activities such as crafts or coloring projects that are handed out to children to do after a brief explanation. Such activities require little if any reflection, interaction, problem-solving, or creativity. I question the value of such closing activities when students go through the motions of completing an activity without engaging their emotions, thoughts, or wills. I get even more frustrated when well-meaning teachers think their students have learned and applied a biblical principle because they have accomplished some token activity that only superficially relates to the theme of the lesson.

The third trap is to follow the same format in closing all their lessons. While in some denominations it is a standard practice to close a service or teaching session with the same kind of response, this may not always be wise. Even Jesus used a variety of approaches to challenge His listeners to respond to His messages. It seems to me that a wiser approach might be to tailor the response to the content of the lesson, the needs of the people, and the leading of the Holy Spirit. While there is security in doing some things the same way all the time, routine can lead to hardness of heart and callousness to the voice of the Holy Spirit.

The point of mentioning these three dangers is simply to keep us pliable and sensitive as teachers to the needs of our students and how the Holy Spirit may be leading them to respond to God's Word. By listening to our students, regardless of their age or level of maturity, we are more apt to design appropriate learning activities and choose meaningful methods to enable them to be more responsive to God's voice in this step of the lesson.

Purposes of the Fourth Step, "Encouraging Heart Change in Life"

While the process of change and spiritual transformation may be gradual, it is often punctuated by specific decisions, crisis experiences, and insights that open us up to new manifestations of God's grace and power. While these points of transformation may occur at any time or place, the Spirit-directed teacher will strive to create moments of transformation in students' lives. The overall purpose of this fourth step in the lesson is to create an optimum teaching and learning environment in which the Holy Spirit is free to work. Under the overall purpose for this step, there are six related goals. These goals are: accomplishing the lesson goals related to volition and behavior, responding at the deepest level possible to the Holy Spirit, making specific personal applications, making choices with freedom, designing action plans, and establishing accountability measures to ensure the accomplishment of action goals.

The first goal of the "Encouraging Heart Change in Life" step is to accomplish the lesson goals related to volition and behavior. The focus of this step is to encourage students to make decisions that will result in changed behavior related to the Big Idea and major principles in the lesson. Since behavioral change is rooted in the decisions of the will, this part of the lesson focuses on these goals. It is wise for the teacher to designate the volitional and behavioral goals they will deal with in this step of the lesson and then to design meaningful methods and learning activities to help students accomplish these goals.

The second goal of the "Encouraging Heart Change" step is to encourage students to respond at the deepest possible level to the voice of the Holy Spirit speaking through the objective principles of God's Word in the biblical text. This process is similar to the prayer in Eph 1:18 (NIV) for believers that "the eyes of your heart may be enlightened" so they would know more of God's blessings documented in His Word. Since the Holy Spirit is the real person who teaches, convicts, fills, and softens hearts, it is imperative that the teacher connects with the Holy Spirit to encourage transformation in students' hearts.

The third goal of the "Encouraging Heart Change in Life" step is to inspire students to make specific, personal applications of the Big Idea or other principles in the text. Rather than impose external responses on students, the teacher's role is to help students focus on the principles they discovered from God's Word and to listen to the Holy Spirit as He instructs them in how to respond. While students will have already wrestled with general applications in the previous step of the lesson, they will now be challenged to respond personally. If this distinction is not made between *we* and *me*, then students will keep God's Word at a theoretical level outside their hearts. This step is an inside-out process in which students reflectively listen and respond to the Spirit of God rather than simply do what their peers or their teacher pressures them to do. Part of the teacher's role is simply to provide a quiet space and time for students to be reflective and meditative so they can hear the voice of the Lord. Given the chaotic environment of so many children's and youth programs, it is no surprise that students are not used to being quiet and reflective before the Lord long enough to hear His voice.

The fourth goal of the "Encouraging Heart Change" step is to provide choices and freedom for students to make decisions on their own without undue pressure from teachers or peers.

I am reminded of an experience in Kenya several years ago that illustrates the need for freedom and choice in responding to a message from God's Word. On one of my trips to Kenya, I had the privilege of being the Bible teacher at a youth camp attended by hundreds of people of all ages. During one of the evening sessions, a guest preacher gave the evening message. The preaching was demonstrative and forceful yet based on shallow biblical content. The longer the man preached, the louder he got, and the more manipulative his message became. By the end of his two-hour sermon, he convinced almost everyone to come forward to be saved. Since the preacher was white and a guest, the leadership team, out of respect, felt hesitant to critique what happened. When I brought it up later that night, the men immediately expressed their disappointment in the way he manipulated the people. Apparently he did this routinely to inflate the number of people he reported to those listening to his radio broadcast back home. The next morning during the teaching time, we decided to rephrase the invitation question by dividing up the types of responses between those who came forward for initial salvation, recommitment, filling with the Holy Spirit, healing, deliverance, and support for an emotional struggle. We had trained elders to counsel each group of people when they came forward to acknowledge the decisions they had made the night before. While there were small groups of people at each station, there were only four people who had actually made a decision to be saved. It was a valuable learning experience for both me and the team of elders at the church camp.

Teachers must be careful not to pressure anyone into a desired response in the last step of the lesson. Students need to be given freedom, choices, and options related to how to respond to the scriptural lesson based on their needs and the conviction of the Holy Spirit.

The fifth goal of the "Encouraging Heart Change" step is to help students structure a plan to follow through with the decisions made. Students are much more apt to follow through with a decision if they plan how they will live out the decision with specific goals and objectives. As we have discussed, Christ's design for discipleship includes His followers not just making decisions to follow Him but rather continuing to follow Him and obeying everything He has revealed. A major part of the last step in every lesson should focus on helping students design specific goals and objectives to live out their commitments in their everyday lives. In some corporate training manuals, this step is called training for "reentry," in which participants map out the steps they will take to become more consistent in implementing what they have learned in their work environment.[1]

When this purpose is not accomplished, students will have little hope of following through with their decisions. Yet if students are given the opportunity to design a structure for accomplishing the goals related to their decisions, they are much more apt to reach them. Scripture is full of practical wisdom relating to the steps people need to take to accomplish the standards of righteousness modeled by Christ. In this part of the lesson, teachers need to help students establish the "scaffolding" they need to climb to the heights of Christlikeness to which they are called.

The sixth goal of "Encouraging Heart Change in Life" is to establish accountability procedures to ensure that students follow through on their decisions to accomplish the goals and plans they established. This is where many parents, teachers, youth pastors, children's workers, and pastors are

---

[1] Melvin L. Silberman and Carol Auerbach, *Active Training: A Handbook of Techniques, Designs, Case Examples, and Tips*, 3rd ed., Pfeiffer Essential Resources for Training and HR Professionals (San Francisco: Pfeiffer, 2006).

shortsighted. They think people will automatically accomplish the plans they set. Yet my experience in all of these ministry roles has convinced me that all people need support in the early stages of learning any new skill or behavior. During this final stage of the lesson, it is essential that teachers network their students with one or more levels of accountability including parents, mentors, role models, peers, and self-monitoring.

It is easy to see how important this step of the lesson is to accomplishing the goal of heart-deep teaching. In this step students are challenged to respond to the Big Idea discovered in God's Word and to decide to put it into practice. If the goals for this step are accomplished in the lives of the students, they will turn from passive sitters in the kingdom of God to active doers, reflecting more and more of the fragrance of Christ in a decaying world.

Teaching Strategies and Learning Activities

The teaching and learning strategies and activities that encourage students to change their hearts in life are built on the six purposes stated above. Teachers should begin the process of choosing which methods and strategies to use by identifying the lesson goals related to this part of the lesson. The main goals connected to this last step usually come from the volitional or behavioral domains since the last step focuses on choosing and doing. As with every other section of the lesson, methods and strategies of teaching or learning should be based on the intent of each lesson goal.

We will look at six categories of learning experiences or methods to reach the lesson goals related to accomplishing the purposes of this step in the lesson. The categories will cover reflective exercises, personal application activities, strategies for encouraging freedom and choice in decision-making, ideas for designing action plans, accountability options, and methods of prayer.

Reflective Exercises

The options for encouraging reflection depend in a large part on the learning environment and context. While it is best if students can get alone to reflect on the passage of Scripture, sometimes this is impossible. The secret is to make use of the space you have. In the last church I served as pastor, we had a beautiful, lofty sanctuary with oak woodwork, stained-glass windows, and deep-red carpet. I used the sanctuary many times for people to wait on the Lord in reflective silence. During Kids Club, which was held in the fellowship hall, we divided the large group into groups of two to five children to reflect on the lesson theme or Scripture. Getting them separated in small groups was essential to remove the distractions of noise and activity. Teachers can divide students individually, in pairs, or in small groups to reflect on that with which the Holy Spirit is challenging them. Depending on the age of students, the weather, and the outside context, it is often meaningful for students to go out of the building to feel closer to the Lord. This is especially true in natural settings.

It is often helpful for students to have a guide to focus their reflection, especially if it is a new experience for them. A guide can be one or two questions, a short passage of Scripture, a statement of the Big Idea, a poem focusing on the theme of the lesson, or a list of challenges based on the biblical text. Sometimes I have found it helpful just to give participants a blank sheet of paper and a pen to jot down what the Holy Spirit says to them.

If students are given a reflective experience like this during a regular class session, they must be allowed enough time to reflect, and they must be given specific instruction as to when to move back to the large group. Yet even five or 10 minutes can be valuable with the proper guidance and preparation.

Personal Application Activities

Students can make personal applications in many ways to the challenge related to the Big Idea or other principles in the text. The options in methodology depend on the age of the student and the goals of the lesson. While the previous step in the lesson focuses on general applications, this step focuses on specific personal applications the students choose for themselves. Students need to be brought to a place where they share the details and needs of their lives in relation to the lesson goals. Skits, pantomimes, or artistic expressions can be a good way for both children and adults to share their feelings and thoughts about a need or situation.

In a lesson with junior high boys related to dealing with bullies, I might have the boys identify characteristics of actual people who are bullying them and to write them down or draw a picture of the bullies' facial expressions. I would then ask them to think of specific things they learned from the Bible related to the lesson about how to respond to bullying. Next I would ask volunteers to demonstrate for the class how they would respond the next time they were bullied. Since junior high boys are usually active learners, it would be more effective to have them demonstrate their applications than to discuss them. In the demonstration of how they have learned to deal with bullies, the boys would learn from one another and the teacher's comments how to refine their approaches.

Simple application questions can also be used to spark students to respond more deeply on a personal level. Such questions, however, need to get students to go beyond general statements to focus on specific, personal applications. It is helpful to have students share their applications with their peers in small groups as long as the details are not confidential.

Sometimes a good way to encourage students to share personal applications is to start with an inspiring short story, testimony, or video related to the Big Idea of the lesson. Yet it is important to keep the methods simple and direct.

Strategies for Encouraging Freedom and Choice in Decision-Making

It is important for teachers to encourage students to depend on the Holy Spirit to speak directly through the biblical text as the main factor in determining their response to the lesson. From an early age, children can be trained to listen to God as He speaks through His Word. While the teacher's role is to give structure so students can accurately discover what the Word is saying, they must be careful not to tell the students how they must respond.

Strategies to encourage freedom and choice in responding to the Big Idea may include giving suggestions for students to choose from, giving alternatives based on different learning styles or multiple intelligences, or giving open-ended options for applications and assignments. When students choose their own applications and responses, they are more apt to follow through.

An example of a learning activity that gives students freedom to decide their own outcomes can be seen in this lesson for high school students that teaches them to reach out in love to people different from themselves. While many youth pastors might simply choose a service activity for the students, an alternative is to let the students choose and plan their own service project. In the third or previous step of the lesson, students could identify and describe all the types of needy or lonely people in their area and research some of the situations of these people. Then in the fourth step of the lesson, they could brainstorm which group they feel the greatest burden to help as a youth group. Since the group had the freedom to make the decision, they would be more apt to carry out the service project.

The same is true for individuals. When teachers give students the freedom to express their own responses to God's Word, they are more apt to follow through. Often the best way to do this is with open-ended questions that students can respond to either orally or in writing.

Designing Action Plans

In this step of the lesson, when people decide to change a habit, start a new behavior, learn a new spiritual discipline, or overcome a temptation, they need help in establishing an action plan to make it happen. Different approaches to establishing action plans might include making a list of steps toward accomplishing a task or dealing with an issue, filling in the steps of a staircase moving toward a desired destination, or labeling the rungs on a ladder to reach the goal that is set. By writing down the steps in an action plan, the process becomes more manageable and definable. Students are able to fill in times and dates and note their progress more clearly. Action plans designed by students are good ways of teaching them to take more responsibility for their own growth.

Action plans could also include home assignments for children and even teenagers to work on at home. Children and their parents could be given assignments designed for them to work on together to strengthen their relationship. This would ensure that the Big Ideas discussed in class were reinforced and practiced in the home.

Accountability Options

By keeping students accountable for their commitments, decisions, goals, and objectives, we give them additional structure and support to help them do what they set out to do. Higher levels of consistency and competency in any task depend on the investments of significant people who come alongside to support and guide. Some of the accountability options include parents, mentors, peers, small groups, and community leaders. Take-home sheets and assignments can be given to students to work on during the week to help them be accountable for their own learning. Social networking sites can be effectively used to help communicate, encourage, and instruct. When working with children and youth, it is essential to partner with the parents, since they are the primary nurturers of their children.

Methods of Prayer

Prayer is an essential component of the fourth step of the lesson. While the whole teaching and learning process must be immersed in prayer, the last step of the lesson is even more crucially connected to a deep communication link with the Father. Teachers need to be in tune with the Holy Spirit to cooperate with Him in encouraging deeper student learning, and students will need to spend time in quiet reflection to discover how to apply the Big Idea to their lives at the deepest possible level. Some approaches to prayer that I have found effective at this stage are individual quiet prayer time, using soft music to encourage prayer, focused prayer in small groups on the things learned from the text, and conversational group prayer.

My favorite expression of prayer in both small and large groups is conversational group prayer at the conclusion of a lesson. I instruct participants to sit in a circle if possible and to express to the Father the needs, desires, longings, and praises of their hearts. Often I suggest beginning with praise and thanksgiving. Rather than share prayer requests prior to the prayer time, I encourage participants to express the needs and desires of their hearts directly to the Lord, one simple thought at a time. Each person is encouraged to listen carefully to each prayer and to empathize with each person in his or her prayer to the Lord. I ask at least two people to respond to each person's prayer by continuing to intercede with them concerning the same request or thanksgiving. People are encouraged to be vulnerable and honest, encouraging and supportive as they pray and lift up others in prayer. This approach not only softens people's hearts individually, but it also brings people together in close spiritual unity. It can be a great way to use God's power in helping people learn and live at a heart-deep level.

Sequencing Learning Experiences in the Fourth Step

Plan the last step of the lesson wisely so that it does not come across to students as either rushed or pressured. Simple is often best. It is best not to have too many complex activities in this last step but rather to sequence the learning experiences so students become soft and open to the leading of the Lord. While it is impossible to accomplish all of the goals of this step of the lesson in a single session, they can be spread out over several lessons. The most important part of this step is that students listen to the Holy Spirit to see how He wants them to change in relation to the Big Idea and to obey Him.

Questions and Applications

1. Why might teachers tend to put less time into planning for the last step in the lesson?

2. State and briefly describe the three traps for teachers during the last step.

3. What are the purposes of the last lesson step: "Encouraging Heart Change in Life"?

4. List the learning experiences from which teachers could choose in the last step of the lesson.

5. What are some important considerations when structuring the learning experiences in the last step?

6. Plan a complete lesson based on a scriptural passage of your choice, implementing the steps and principles discussed in the book.

The Challenges and Benefits of Heart-Deep Teaching

The first time I went whitewater canoeing I was scared to death. As I looked downstream, I saw churning rapids, exposed rocks, and swirling whirlpools. Yet a spirit of adventure inside drove me into that canoe with a trusted friend to conquer my fear.

While you may approach the challenge of heart-deep teaching with a similar feeling of fear or apprehension, the benefits will far outweigh the challenges. This last chapter suggests reasons many teachers hesitate to teach at a heart-deep level. It takes considerably more preparation, emotional energy, and personal integrity on the part of the teacher. This type of teaching might even scare away some students who would rather remain at a nominal level. Yet the benefits far outweigh the challenges.

Challenges

Preparation Time and Effort

The first challenge of heart-deep teaching is the amount of time it takes to prepare for a class. I talked recently to a curriculum specialist for a major Sunday school publisher who told me that teachers spend an average of half an hour or less preparing for a class. It's no wonder Christian young adults are so anemic spiritually.

Emotional Energy

The second challenge of heart-deep teaching is that it demands teachers get to know their students not only on a deeper spiritual level but also on a closer emotional level. This will demand deeper interpersonal intimacy with students to identify and empathize with their struggles, temptations, doubts, and challenges. In a culture dominated by fast food, high-speed Internet, and instant messaging, this trend certainly is countercultural.

Personal Integrity

One of the biggest drawbacks to this approach to teaching is that it demands a high level of personal integrity on the part of the teacher. While the standard may be shy of perfection, it has the aura of a standard just a little higher than the typical Christian leader in popular culture. Many teachers resist setting such high standards for fear of having to reveal their failures and inconsistencies.

Lower Popular Appeal

One of the comments I hear from both Christian and secular educators who hold to high standards is that students today do not want depth as much as they want power, grades, and prestige. Even school administrators may be tempted to lower their standards of excellence to satisfy the realities of the bottom line and to please students and parents. Furthermore, teachers who challenge their students to think, wrestle, work, and grow may not initially attract many students. After all, who wants to teach a class with just a few good men and women?

Benefits

In wrestling with what to mention as the benefits of heart-deep teaching, I was tempted to start with the joys of teaching, the experience of seeing people grow, the feelings of accomplishing something worthwhile, or the adventure of taking up a challenge. But I backed off from these after I realized the benefits that drive me to enter this adventure of teaching others are much deeper. They relate more to the intense pleasure I enjoy when I simply do what is right, based on what is true.

Biblical Truth

I am convinced that the greatest joy and pleasure in the universe is revealed in God's objective revelation to humankind through the written and living Word of God. Helping others to discover and use the treasure in God's Word brings me more pleasure than just about anything else in life. Knowing and reflecting God and His truth are the supreme benefits of heart-deep teaching.

Philosophical Truth

I get great pleasure in realizing that heart-deep teaching incorporates all the ways of knowing used by humankind while affirming the reality that we serve and follow a God and Savior who is eternally stable. He has revealed Himself to humankind and given us all the riches of wisdom and knowledge to use for His glory. The depth of the universe is found in the depth of God.

Educational Truth

The more I am learning about how people learn, the more convinced I am that the wisdom found in Scripture parallels the most empirically grounded principles of education. It has been exciting for me to see how principles in God's Word affirm many of the most proven educational strategies. A major benefit of heart-deep teaching is the security that it is based on a theoretical foundation reinforced by some of the most tested educational research findings.

Practical Benefits

In my mind the practical benefits are the blessings that come from living in line with biblical, philosophical, and educational truth. The older I get, the more appreciative I become of the things in life that bring the greatest pleasure over the longest duration. When I think of the joys of my life so far, there is no question that I would put Jesus Christ and my family at the top of the list. Living, loving, and serving with my wife and camping, canoeing, and ministering with my three boys have brought me deep, lasting joy. Yet I recall the boys and girls I taught at the Salvation Army in Wellsville, New York; the teens with whom I worked at a little church in Angelica, New York; the children and teens I taught at churches in Chicago and Marietta, Pennsylvania; the church families I served in Littleton, Colorado, and the Indiana towns of Upland, Milgrove, Huntington and Columbia City; and the many at-risk kids and their families to whom my wife and I ministered in both Marietta and Huntington, Indiana.

The blessings of heart-deep teaching come from the deep and lasting joys of living and serving from a foundation of rich truth. As J. P. Moreland concludes in his book *The Kingdom Triangle*, "These are unprecedented times for the church to fill the huge void in our culture that has resulted from decades of secularization. We actually have 'the way, and the truth, and the life'

(John 14:6)."[1] Yet he goes on to lament the fact that because the church has lost its cutting edge in contemporary culture, we are in danger of losing our distinguishing beacon. Heart-deep teaching will enable the church to regain her foothold within contemporary culture by lifting high the banner of truth and helping people of all ages know and live it deeply.

---

[1] James Porter Moreland, *Kingdom Triangle: Recover the Christian Mind, Renovate the Soul, Restore the Spirit's Power* (Grand Rapids: Zondervan, 2007), 195.

Bibliography

Anderson, Lorin W., David R. Krathwohl, and Benjamin Samuel Bloom. *A Taxonomy for Learning, Teaching, and Assessing: A Revision of Bloom's Taxonomy of Educational Objectives*. Complete ed. New York: Longman, 2001.

Anthony, Michael J. *Introducing Christian Education: Foundations for the Twenty-first Century*. Grand Rapids: Baker Academic, 2001.

Barna, George. *Transforming Children into Spiritual Champions*. Seminar ed. Ventura, CA: Issachar Resources, 2003.

———. *Transforming Children into Spiritual Champions*. Ventura, CA: Regal, 2003.

Blackaby, Henry T., and Claude V. King. *Experiencing God: How to Live the Full Adventure of Knowing and Doing the Will of God*. Nashville: B&H Publishers, 1994.

Bloom, Benjamin Samuel. *Taxonomy of Educational Objectives: The Classification of Educational Goals*. 1st ed. New York: David McKay, 1956.

———. *Taxonomy of Educational Objectives: The Classification of Educational Goals*. 1st ed. New York: Longmans, Green, 1956.

Borthwick, Paul. *New Directions for Small-Group Ministry*. Loveland, CO: Vital Ministry, 1999.

Bransford, John, National Research Council (U.S.) Committee on Developments in the Science of Learning, and National Research Council (U.S.) Committee on Learning Research and Educational Practice. *How People Learn: Brain, Mind, Experience, and School*. Expanded ed. Washington, DC: National Academy Press, 2000.

Brown, Colin. *The New International Dictionary of New Testament Theology.* 3 vols. Grand Rapids: Zondervan, 1975.

Brown, Colin, and Lothar Coenen. *The New International Dictionary of New Testament Theology.* 3 vols. Exeter, Devon, U.K.: Paternoster Press, 1975.

Bultmann, Rudolf Karl. *Theology of the New Testament.* New York: Scribner, 1951.

Downs, Perry G. *Teaching for Spiritual Growth.* Grand Rapids: Zondervan, 1994.

Ford, Le Roy. *Design for Teaching and Training: A Self-Study Guide to Lesson Planning.* Nashville: Broadman Press, 1978.

Fowler, James W. *Stages of Faith: The Psychology of Human Development and the Quest for Meaning.* 1st ed. San Francisco: Harper & Row, 1981.

Groothuis, Douglas R. *Truth Decay: Defending Christianity Against the Challenges of Postmodernism.* Downers Grove, IL: InterVarsity Press, 2000.

Holmes, Arthur Frank. *All Truth Is God's Truth.* Grand Rapids: Eerdmans, 1977.

Issler, Klaus Dieter, and Ronald T. Habermas. *How We Learn: A Christian Teacher's Guide to Educational Psychology.* Grand Rapids: Baker Books, 1994.

Jensen, Eric. *Brain-Based Learning and Teaching.* Del Mar, CA: Turning Point, 1995.

———. *Brain-Based Learning: The New Paradigm of Teaching.* 2nd ed. Thousand Oaks, CA: Corwin Press, 2008.

———. *Enriching the Brain: How to Maximize Every Learner's Potential.* The Jossey-Bass Education Series. 1st ed. San Francisco: Jossey-Bass, A John Wiley & Sons Imprint, 2006.

Jensen, Eric, and LeAnn Nickelsen. *Deeper Learning: 7 Powerful Strategies for In-Depth and Longer-Lasting Learning.* Thousand Oaks, CA: Corwin Press, 2008.

Kohlberg, Lawrence. *The Philosophy of Moral Development: Moral Stages and the Idea of Justice.* Essays on Moral Development. 1st ed. San Francisco: Harper & Row, 1981.

Kolb, David A. *Experiential Learning: Experience as the Source of Learning and Development.* Englewood Cliffs, NJ: Prentice-Hall, 1984.

Lee, James Michael. *The Content of Religious Instruction: A Social Science Approach.* Birmingham, AL: Religious Education Press, 1985.

LeFever, Marlene D. *Creative Teaching Methods.* Elgin, IL: D. C. Cook, 1985.

———. *Learning Styles: Reaching Everyone God Gave You to Teach.* Colorado Springs: David C. Cook, 1995.

Lewin, Kurt. *Field Theory in Social Science: Selected Theoretical Papers.* 1st ed. New York: Harper, 1951.

McCarthy, Bernice, and Dennis McCarthy. *Teaching Around the 4mat Cycle: Designing Instruction for Diverse Learners with Diverse Learning Styles.* Thousand Oaks, CA: Corwin Press, 2006.

Merriam-Webster's Collegiate Dictionary. 11th ed. Springfield, MA: Merriam-Webster, 2003.

Moreland, James Porter. *Kingdom Triangle: Recover the Christian Mind, Renovate the Soul, Restore the Spirit's Power.* Grand Rapids: Zondervan, 2007.

Moreland, James Porter, and Klaus Dieter Issler. *In Search of a Confident Faith: Overcoming Barriers to Trusting in God.* Downers Grove, IL; Nottingham, England: InterVarsity Press, 2008.

Nouwen, Henri J. M. *The Way of the Heart: Desert Spirituality and Contemporary Ministry.* New York: Seabury Press, 1981.

Plueddemann, Jim, and Carol Plueddemann. *Pilgrims in Progress: Growing through Groups.* Wheaton, IL: Harold Shaw Publishers, 1990.

Richards, Larry. *Creative Bible Teaching.* Chicago: Moody Press, 1973.

———. *A Theology of Christian Education.* Grand Rapids: Zondervan, 1975.

Richards, Larry, and Gary J. Bredfeldt. *Creative Bible Teaching.* Chicago: Moody Press, 1998.

Ridderbos, Herman N. *Paul: An Outline of His Theology.* Grand Rapids: W. B. Eerdmans, 1975.

Robinson, Haddon W. *Biblical Preaching: The Development and Delivery of Expository Messages.* Grand Rapids: Baker Book House, 1980.

Rogers, Cleon. *The New Linguistic and Exegetical Key to the Greek New Testament.* Grand Rapids: Zondervan, 1998.

Schaeffer, Francis A. *True Spirituality.* Wheaton, IL: Tyndale House Publishers, 1971.

Shoemaker, Samuel M. *How to Become a Christian.* 1st ed. New York: Harper, 1953.

Silberman, Melvin L., and Carol Auerbach. *Active Training: A Handbook of Techniques, Designs, Case Examples, and Tips.* Pfeiffer Essential Resources for Training and HR Professionals. 3rd ed. San Francisco: Pfeiffer, 2006.

Sylwester, Robert. *The Adolescent Brain: Reaching for Autonomy.* Thousand Oaks, CA: Corwin Press, 2007.

———. *A Child's Brain: The Need for Nurture.* Thousand Oaks, CA: Corwin Press, 2010.

Tozer, A. W. *The Divine Conquest.* Bromley: STL, 1979.

Traina, Robert A. *Methodical Bible Study: A New Approach to Hermeneutics*. Wilmore, KY: Zondervan, 1980.

Vella, Jane Kathryn. *Taking Learning to Task: Creative Strategies for Teaching Adults*. The Jossey-Bass Higher and Adult Education Series. 1st ed. San Francisco: Jossey-Bass, 2000.

Watson, David L., and Roland G. Tharp. *Self-Directed Behavior: Self-Modification for Personal Adjustment*. Pacific Grove, CA: Brooks/Cole, 1989.

Weimer, Maryellen. *Learner-Centered Teaching: Five Key Changes to Practice*. The Jossey-Bass Higher and Adult Education Series. 1st ed. San Francisco: Jossey-Bass, 2002.

Wiersbe, Warren. *The Bible Exposition Commentary, Old Testament* (Seattle: Biblesoft), Commandment V. 5.

Wilhoit, Jim. *Christian Education and the Search for Meaning*. Grand Rapids: Baker Book House, 1986.

———, and Leland Ryken. *Effective Bible Teaching*. Grand Rapids: Baker Book House, 1988.

Willard, Dallas. *Renovation of the Heart: Putting on the Character of Christ*. Colorado Springs: NavPress, 2002.

Williamson, Marianne. *Illuminata: A Return to Prayer*. 1st Riverhead ed. New York: Riverhead Books, 1995.

Wolterstorff, Nicholas, and Christian Schools International. *Educating for Responsible Action*. Grand Rapids: CSI Publications; Eerdmans, 1980.

Yount, William R. *Called to Teach: An Introduction to the Ministry of Teaching*. Nashville: B&H Publishers, 1999.

Zuck, Roy B. *Teaching as Jesus Taught*. Grand Rapids: Baker Books, 1995.

———, and Charles R. Swindoll. *Spirit-Filled Teaching: The Power of the Holy Spirit in Your Ministry*. Swindoll Leadership Library. Nashville: Word, 1998.

Name and Subject Index